UNCOMPETE

UNCOMPETE

Rejecting Competition
to Unlock Success

Ruchika T. Malhotra

VIKING

VIKING
An imprint of Penguin Random House LLC
1745 Broadway, New York, NY 10019
penguinrandomhouse.com

Copyright © 2025 by Ruchika Tulshyan

Grateful acknowledgment is made for permission to reprint the excerpt by
Alok Vaid-Menon, author, on pages 242–243.

Designed by Nerylsa Dijol

LIBRARY OF CONGRESS CONTROL NUMBER: 2025022565
ISBN 9780593832158 (hardcover)
ISBN 9780593832165 (ebook)

Printed in the United States of America
1st Printing

The authorized representative in the EU for product safety and
compliance is Penguin Random House Ireland, Morrison Chambers,
32 Nassau Street, Dublin D02 YH68, Ireland, https://eu-contact.penguin.ie.

For Mum, of course.
For Ra and S, because.
For P and V, always.
Om Tat Sat.

"i am a dream still dreaming."

NAYYIRAH WAHEED, *SALT*

CONTENTS

UNCOMPETE

Competition Is the Thief of Joy

Nadya and I started our job at the magazine on the very same day. She'd had a nontraditional route through customer service to land the job, whereas I had dreamed of being a journalist for years. On our first day, our boss told us how much this team valued collaboration and kinship, and that office socials were a big part of the culture. Nadya and I ramped up together, bouncing ideas off each other and cheering each other on—being on the launch team of a brand-new magazine for an established organization was no small feat. I was excited to have a "work wife" well before the term became trendy, and we shared personal and professional wins and grouses with each other.

But as the weeks went on, I started noticing that Nadya would often meet with my boss and colleagues alone, and also leave me out of emails. When I entered our meetings, she would switch over to Mandarin, a language that everyone else on the team spoke but I didn't, for the pre-meeting banter. One day, my boss called me over to share a cool new idea that Nadya had impressed the team with—an advice column where people could write in for career solutions. It was a smart idea that focus groups were already showing would increase readership. It would be a fun column with great visuals, one that would help transform the bureaucratic, boring perception of the organization.

The only problem? That idea was mine.

Over two decades have passed since that incident and that job. In that time, I've learned a heck of a lot about how competition and rivalry show up in our professional and personal lives. We've all strategized about how to get promoted by beating out our rivals. We've rooted for our favorite Kardashian on reality TV as they throw a member of their family under the proverbial bus so that they emerge as more popular. We've secretly relished when a friend who always seems to be winning at life confesses she's going through a rough patch because that somehow makes us feel like we're better.

Incidents like these are so common and acceptable that we rarely give them a second thought. In fact, we're deeply suspicious of people who *aren't* constantly striving to improve themselves and get a leg up against others. It's not enough to have gotten a new job—the natural next step is to already be planning when and how to get promoted. It doesn't matter that we trained hard to run a marathon; we'll immediately be asked when our next one is. The next time, we'll not only be trying to beat our last running time; maybe we could also qualify for one of the famous city marathons and compete against others as well? On and on it goes.

Even if it's crossed our minds briefly to question this narrative, we still fall back on the idea that there simply isn't another way to live, advance, and succeed. Competition is a fact of life, an unspoken rule that most of us don't even think to challenge, no matter where in the world we live, who we are, who we love. It's in the air that we breathe and the water we swim in: We're paddling so hard that we don't even have the bandwidth to understand how strong the tides are and what's at stake. It surrounds us in every facet of our lives, and we automatically believe that staying competitive is the surest way to succeed. So pervasive is this narrative that we've simply accepted the validity of long-held beliefs like these: *Competition makes me better, smarter, more innovative. If I don't compete, others will get ahead. I can't escape it anyway; humans are biologically hardwired to compete.*

But what if this isn't true? What if the cost of trying to constantly get ahead is far too high? What if competition isn't the best way or the only way to progress? And most of all, what if we started questioning *who really wins* when we compete? We don't leave behind competition and rankings when we graduate from school or college. A competition mindset and approach not only follow us all our lives but also become more insidious, harmful, and toxic as we age. I know this because I long upheld the idea of pushing myself hard to be the very best to get ahead, no matter the cost—mental, physical, financial, spiritual. That is, until a series of eye-opening incidents occurred in my life to show me not only how flawed the idea that outcompeting others would get me ahead was but that it was also irrevocably burning me out.

In economics we're taught that there's a scarcity of opportunities and resources, so we must compete for them. From wealth to opportunities to educational advancement to status, recognition, and power, we've been indoctrinated to be in constant rivalry with others, to believe that the only way to win is to ensure that your opponent loses. We're taught to believe that we must cajole, elbow, fight, and ultimately take down our opponent at all costs and that winning justifies all means. Win a race, the ranking of "best of," the contract, the promotion, the unspoken contest in society to be most attractive, have the bigger home and paycheck, have the most brilliant kids . . . you can see that the competition is nonstop.

But we rarely admit that this mindset has serious downsides. That competition is making us sick, anxious, exhausted, isolated, and worse off in every way. Sure, sometimes there's a short-term gain to being competitive: Maybe a new product is created or someone works tremendously hard to qualify for a marathon. But in the long term, always-and-at-all-costs competition depletes us instead of giving us the purported upsides we're conditioned to believe in. As you'll learn through data, stories, and my own experiences, almost no one truly wins in a competitive system.

The deleterious impact of competition is far-reaching on the individual, the community, the society, and the environment. For women and people of color, competition is exploited to divide us, and its impact proliferates significantly more harm in our lives compared with our dominant-group peers. In any society built on competition, rather than supporting humans as they navigate very human experiences such as childbirth, caregiving, disability, and chronic illness, we literally shut them out for not being "hardworking" enough. If they raise the alarm about experiencing sexism, racism, ableism, or any other form of bias in the workplace, we write them off for being timid and therefore not wanting to win badly enough to ignore what ends up being even egregious harm. We're often pitted against one another to compete for scraps, which has us competing against the very people we should be building coalitions and solidarity with.

And it doesn't end in the workplace, either. Societally, competition has been particularly harmful for those of us most disenfranchised by racism, patriarchy, and oppression, all of which are thriving as functions of the hypercompetitive, late-stage capitalist societies that we find ourselves in. Competition has had disastrous consequences on a personal, organizational, and societal level, and the myths that uphold it pose significant challenges to creating a more just, equal, and antiracist world. We are living in a deeply polarized world where a winner-take-all competitive political system has given rise to charlatans, demagogues, and oppressive dictators. Add to this the fact that far too many of us are too overwhelmed trying to keep up in a hypercompetitive system and consequently are unable to fully participate in our civic duties, which has contributed to the steady erosion of our democracy. All these factors have also ravaged the environment—profit over planet has created and exacerbated a climate crisis.

If you're wondering, I didn't come to this work by chance. My interest in competition is deeply influenced by my role as a diversity, equity, and inclusion (DEI) practitioner. I've advised organizations big and small—many are household names—on how to create a culture that supports and empowers women, people of color, and people from other historically excluded backgrounds, often at the intersection of multiples of these. My company does this through data collection and through awareness and education regarding how bias and exclusion have long-lasting impacts on the hiring, retention, and advancement of nondominant groups of people.

In my practice, one of the consistent lines of pushback I hear from corporate leaders, no matter how well-intentioned they are, is that DEI interventions mustn't ruffle the feathers of people already established

5

within the organization: typically, white men. "We believe in the importance of women, people of color, and all marginalized groups making gains," I hear. And then, invariably, "But . . . we fear that a women's sponsorship initiative or trying to hire more people of color would be seen as unfair for the white men who've worked so hard to get here." Never mind that any modest gains made by historically marginalized communities would come nowhere close to overturning centuries of systemic oppression. What we're seeing now—a pernicious, vicious attack on corporate and educational DEI programs across the United States—is basically a turbocharged version of this belief. In my practice, I'm constantly being reminded how pervasive the belief is that one community's gains can come only through another's losses—that even equality is a zero-sum game.

In my own way, I also bought into that narrative for a long time; I had my sharp elbows out earlier in my career to succeed as an ambitious woman. I'm often asked why women don't support one another or are often perceived as being maliciously competitive with one another. Are women just naturally more competitive than men? The data shows that we're not. But we *are* exponentially more harmed by competition in the context of a sexist, racist, and biased society. In a gender-imbalanced environment, women are signaled that they should make rivals of other women to succeed for that one coveted spot. So they do, sometimes viciously and devastatingly. And to uphold the power dynamics fostered by racism and competition, we often see white women isolating women of color. In all my work, I've looked at how systems of oppression create challenges to inclusive, equitable, and diverse workplaces, rather than individuals being to blame.

Personally, I believe we are seeing the worst of this kind of competition, exacerbated by the comparison fueled by new digital technologies and social media platforms. Particularly for humans socialized as girls and women, a patriarchal system that has pitted us against one another continues to fan the flames of a competitive mindset and perpetuate an endless cycle of comparison. These kinds of behaviors are especially toxic in a world where social media algorithms depend on us competing against one another and comparing our regular lives with other people's "highlight reels." Constant competition can spread wide-ranging feelings of sadness, pain, and trauma on a global level. Why are we so likely to compare ourselves to another person? Why are we always looking over to the proverbial grass on the other side to see if it is indeed greener? Where do these cycles of competition come from?

Our minds have long been colonized by systems of oppression—the idea that the "best" person will win, that meritocracy is real and competition is natural. This book intends to carefully dismantle these long-held beliefs. There is another way to live, and when we actively choose this other way, individual happiness, joyous communities, and a society where suffering isn't a measure of success are possible.

TO COMPETE—OR NOT—IS A CHOICE

I was born into a household of modest privilege that eventually grew to one of financial abundance as I got older. My father was an entrepreneur who moved from India to Singapore and was able to enjoy many of the economic successes of a nation that had recovered relatively quickly from the ravages of colonialism. My parents had an arranged marriage, and my mother moved to Singapore from India at the age of twenty-one. Both of my parents had grown up in lower- to middle-class families in India characterized by varying degrees of financial scarcity. Whether it was scarcity in education, resources, or not being able to spend time doing leisure activities, my parents' worldviews were affected by living in these environments. But they each took a very different approach toward life.

My father was a greedy capitalist who constantly believed that the way to get ahead was to undercut others. His approach to life was about sizing other people up and constantly worrying: *How do they compare against me? Are they wealthier than me? Are they better looking than me? Are they more sophisticated than me? Do they have a better life than me?* He believed that success was incumbent upon elbowing others out of the way, that power had to be fought for, and that any means justified the ends for amassing personal financial gains.

My mother showed me an opposite path in every single encounter. Although our culture in the Indian diaspora, like so many others, rewards competition and comparison, my mum would actively advocate for other women and would never have an unkind thing to say about others in our community no matter how much they tried to denigrate her. My mother always approached life with the belief that a healthy society is one where everyone thrives, believing that an abundant community was worth celebrating much more than the financial wealth that my father tried to amass. For her, success meant peace of mind for herself and joy for others. She would discourage my younger siblings and me from competing with other children or even with each other. We were encouraged to celebrate one another's unique strengths and prioritize our long-term relationships over point-in-time rivalries of the type that often end up corroding sibling relationships in adulthood. She met new people with an open-minded outlook, and I remember her frequently asking people "How can I help?" or making connections without even asking.

I could see over the years that my father's constant stack ranking and wealth hoarding were incredibly damaging to his relationships both in and out of our home and that these habits created challenges for him, including later falling into debt and financial crime. That doesn't even account for the emotional havoc it wreaked on me, my siblings, my mother, and, I'm sure, many other people past and present in his life. His winner-take-all approach to life left a path of destruction for almost everyone he was in contact with. In the years we lived with him, he created intense emotional dysregulation and fear in my mother, my siblings, and me that we are only now starting to understand and work to undo. It is what led me to writing this book, which is equal parts a cautionary tale and a manifesto for choosing a radically different way of being.

As I began my own journey into adulthood, I came to understand that you can compete all you want, but when you regularly push people out of the way, all you find is loneliness at the top—if you even make it to some version of "the top." The reality is that many of us have been denied an idealized state of "making it" or achieving our version of the American dream yet were blamed for this as an individual failure without looking at how our systems make it so hard to prosper.

And living a life ranking yourself in relation to others is simply ensuring that you will never be satisfied: There will always be someone who is more *fill in the blank* than you. Most of all, though, growing up with these two drastically different approaches seeded in me the idea that engaging in competition is a choice.

INTRODUCING UNCOMPETE

Uncompete is built on the unyielding belief that there's more than enough room for all of us to succeed. If competition tells us that two or more parties who want the same thing need to fight it out for one to be declared the winner, to uncompete tells us the exact opposite. It requires us to intentionally push back on the idea that in every situation there are only finite opportunities and just one winner. To choose collaboration over competition, abundance over scarcity, long-term gains over short-term wins. To know that success must be measured on the gains of a community over individual wins.

To uncompete doesn't mean never taking a job or forgoing ambition or a desire to build wealth. On the contrary, when we uncompete, we often find more wealth and opportunities come our way, as my own story and those of others will illustrate in these pages. But it *does* mean opting out of competition that rests on a zero-sum, scarcity, winner-take-all, any-means-necessary approach. We must deliberately resist the many beliefs about success we've been conditioned with so that there can be a path to liberation, opportunity, and peace for *all* that has long evaded us.

This book is structured into three parts to guide you: **Choice,**

Action, and **Resistance**. Only when we understand how a competitive system has been designed to fail us can we begin to make **choices** and take **actions** that ultimately allow us to **resist** this system. When we uncompete, we intentionally:

- **Choose** what's best for the group and environment *as well as* (not *instead of*) the individual.
- **Act** in the spirit of collaboration, curiosity, and consideration.
- **Resist** cultural norms that are rooted in the domination and exploitation of others, especially marginalized communities.

I'll outline some of the most prevalent myths about competition that we often take for granted, then show you how I'm rewriting them in my bid to uncompete. When we can decolonize our mind from the "truths" we've believed for so long, we begin the work of thinking differently and behaving differently. That's where the five principles of uncompete come in. Each guides us on a tangible way to approach our lives: **collaboration, an abundance mindset, radical generosity, inclusion**, and **solidarity**. I truly believe that if people in my society are hungry, poor, and sick, that is the yardstick I should be using to measure my (lack of) success. In a thriving society, we are responsible for one another. We work to uplift one another so that none of us are without basic needs and care.

To uncompete is to redefine what success means, on our own terms, for ourselves. And constantly, doggedly pushing back against the idea that there's only room for one person (or a few) to win. Although the existing narrative tells us "competition is the only way," the reality is that in every facet of life—nature, business, social, and even sports—

success is usually predicated on collaboration. In fact, the more hairy and audacious the goal, the more we need to be in sync with one another.

The hardest part of practicing what it means to uncompete is making *daily* choices to opt out of competition and build collaboratively. This is where the real work begins. To uncompete is about agency and building collective power. It can range from choosing to behave joyfully toward someone who actually makes you feel envious, to revealing your salary to a coworker instead of believing that if you do, she'll somehow get an edge over you. To uncompete can range from choosing *not* to undercut your biggest competitor in the office to actively advocating for an often-overlooked colleague to lead a big project at work, rather than viewing success as simply your individual career progression. It essentially means thinking, believing, and behaving with the core premise that dismantling larger systems of competition and scarcity requires us to act on a multitude of small, daily choices. To take the long view of the society we want to create, rather than the short-term behaviors that we often cycle through on autopilot.

To uncompete, we must make intentional choices that require us to step away from the belief that "competition is the only way." Although it's bold and revolutionary in theory, it's also deeply practical. Here are the eight practices of uncompete that I'll detail in this book:

1. Reset Our Mindset
2. Reframe Comparison
3. Choose Joy
4. Create an Abundant Community
5. Build Collective Power

6. Liberate Our Bodies
7. Redefine Success on Our Own Terms
8. Seek Peace

As you can imagine, none of this is the default or made easy in our current system. To uncompete requires us to courageously choose a different path than many laid out in our Western paradigms, although there is evidence of its wisdom in many Native, Indigenous, and Eastern traditions, and in many more traditions that have been lost in the annals of history within cultures and communities that were wiped out by settler colonialism, slavery, and genocide.

Many of us may find that we're actively met with opposition or suspicion when we undertake this journey. We've all been taken hostage by the seductive pull of competition—particularly the idea that there's no harm in constantly advancing yourself. That's precisely why we must be so deliberate, and we have to do it together, taking turns to hold space for one another as we begin this work in community.

In any of the series of early actions I took in my own life to uncompete—from choosing to leave a lucrative corporate job, to prioritizing rest, to building power collectively instead of individually—I have often been questioned, ridiculed, ignored, and even actively blocked. Sometimes, even people I loved and trusted second-guessed me. But as there became clear evidence of how much I gained from this new approach, the naysayers fell to the wayside, one by one.

I've noticed time and again that the leaders I have worked with who deliberately moved away from a competitive mindset have constantly been more successful than their peers—in creating innovative organizations, new products, and work cultures that employees actually want to be a part of. I learn time and again that to uncompete is the only way to create a win-win scenario.

WHAT CAN THIS LOOK LIKE IN PRACTICE?

When I was putting together the proposal for my last book, *Inclusion on Purpose*, I heard (both subtly and explicitly) from literary agents, editors, and industry experts alike that books by women of color were not saleable. That there wasn't a market for our stories. Many would apologetically say that even though they *believed* in the need for stories from a diversity of authors, they couldn't argue with the fact that book sales mattered more. Indeed, a report published in *The New York Times* found that close to 90 percent of books published by traditional publishers are by white authors.

Although my book proposal attracted multiple bidders, it did not command a high advance. Even then, the advice was to keep my cards close to the vest—to be grateful for this opportunity that's so rare for people like me and to jealously guard all my lessons, contacts, and book ideas. But rather than view other books by women of color as my competition (for that coveted "one spot"), I took a different approach. I wished (and fervently continue to) that there were plenty more authors like me that the industry could have turned to as proof that we can write successful books. I didn't fiercely guard my ideas or keep my work secret, as many authors are advised to do. I celebrate the wins of other aspiring authors of color when they get book deals, believing that their successes mean there is more proof for my book's existence, not less.

Inclusion on Purpose went on to exceed all expectations when it published. It became the number-one bestselling book for my publisher for the year it was published, earned back its advance within three months, and spurred several aspiring authors who have since contacted me to let me know that the success of my book has allowed them to secure higher advances and book deals. I've liberally sent my book proposal to women of color who are aspiring authors in sincere hopes it can help guide their proposals, too. Not only for altruistic purposes, but because I truly believe that having stories from more of us out in the world *expands the pool, not narrows it.* It means that there's less of a burden on people from underestimated identities to prove there's a "market" for our work.

I've seen this hold true in other spaces, including the corporate world; current systems of oppression tell us that the prize is in being the *first*: the first in class, the first female CEO, the first Indian woman to break barriers. But when I interview the "first" or "only" of any kind, what I've often heard is stories of pain, loneliness, and exhaustion from needing to constantly prove you belong. Many leave, broken down and disillusioned.

A book by my friend Deepa Purushothaman, *The First, the Few, the Only: How Women of Color Can Redefine Power in Corporate America*, highlights these stories well. Deepa and I have also done for each other what any traditional industry would tell us not to—rather than see each other as rivals, as Indian women in America "fighting" for the same book audience, we've deliberately championed each other, recommended the other's books to our audience, steered each other toward huge opportunities, and generally refused to give in to the idea that there's only one spot for one winner. Because like so many more women of color, I'm tired of it all. Of being told to compete against people I would most benefit from collaborating with. I'm exhausted from being the "first" or "one of the few." I'm devastated that my "wins" should come at the expense of others losing. And not when the stakes are low, like at my fourth grader's recreational soccer games, but in life-changing circumstances, such as making other women feel bad about themselves when I share only big wins on social media, undercutting my "rival" at work so that I get the promotion, and raising or strategizing against someone else to bolster myself up. I've seen how much that scarcity thinking harms me and others, and I want a different way. I know you do, too.

WHAT WE WIN BY CHOOSING TO UNCOMPETE

In these pages you will learn from incredible leaders, particularly women of color at various intersections (they may be part of the LGBTQ+ community, disabled, caregivers, socioeconomically diverse) who are leading the way on how to uncompete because we've long had to imagine, dream, and create our own worlds as we navigate systems that are not built for us or are even actively trying to harm us. In finding community care and a world in which we don't stack-rank others or leave anyone behind, we begin the possibility of healing. By refusing to see opportunities, advancement, and even joy as zero-sum issues, we begin to walk toward redemption and justice. I no longer believe that we must suffer to be considered worthy. It's taken me decades to unlearn the idea that my body is worthy only when it's producing. I think the hustle culture that competition imposes on us takes so much more away from us than it imparts to us.

The good news is we already have some guidance on what it looks like to uncompete. It's Jamie Lee Curtis jumping out of her seat to cheer on Michelle Yeoh (the first Asian woman to win the Oscar for best actress) rather than being threatened by a fellow actor's win. It's the solidarity that Oprah Winfrey demonstrated when she looked at Meghan Markle on national TV and asked, with deep empathy, "Were you silent, or were you silenced?" In a culture where the "Queen Bee" trope of older women undercutting younger ones is commonplace, which I'll explore in chapter 2, Oprah showed us what it meant to publicly stand up for Meghan—against the British royal family, no less! It's the way that Michelle Obama amplified Beyoncé's daring new album *Homecoming* by using her star power as First Lady of the United States to call her a "queen" and tell her she was so proud of her in a public video. We can do this for others—not just people with our shared identities, but particularly those who have been most harmed by racism, sexism, and systemic oppression. In solidarity, in collaboration, with unapologetically radical generosity.

WHY I HOPE YOU'LL JOIN ME

The first person who inspired me to put these ideas together was my mother. I saw her doing naturally so much of what I've managed to finally capture in these pages. Seeing what it means to uncompete play out over the nearly four decades I've known her, I believe she embodies a type of magic that we can all learn from. It's not easy, nor is it the default. But it is worth it.

I saw it modeled most in the courage she found to move from a hypercompetitive community that berated her for breaking traditional norms by divorcing her husband at fifty and building an abundant community around her. My mum suffered financially by leaving her marriage, and she lost many friends and family members who didn't want to be associated with a divorced woman or her kids. Slowly, however, she sought out friends who celebrated her courage and single status, people who believed that women deserved to be joyous. Her new community exemplifies what it means to uncompete and has mutually flourished with her. What I see as I reflect on her life now: Joy comes from belonging authentically to a community. Her form of resistance was leaving a toxic marriage built on patriarchy, competition, and capitalism. And what she won wasn't the "financial half" promised by a competitive system: Anyone who knows the law will know it's not set up to support the vulnerable.

But what she gained was far greater: mental peace. She has since coached dozens of women in our traditional Indian diasporic community who are leaving toxic marriages or are facing major health issues and other challenges. I've seen unleashed in her an opportunity to catalyze a community of immigrant women who show up for one another, celebrate and uplift one another. Inspired by her, I'm trying to do the same among a community of diverse women of color I'm building in person in Seattle and, thanks to digital technology, all over the world. My approach is simple: I want them to win, too. My joy is intrinsically linked to their joy.

After all, I learned that my mum was right all along. When you uncompete, you live up to the promise of a world where everyone wins. And not just you, but your community, your society, and the world. I'm so ready for a radical new way to live my life away from fear, stress, and scarcity. Won't you join me?

PART ONE
CHOICE

CHAPTER ONE

Competition Is
the Water We Swim In

I grew up in Singapore—it's a city, a state, an island, *and* a country of just 275 square miles. My home country prides itself on becoming a competitive financial juggernaut, "from third world to first within three and a half decades," according to its first prime minister, after navigating postcolonial independence from Malaysia in 1965. As in much of the world, Singaporeans are taught from a young age— through societal messaging, education, and workplace norms—that the only way to get ahead is to work hard or risk falling behind. It was, and remains, well understood that if you didn't outwork everyone around you, there wasn't room for you to succeed. In a high-pressure environment of grades and examinations, against the backdrop of a rapidly modernizing country that experienced monumental economic growth only won by sheer grit, we didn't even think twice about whether competition was a good thing or not: It was just the only way. The message was reinforced as I went on to obtain elite college degrees and work as a professional journalist and DEI strategist in places like London, New York, Mumbai, Atlanta, and Seattle.

Now, as the mother of an elementary schooler, I'm finding that the cycle is repeating. Rankings, tests, and stress about which college my son will "beat out" others to get into a decade later are a normal part of conversations I have with my family, friends, and even strangers. With other parent friends—including ones who don't live in the same country—there's an omnipresent "sizing up" of who is doing better in ensuring that their kids have a leg up: *How many extracurricular activities does your child do? How many languages do they speak? Is your child reading at above grade level? How many countries have they traveled to?*

It's not an exaggeration to say it feels like competition touches every facet of our lives: as professionals, as caregivers, as people.

But we didn't become competitive by happenstance. A variety of economic, political, and social factors coalesced to ensure that we were in constant competition with one another in school and then in the workplace, ultimately conditioning us to compare our wealth and status in society with our peers. This isn't who we innately *are*, but it is the way we're taught to navigate the waters we swim in.

I have come to realize that it's not a personal failing or an issue that affects some of us and not others. Competition is everywhere, every time, with and within everyone. It is simply the default mode we're socialized to operate in to advance.

Below are five widespread beliefs about competition that we rarely consider or question, yet are ubiquitous in our lives. They seem benign and even positive in many cases. It's only when you slow down and begin to unpack them that you realize how insidious and harmful they can be.

Belief 1: We're Hardwired to Compete

Like most, I learned about Charles Darwin and the *survival of the fittest* theory in school. From the dawn of time, our earliest ancestors were built with a primal instinct that can be best described as "Eat or be eaten." To put it another way, if you aren't the predator, stalking your next kill, then you'll be preyed upon and meet your demise. This battle for dominance isn't about just staying alive. Darwin asserted that natural selection is what forces creatures to evolve and thrive. When one species defeats another, the victor's offspring gains new traits that will help keep it powerful and secure. Although this ideology was formulated in the 1800s, we still see it alive and well in our modern world.

We're taught that those primal instincts are baked into our DNA. They just show up differently now that we've made it into the twenty-first century. Our way of life and the road to success seem fundamentally dependent on our competitive instincts. On whether we can outwit and outlast those who are weaker than us—in our workplaces and in our personal lives—to survive and thrive. Our history textbooks have given us countless examples which prove that our winner-take-all nature is what drives us to learn, invent, accomplish, and flourish. There is no shortage of stories that show how our innate need to outwit and outlast is what breeds survival, ingenuity, and excellence.

Belief 2: Competition Brings Out the Best in Us and the World

In seventh grade I learned about a remarkable, Earth-defying feat born from one of the most intense competitions in history. The United

States succeeded in putting men on the moon during the Cold War, after a five-decades-long space race for world dominance with Russia. After World War II, the two countries were trying to prove their global superiority through physical and technological battles. They then set their sights on the universe, where each nation spent billions of dollars to further advance into space. Russians, Americans, and the rest of the world watched with bated breath as the two nations competed to see who could put a man (yes, *only* men) into space, then to orbit the Earth, and finally to land on the moon. To win this competition, teams at NASA worked round the clock and eventually achieved the unlikely goal of a moon landing. The pressure that led to innovation of this magnitude was possible only with fierce competition. As a person born in Southeast Asia, in a nation formed in 1965, I was unequivocally taught that America *had* to win the competition so our nation and others in our region could thrive. The Soviets' dominance would mean the end of the free world. In July 1969, when US astronauts Neil Armstrong, Buzz Aldrin, and Michael Collins made a lunar landing, more than half a billion people around the world watched the historic moment on television. Americans definitively "won" the space race.

See? Competition was, and is, necessary for democracy, innovation, and world peace! Throughout history, contests have been known to spur innovation. In 1795 Napoleon offered a 12,000-franc prize to drive innovation in food preservation, which led to the invention of canning to prevent food spoilage. As I crack open a can of garbanzo beans for weekly dinners to save me precious time, I'm reminded that competition made it possible.

Even in more contemporary examples, we've been sold on the idea that competition can bring out the best ideas. Challenge.gov lists federally funded contests to innovate for public betterment, and companies like Amazon, Tesla, and Uber all cite outwitting their competitors as a key factor of their business success. Competition = innovation.

Belief 3: There's Only Limited Success to Go Around

Sia Singh had been a publicist for a decade. She was the only South Asian woman in her organization and prided herself on bringing clients from marginalized backgrounds to diversify the overwhelmingly white roster of clients they worked with.

One day her manager, Marc, called a meeting with Sia and two other senior publicists in the company, Henry and Tess. The three of them made a solid team, and up until now they'd all been collaborative and supportive of one another. At the meeting, Marc told the group that he intended to promote one of them to a senior publicist position that would report up to him but that he would make that decision based on who performed the best over the next quarter. A little healthy competition would encourage everyone to bring their A-game, right? Everyone nodded along, strategizing how they would win.

For months, Sia worked her fingers to the bone, doing everything she could to dazzle Marc and outshine Henry and Tess. At every turn, Henry and Tess were on Sia's heels. Their client list was more robust than ever, but the camaraderie that had previously existed among them was beginning to vanish. Meetings that were once constructive were becoming more like gladiator-type battles where they'd try to destroy one another's prospects with harsh criticism. They stopped having lunches where they'd brainstorm how to bring in new business and instead ate at their desks while they hustled away. Sia was particularly tormented by how her burgeoning relationship with Tess was being destroyed. She was so excited to work with another woman of color when Tess was hired, and she envisioned them becoming close friends and cheering each other on. That was clearly impossible now.

At the next company-wide meeting, an exhausted, burned-out Sia tried to stay awake in her chair.

"I am really happy with the contributions everyone has made. Our sales revenues have almost tripled. The stakeholders couldn't be more excited about our performance," said Marc, beaming.

But she had this nagging feeling, like the other shoe was about to drop.

And it did.

Their recent success proved to Marc that he didn't have to promote any of them to get the business results he wanted. All he had to do was pit his staff against one another and reap the rewards of their productivity without having to give them anything but a bit of (false) incentive.

It's safe to say that we've all been in Sia's shoes at some point in our careers. Whether or not our manager has thrown down the gauntlet like Marc, we've elbowed our way through the crowd so we could ascend the corporate ladder with little interference. Like Sia, I've bought into the idea that success isn't widely available—it must be fought for to be earned. It feels innocuous, benign, just the way of a world where there's limited resources.

Belief 4: When Someone Else Wins, I'm Losing by Comparison

We are conditioned to believe that if another person achieves or accesses something valuable—a raise in salary, a corner office, an ambitious project, a leadership position, a merit bonus, a service award—then that comes directly or indirectly at the cost of another's loss.

People will fiercely compete to protect and hold on to the things they've worked so hard to achieve. And, in doing so, try to ensure others don't get a "leg up" on them. If we believe there's a limited pie to be divided up, then when someone else gets a "big piece," we've automatically got the smaller piece. Of course, we see this most clearly in the way hierarchies are structured. At school, there can only be one class valedictorian. Companies have only one CEO, a person who was chosen above all others to lead. There can be only one president or prime minister of a country, who wins by defeating their opponent. Even in our personal lives, we must "win" the affection of our partners above all other suitors so that they choose to commit to us.

So of course we're taught at every stage of our lives that being a winner automatically requires others to be losers. And no one wants to be a loser.

On May 31, 2000, when I was thirteen, a new reality TV show took the world by storm: *Survivor*, a show where contestants stranded on a desert island would compete against one another in a series of challenges to ultimately win a prize of $1 million. *Who Wants to Marry a Multi-Millionaire* and its successor, *The Bachelor*, were also starting to gain traction, imparting the idea that women needed to be more attractive, more strategic, and more ruthless to win the "prize" of marrying a rich, handsome man. Suddenly, there were competitions on television for everything: singing (*American Idol*), modeling (*America's Next Top Model*), cooking (*Top Chef*), and . . . I'm not sure what *Big Brother*'s winners are assessed on, but I remember reading that more young people voted for who they wanted to cut out of the competition than voted in the UK general elections over multiple years. What stands out is that unlike TV game shows popularized in the past, such as *Wheel of Fortune* and *Jeopardy!*, where contestants play for a finite amount of time, the newer iterations of television competition, which have now become ubiquitous, reiterate the idea that *every day and every interaction* is a competition to be won. Instead of a thirty-minute slot of good-natured play where the rules were clearly defined, what we've normalized and internalized is that being ruthless, dramatic, and messy toward our "rivals" in any arena can make us winners. If all others lose, we win, and if someone else is winning, we're losing by default.

Belief 5: Competition Is Inevitable

As a teenager, much of what I learned about the rules of success—especially for women—was guided by American pop culture. Watching popular law-firm TV shows like *Ally McBeal* and *The Practice* and movies like *Mean Girls*, *Bring It On*, and *Legally Blonde* drew me into a world that was fascinating, foreign, and feral. There was something about the female characters that intrigued me. The protagonists were peers and colleagues, but they were also fierce competitors, vying for the best opportunities, the coveted promotions, and often the romantic love interests, too. They might play nice with one another when the chips were down, but the gloves would always come off whenever they had to fight for a seat at the bargaining table and a place at the top. Female rivalry seemed to be par for the course for success, I internalized, especially in the workplace.

Now, as I reflect on my own career of two decades spanning three continents, I've seen this play out in various ways. In my early career, I'd think nothing of competing with other young professionals for a limited number of internships or of getting on my boss's good side to be considered for a promotion over a peer. I thought it was just a rule of getting my foot in the door, and when I would get ahead, I wouldn't play "the game" to tear others down like I'd seen on TV or observed around me. But as I progressed, the competition got even stronger as the stakes got higher. Even when I often saw relationships suffering as collateral damage in this "inevitable" competition, it just felt unavoidable. Like there wasn't much I could do to opt out without risking my own security or success. In fact, some of the most competitive experiences I've had in and out of the workplace have involved other women of color.

That's precisely why competition-at-all-costs beliefs are so harmful. They lull us into a false sense of security—play and you'll have a shot at winning. It's only when we begin to peel back the layers and question whether competition is truly the best way, the only way, and the inevitable way that we begin to see a different path. We must decolonize our minds from these long-held beliefs and defaults that divide us, stress us out, and keep us powerless.

Here's how.

Unpacking Belief I: We're Hardwired to Compete

We've internalized the idea that (1) competition is unavoidable because it's in our DNA and (2) it's what makes us great because we're the product of winners who beat out their competitors. The place where these beliefs have the most impact is at work because our ability to afford a home, feed our families, and seek medical help when we're sick (to put it simply: survive)—as well as demonstrate our worth, acquire social status, and distinguish ourselves from the pack (to excel)—is inextricably linked to our performance in the professional arena.

What might surprise you is that these ideas aren't exactly rooted in facts, or at least not the facts as we know them to be.

Let's consider the idea of "natural selection" that's attributed to Charles Darwin. Although the idea of natural selection has been around since the mid-1800s and explains that predators outlived their prey because the law of nature "kills off" those who can't compete to stay alive, many contemporary scientists have found evidence shifting us away from the "born to compete" theory and toward a more holistic view of human nature. Two are Australian science writer Vanessa Woods and Duke University evolutionary anthropology professor Brian Hare, who coauthored the book *Survival of the Friendliest: Understanding Our Origins and Rediscovering Our Common Humanity.* In their research, they found that Homo sapiens outlived every other early human species not because we were more competitive but because of our unique collaboration skills. Some of their evidence also comes from others within the animal kingdom—species like bonobos and orcas, which problem-solve in teams instead of exploiting one another's weaknesses to gain power. These findings support the thesis that humans made it

32

out of the Stone Age because we similarly realized through experience that working together gets us much farther in the world than competing does. Survival of the "fittest" refers to the ability to *reproduce*—not to compete.

But even if our human predecessors *did* compete to some extent to stay alive in our hunter-gatherer years, that doesn't mean we can't choose collaboration now in our modern era. What worked for us then isn't going to work for us now, and we can *choose* a different way because collaboration does benefit us so much more than competition right now. We aren't constantly in fear of being eaten by a lion in our modern lives, so why should we subscribe to beliefs that aren't relevant to our lives right now?

One of my favorite modern examples of designing for collaboration is from a group of Silicon Valley technology entrepreneurs who were part of a prestigious start-up accelerator program. The accelerator encouraged collaboration among the entrepreneurs with the goal of fostering ideas and resource exchange that would lead to more innovative, higher-quality products. But in practice, the researchers found collaboration wasn't a given—it had to be built into the system. When entrepreneurs engaged in "tournament-style" progress-update meetings, where they felt they needed to show off their strength compared with their peers, it "generated an expectation among entrepreneurs to be strategic in exchanging resources with peers," wrote the researchers. When these entrepreneurs approached peers for help, they often declined because helping others was not seen as valuable. But entrepreneurs who didn't engage in these competitive progress-update meetings, and instead met their peers for informal team-bonding opportunities, were more comfortable asking for help and also received help from peers who didn't expect anything in return. "This giving-gratitude cycle eventually resulted in a thriving community of giving and a dense network populated by affective relationships," said Rekha Krishnan, one of the researchers who studied the group. Basically, the entire start-up ecosystem benefits when people choose collaboration over competition.

Ultimately, we have a choice about whether to engage in the rules of competition. We might have been taught to buy into the myth that competition is a default biological setting of ours, but there's evidence to the contrary. Newer beliefs support that it's collaboration and cooperation that have led us to survive and prosper despite our predators.

The idea that competition is what fuels humans' success as a species has long exploited racial pseudoscience to create hierarchies and justify inequality. Not only was scientific racism used to justify horrific inequality such as chattel slavery and the Holocaust in the past, but to this day, many prominent people still believe, despite scientific evidence to the contrary, in inherent differences among the races—which, in their view, justifies unequal treatment or even exploitation. As University of Pennsylvania law professor Amy Wax declared in 2019, "Our country will be better off with more whites and fewer nonwhites." She still holds tenure at her institution. Today's version of *survival of the fittest* justifies leaving by the side of the road people who don't have the means to advance. We've seen it in horrific, racist policies, in eugenics and genocides, and even in the COVID-19 pandemic with uneven access to treatments and vaccines that disproportionately prioritized Western, white, nondisabled, and wealthy lives.

I also often hear that competition helps level the playing field so marginalized people have opportunities to get ahead. It does not. A

competitive system that has long been rigged against us will never result in us reaching equality or undoing the injustices of the past. Author
and activist Kimberly Latrice Jones put it beautifully (and painfully)
by explaining progress using the analogy of a game of Monopoly. In
her analogy, white people have been playing Monopoly against Black
people for 450 years (the history of modern America). For four hundred rounds of play, Black people weren't allowed to have any money
or assets on the board. Then for the next fifty rounds, any economic
progress that Black people earned was willfully taken away from them
(as in the 1921 Tulsa Race Massacre and the 1923 Rosewood Massacre,
where white supremacists destroyed centers of Black economic wealth).
Despite all that history, Black people are expected to "catch up" today,
Jones says, which is impossible. There's no way to win under the current rules:

> Now, at this point, the only way you're going to catch up in the
> game is if the person shares the wealth, correct? But what if every
> time you shared the wealth, then there's psychological warfare
> against you to say, "Oh, you're an equal opportunity hire." So if
> I played 400 rounds of monopoly with you and I had to play
> and give you every dime that I made, and then for 50 years, ev-
> ery time that I played, if you didn't like what I did, you got to
> burn it like they did in Tulsa and like they did in Rosewood,
> how can you win? How can you win? You can't win. The game
> is fixed.

When we talk about competition as a fact of life and what makes us
human, we're ultimately saying that it is morally acceptable to block
and stunt the progress of *some* humans so that *others* can "win."

Unpacking Belief 2: Competition Brings Out the Best in Us and the World

We believe that without competition, we wouldn't grow to our full potential. But in this belief, we often don't face an important question: *Who really benefits, and who loses?* In attending elite schools and colleges, as well as often returning to speak to students as an adjunct professor, guest lecturer, or speaker, I hear time and again of an ever-growing number of students at every age and grade level who face severe stress, anxiety, depression, or other mental health crises. Many share that they worry constantly about falling behind in grades, rankings, internships, job opportunities, and life events (partnering up, buying a home, having children, etc.) compared with their peers and predecessors. Even if students find ways to cope throughout their academic careers, it can often breed lifelong habits of stress, anxiety, and perfectionism.

The competition that's supposedly designed to bring out the best of us at work is often not doing that either. We are more stressed, burned out, and afflicted with mental health challenges in the workplace now than ever before. Rather than resting, seeking help, or opting out, we're taught to double down and "just deal with it" because competition is seen as the best way to thrive. One of the results of this belief that I'm deeply concerned about is how many professionals endure—then ignore—the all-too-real physical symptoms of work-related stress.

According to the Centers for Disease Control and Prevention, a variety of chronic illnesses stem from anxiety-inducing experiences, including working at jobs within highly competitive and sought-after fields. Here's a short list as a sample, which is just scratching the surface:

- fatigue

- a weakened immune system

- brain changes that can contribute to anxiety, addiction, and depression

- gastrointestinal issues

- musculoskeletal disorders, such as carpal tunnel syndrome, tendinitis, and tension neck syndrome

- sleep abnormalities, including insomnia

- cardiovascular problems, including an increased risk of heart disease and heart attacks

Many of these symptoms and illnesses can be linked to or exacerbated by increased cortisol, a steroid hormone that's released from our adrenal glands throughout our body whenever we're in flight-or-fight mode. In fact, studies have shown that measuring our cortisol levels on the job can provide valuable insights into the types of occupational stressors we face and how we can minimize them. One study on work stress in nursing found that average cortisol levels on workdays were 60 percent higher than during off days. And another study that measured stressors at work concluded that "it was common for participants to feel emotions involving stress, frustration, anger, anxiety, and being overwhelmed." That's how strong the correlation is.

Our mental and emotional health are also severely threatened by the debilitating work stress that's brought on by everything from passive-aggressive coworkers baiting us into doubling down on competitive behaviors to hostile corporate takeovers that result in creating industry monopolies and triggering thousands of layoffs. However, what sends us careening into despair—regardless of the source of stress—is loneliness.

We often see the effects of how competition is designed to break down trust and breed suspicion so people can be at a disadvantage and overpowered. Competition often forces people into corners and behind closed doors because they're scared of being seen as weak and vulnerable. The loneliness that is born from that kind of self-imposed isolation can often feel insurmountable. Close to 50 percent of American adults report experiencing loneliness. This partly explains why several health experts, including former Surgeon General Vivek Murthy, have sounded the alarm on mental health struggles in the United States, categorizing them as a growing epidemic. One in eight Americans now takes an antidepressant. Suicide rates have risen by close to 30 percent since 2000. In 2022, just 31 percent of US adults considered their mental health to be "excellent," down 12 percent from two decades prior.

A significantly increased cognitive load underpins the workplace experiences of most women, people of color, LGBTQ+ individuals, and other marginalized groups. It is already stressful enough facing bias in tangible ways: exclusionary behaviors (one that stood out often for me was having my name mispronounced by colleagues I'd worked with for years), being among the few or only of your identity in the workplace—and often feeling the pressure to represent your entire group—and, of course, facing pay and promotion gaps compared with white male peers. In short, the mental duress of a competitive workplace compounds the situation of too many of us who also navigate being the first, the only, or one of the few at work. And even if, in some isolated cases, competition has brought us scientific advancements and pushed individuals to greatness, we are vastly underestimating the enormous human potential that is lost to the suffering, loneliness, stress, poor health, and burnout that it brings most of us on a much more regular basis. So, no, competition doesn't bring out the best in us; if anything, it makes most of us worse off.

Even if we take a critical look at the space race, there's no denying that innovation and progress were made at the expense and erasure of so many, while glorifying extremely problematic individuals. From historian Fraser MacDonald's book *Escape from Earth: A Secret History of the Space Rocket*, I learned that many engineers pivotal to space technology were written out of history, including Frank Malina, who founded the Jet Propulsion Laboratory, because he had joined the Communist Party to protest against racial segregation. On the other hand, 1,600 German engineers, many who were Nazi Party members, were brought to the United States to advance engineering that was pivotal to American space domination. One of the most controversial yet celebrated people involved here is Wernher von Braun, a staunch member of the Nazi Party.

And if you, like me, hadn't learned about the incredible Black women who were key contributors to the space race until the 2016 movie *Hidden Figures*, you're not alone. Often, the flawed narrative of the winner willfully erases so many others because they're the "wrong" gender, race, or nationality to deserve being celebrated among the "best" that competition is supposed to uncover in a biased society.

As it stands, competition cannot overturn entrenched biases to bring us toward a more just future. A Stanford University study of 1.2 million PhD recipients over three decades found that even though students from racial- and gender-marginalized backgrounds innovated at higher rates than dominant-majority students, their contributions were discounted and less likely to help them secure lucrative academic careers, compared with their male and white peers. Competition fortifies existing barriers instead of democratizing opportunities for people already disenfranchised in our society.

Furthermore, we must critically examine what type of innovation we mean when we say "competition unlocks innovation." If innovation *only* means greater shareholder returns, then maybe we can argue that competition results in innovation. But my question to this is: innovation *for whom*? Do we really need another faster food-delivery app that requires an underclass of lower-wage workers forced to beat the food-delivery times of their competitors, risking their health and safety? Does innovation mean lining the pockets of rich white male executives who come up with new ways to make us buy more things that we don't need and can't afford? Does innovation mean colonizing Mars instead of saving the planet we live on? Does innovation mean making mass-produced, cheap goods in foreign countries where workers are exploited so that domestic consumers can buy more, while domestic factories shut down?

I would argue that competition as we see it today stifles or even actively discourages true innovation around every issue that desperately requires it, from solving poverty and food insecurity to racism and the climate crisis. Even technologies such as artificial intelligence, which is often touted as the future of innovation, have already come at significant costs. A lack of diversity in its creators has led to biased AI that doesn't detect darker-skinned faces, gives women lower credit card limits than their husbands, and is more likely to incorrectly predict that Black defendants will commit future crimes than white defendants. There's the eye-watering exploitation of AI content moderators and data annotators from poor communities—some who are paid under two dollars an hour to work in this field. Content moderators in countries like Kenya have reported experiencing severe trauma, anxiety, and depression from watching videos of child sexual abuse, murders, rapes, and suicide to train AI apps like ChatGPT to identify explicit content. There's also evidence that AI acts unethically when its winning-at-all-costs programming has no guardrails. According to a Palisade Research study, when AI models were tasked with beating a bot at chess, they were likely to cheat or use other unethical methods to win if they started losing a game. As I write these words, there's no regulation on the creation or use of AI, despite many prominent technologists emphasizing how urgent regulation is.

If "competition = innovation" led to the creation and mass adoption of solutions to poverty, childhood hunger, homelessness, addiction, and other social challenges, I'd consider dropping this argument right here. Unfortunately, the race to innovate too often focuses on innovations that make the most money, not ones that equalize progress. A *Nature* magazine article states that medical research (and, therefore, corresponding innovations) in diseases that largely affect women are significantly underfunded compared with diseases that affect a similar proportion of men. In short, without the context of who benefits from innovation—and are the largest share of people prioritized in these innovations—I don't buy that competition is the only way to bring out greatness. In fact, I would say the case for *collaboration* over competition in fostering transformation is deep and compelling. From start-up hackathons to large-scale collaborations like the Human Genome Project, Wikipedia, and Linux, there is more compelling evidence that working *together* can unlock the greatest value for the greatest number of people, not just the already wealthy.

Unpacking Belief 3: There's Only Limited Success to Go Around

At the core of the belief that there isn't enough to go around is a scarcity mindset. We're trained to believe that if we don't comply with the rules of competition, we'll lose everything. Scarcity threatens our very sense of security. So we continue to compete with one another for every shred of security there is, wherever we can find it. To be sure, our fear of scarcity couldn't be more valid. Scarcity is literally *everywhere* we look. If we belong to a privileged group, we're usually made to believe we must cling to every last thing we have because there's a scarcity of where it all came from, that someone will snatch it away from us if we get complacent or too generous. If we come from a marginalized background, the threat of scarcity isn't theoretical or hypothetical—it is gut-wrenchingly real. For those who live below the poverty line, the effects of true scarcity are far-reaching and can create insurmountable obstacles—from getting a mortgage (which is particularly hard for Black applicants because of systemic racism), to getting a job, to living in a neighborhood with access to good schools, parks, healthy food, and even clean water. Devastatingly, there's growing evidence of the costs of poverty to children's neuroendocrine function, early brain development, and cognitive ability.

It may sound simplistic, but it's at the core of every institution today: For our late-stage capitalist society to function as designed, everyone must believe there's not enough of anything, so we're constantly striving to get more while trying to outwit our peers so they get less. Schools constantly rank children through standardized testing, so kids (and their parents) face constant pressure to get better grades, believing that intelligence is linked to test scores and learning that future opportunities are closed off without top grades. Universities like Harvard boast an acceptance rate under 4 percent, advertising that there are such few spots and only the "best" make the cut. Lucrative, high-paying jobs ruthlessly create an atmosphere of scarcity in the application process, so applicants constantly feel like they're lacking. Just ask anyone who has been through an interview process at a prestigious company like Google (I didn't even get rejected, just ghosted after multiple rounds of interviews), Amazon, or similar.

And to be clear, there can be a scarcity of resources in some situations. Not because there has to be, as I'll address in future chapters, but because people in power benefit from creating limited opportunities and having us compete for those spots.

I waited almost a year for my son to get a place in day care because I made the "mistake" of not getting on a waiting list the moment my pregnancy test was positive. Many parents, including me, are taught to believe that there's just no other way but to elbow out others as soon as possible for those coveted spots. Rather than band together to find solutions, we often just use every means necessary to advance our own position. There's news of parents enlisting CEOs and celebrities to write letters in support of getting their children admitted to certain elite Manhattan private preschools. A longer conversation for a future chapter is how overwhelmed we are navigating competition in a system that keeps us lonely and fearful.

Many childcare specialists I've spoken to admit that there's no urgent financial incentive to fix the childcare system by creating enough supply to match the demand for day cares and other childcare options. Bogged down by political gridlock, it's the families that suffer, struggle, and compete for limited slots, whereas those who could address the shortages—those who control federal and state funding—don't. Just consider that when it comes to ending food scarcity, we have the tools to end hunger, but we don't consider it an important enough priority. The UN Environment Programme found that households wasted more than a billion meals per day in 2022, but in that same year 783 million people experienced hunger, and a third of humanity faced food insecurity. Most experts say world hunger isn't a problem of the scarcity of food supplies but is rather a result of the absence of international cooperation, the rise of conflict and climate disasters, and other reasons that have nothing to do with actual availability of food. Yet the narrative persists that success is limited and, by definition, feeds (pun intended) into the next belief—that there inherently must be winners and losers.

It's worth spending time reflecting on these questions to consider the validity of scarcity: *When I believe there's a scarcity of everything, is this true? Where does it come from? Who benefits from it when I believe in scarcity, and who loses? What would happen if I stopped believing in scarcity?*

Unpacking Belief 4: When Someone Else Wins, I'm Losing by Comparison

Across the many organizations I've partnered with in my work as a DEI practitioner, the biggest barrier that people at all levels need to overcome is zero-sum thinking. Simply put, it's the belief that if *your* group is making gains, it's at the cost of *my* group's success. Never mind that the biological differences between the sexes and races are negligible. A women's leadership program threatens men who don't have their own advancement program. People of color forming an employee resource group take resources away from white people.

Zero-sum thinking stokes resentment like a wildfire. When we see a junior colleague rising through the ranks, we don't see their talent or determination—we see them as a threat, someone who's stealing from *our* talent and determination. When our manager decides to give an important client to someone with less seniority, we don't see their actions as an attempt to build confidence in a member of the team—we see them as coconspirator in a crime against us.

When you factor race and gender into this equation, these irrational fears intensify exponentially. Some of the strongest calls to stall or even reverse progress for the marginalized come from people who have always had their rights protected.

In DEI, zero-sum thinking mandates that people with the most privilege (most often, cis, straight white men) will have to let go of some of their power so marginalized groups are given their fair share. As a result, there can be an angry backlash against employees from underestimated backgrounds. That anger might manifest itself as openly hostile behavior or in a series of microaggressions (or what I call "exclusionary behaviors" because I don't see them as "micro") that make marginalized people feel unwelcome and unsafe. Perhaps even worse is this more subtle camouflaged "concern" from "allies" who claim to be in favor of DEI initiatives but don't want to alienate privileged groups. I heard this kind of comment countless times during my corporate DEI advisory days, and it drove me crazy: "We believe in inclusion and equity for all in theory. But we don't want men or white people to feel like these efforts are leaving them out. So what can we do to create change without white people and/or men having to lose anything?"

Zero-sum thinking exacerbates fears by making the minuscule gains of people who've faced systemic and generational bias and racism feel threatening.

Our cognitive biases are often to blame. These are shortcuts that our brains take to process information, particularly when we need to make decisions quickly. And of course, in some very limited situations, zero-sum is the name of the game—as when there really is only one winner and that winner can be determined only by an opponent losing. For example, only one team can win the soccer World Cup; all other teams must lose. And there can be only one winner of an Olympic gold medal. But it's forgivable to some extent in those cases because the rules are clearly defined and agreed upon, and typically you're having people of very, very similar athletic abilities compete (although I would still question the pitting of athletes in the West who train in specialized facilities against so many Olympians who've literally trained barefoot because they couldn't afford shoes). These are special cases, not the norm, as we've come to believe. In real life, very few things can be so neatly decided like a sports competition. Real life and even our workplaces can't truly be carved out into measurable slices of a pie that can be compared by the same metrics. Our colleague may get promoted and get a big raise, but perhaps that "big job" makes them feel miserable and like they're losing their soul. Does that mean they've won or lost? By whose metrics? It's almost impossible to make an apples-to-apples comparison on anything in our messy, chaotic lives, yet we believe if someone gets *this one thing we wanted*, we've automatically lost out, rather than taking a holistic, longer-term view on our lives and successes.

But when we believe *every* situation is zero-sum—even when it's not—it can lead to more bias and even the perception of unfairness. Other cognitive biases often exacerbate this thinking. Have you noticed how when your coworker is late to work, you believe they're lazy or disorganized, but when you're late to work, it's because of traffic? That's called fundamental attribution error, another cognitive bias, which again makes it harder to critically assess a situation. I've most often seen fundamental attribution error at play when white men challenge DEI programs; they believe they're deserving of opportunities because of their own merit, but when women and people of color advance, those same gains are characterized as unfair and unmeritorious. If we believe that *every* opportunity is zero-sum, I can see why people with privilege see advancement for another group as a loss for their own.

But let me set a few things straight. We can—and should—stretch ourselves beyond the neurological coding inside our brains. When we do, so much can be accomplished. In the DEI space, I've seen firsthand that when corporations encourage their executives to turn zero-sum thinking on its head and prioritize a more diverse representation of people and ideas, a better workplace is created for everyone.

Zero-sum thinking is made more dangerous by the prevailing myth of meritocracy. We use it to automatically discount people facing any challenges in society because we believe they aren't working hard enough and/or lack innate talent. The idea that only the "best" succeed and you get what you deserve is widespread and plain wrong. In the United States, research finds that your skin color is a larger determinant of your household income than your education. On a smaller scale, think of performance reviews—if your manager raves about and commends you, then you obviously earned all the praise and rewards that come with it. But if your colleague receives lower marks, then clearly they didn't work hard enough. This all-or-nothing approach reduces and dilutes the environment we work in and makes every person we encounter an "other" who is on the opposing side. In the long run, zero-sum thinking fuels and exacerbates the additional underpinnings of competition—survival of the fittest, scarcity thinking, and divide and conquer. It has us seeing people we should support and collaborate with as adversaries, even if there isn't a true scarcity of resources.

We see this play out during every US election cycle for sure, as well as increasingly in other countries where nationalism and far-right political ideology are gaining traction. Many social scientists state that political polarization in the United States has more to do with the zero-sum approach of hating the "other side" than with major divergence on policy preferences. If there was, say, a consolation prize for the presidential candidate who didn't win—rather than a total loss—experts say we'd be less likely to see such strong political divisions.

Unpacking Belief 5: Competition Is Inevitable

Competition was never inevitable. The insidious truth is that it is a system manufactured by powerful people to keep people with similar identities and interests apart so they can be divided and then conquered. "Divide and conquer" (also called "divide and rule") is a centuries-old political strategy, especially used in European colonies to pit groups of people who would be stronger and better together against each other as adversaries in order to weaken them. There is no shortage of examples in our bloody history: Hindu and Muslim Indians were torn apart by British colonizers; poor Black and poor white communities in the United States have been pitted against each other by the white wealthy classes in power for more than a century; the divisions sowed among Hutu and Tutsi people in Rwanda by Belgian colonial rule led to the horrific genocide of 1994. These are just the tip of the iceberg.

Let me be explicit here: Divide and conquer *always* benefits only the people in power. In the business world, those people are CEOs, investors, and members of the C-suite class. But throughout the course of history, the benefactors of divide and conquer have been imperialist kings and totalitarian rulers who deployed the strategy to ruthlessly dominate and violently colonize non-European civilizations. It's a strategy used throughout history to separate people of color, who should be united in solidarity, to weaken them. As far back as 360 BCE, Philip II of Macedonia used *divide et impera* to strengthen his reign in the Roman empire, and the same exact tactics are alive and well today, the world over. In modern US domestic and foreign policy, we need not look any further than the Jim Crow laws of the 1960s or the post–Iraq War conflicts in the Middle East. Because I grew up in Singapore, which was part of the British Empire, and because I've heard painful stories from family members who were terrorized when India was partitioned by the British in 1947, divide and conquer isn't history to me; it's very much part of my today. As an Asian woman in America, I've been devastated to discover how the pernicious "model minority" myth was manufactured to highlight anti-Black sentiment in US society by pitting the success of "good" Asian immigrants against Black communities that suffered because of centuries of oppression.

Divide and conquer is alive and well in our workplaces today—as we saw in the previous example of how Marc treated his subordinates.

We see it when colleagues are pitted against one another for limited opportunities, when women don't support each other in the workplace because we believe there's only room for one woman in leadership, when people of color choose to keep white-supremacy ideals alive rather than band together to create racial equality.

The fact that the divide-and-conquer system has permeated our places of work shouldn't be a surprise. It was constructed so the haves could continue to hoard wealth and resources while the have-nots would suffer every indignity as they fought tooth and nail against one another for the scant leftovers.

Reckoning with the reality that many of the company leaders we work for (and with) are perfectly content clinging to competition strategies like divide and conquer can be tough, especially when we take into account how deeply rooted these rules are in colonization and white supremacy. But if we don't acknowledge and doggedly push back against the rules, then we're just going to keep allowing these tactics to enrich the upper echelons of society, who will do whatever it takes to protect their interests.

SO WHAT'S NEXT?

When we begin to dive deeper into these beliefs and question their origins and relevance, we can disrupt the idea that "competition just is the way it is." Even though competition (upheld by beliefs like the ones detailed above) has been around for as long as we can remember, it truly doesn't serve the majority of us.

Instead, the rules of engagement around competition often:

- Drive a wedge between us and our colleagues when we try to surpass one another.

- Are historically rooted in harmful, problematic ideologies that have been used to oppress and manipulate marginalized groups—and they still negatively affect those groups disproportionately.

- Are steeped in fear that if we don't participate, we won't have or be enough and we'll lose our security. The rules were designed this way to keep us fighting for our livelihood, but ultimately they hurt us more than help us.

- Might be part of the way we've been conditioned, but that doesn't mean we're powerless and can't choose another path to live happy, healthy, whole lives within a thriving community.

When we don't actively, intentionally, proactively opt out of competition, we end up lonelier, sicker, less liberated, and less joyful than we can be. We don't have to live like this. In fact, there are individual and community practices that enable us to thrive without the scourge of competition. We have an opportunity to live collaborative, joyful, and abundant lives if we choose a different way. That way is to uncompete.

CHAPTER TWO

What It Means
to Uncompete

When I tell people I'm writing a book titled *Uncompete*, many stop in their tracks and ask me with wide, interested eyes, "Wait, *un*compete? Did you make that up? What does it mean?"

Yes, "uncompete" is a made-up word. (In fact, as I write this book, my laptop is desperately trying to autocorrect it to "noncompete," and there are red squiggles under it everywhere.) But uncompete is so much more than a pithy catchphrase. It encompasses an intuitive yet radical view that I passionately believe can change the world.

Some might assume that uncompete means throwing our hands up in frustration, opting out of engaging in society, and essentially doing nothing. Others might guess that uncompete is the *opposite* of competing. So rather than race against our colleagues, neighbors, and friends to accumulate rewards, prosperity, and security, we just renounce all material possessions and live on a commune together. (Which wouldn't be the worst thing, honestly. It can be very cruel out there!)

Although neither assumption is right, there is something we can take from each of them. When we uncompete, we commit to actively rejecting the rules of competition—but not because we're giving up in resignation. Instead, we intentionally shift our mindset and move into a new era of our lives with redefined values that run deep. When we uncompete, we recognize that the only way we can sustainably accomplish our dreams and goals is by working toward them in community, without zero-sum and scarcity thinking.

If the definition of *competition* is "a rivalry where two or more parties strive for a common goal which cannot be shared and where one's gain is the other's loss," to *uncompete* is to instead strive toward a goal where success is measured by a positive benefit to the individual, to the community, *and* to society. We can uncompete as individuals or in collaboration when there are two or more parties.

The philosophy behind uncompete centers on being *relational*, not transactional, as my friend Aiko Bethea says. It's not the quid pro quo, "you scratch my back, I'll scratch yours" approach. Instead, it emboldens us to rely on our interconnectedness—not our dominance or assumed superiority—to achieve everything we desire and deserve.

We already have a beautiful blueprint for this in our natural world. Social justice activist and *New York Times* bestselling author adrienne maree brown fleshes this idea out further in her critically acclaimed book *Emergent Strategy*. She writes:

> Humans so far have generally deified and aligned with the "king" of the jungle or forest—lions, tigers, bears. And yet so

many of these creatures, for all their isolated ferocity and alpha power, are going extinct. While a major cause of that extinction is our human impact, there is something to be said for adaptation—the adaptation of small, collaborative species. Roaches and ants and deer and fungi and bacteria and viruses and bamboo and eucalyptus and squirrels and vultures and mice and mosquitos and dandelions and so many other more collaborative life forms continue to proliferate, survive, grow. Sustain.

The longevity of collaboration always surpasses the shortsightedness of competition.

Another defining quality of uncompete is *imagination*. So many of the hardships we face at our jobs and in our personal lives are caused by our failure to believe that we can do more—and better—things when we lean on and root for one another. We lack the ingenuity to build and create a society founded on interdependence and filled with abundance because we're just too exhausted trying to survive and we've been taught our efforts would be futile anyway. That's just a silly fantasy to imagine anything else, we've been told repeatedly.

But adrienne couldn't disagree more, and I'm 100 percent with her. In fact, she even asks: What would happen if we didn't think that our goal in life was to compete with or beat out an opponent, but to increase our love toward them? Here's another gem from *Emergent Strategy*:

If the goal was to increase the love, rather than winning or dominating a constant opponent, I think we could actually imagine liberation from constant oppression. We would suddenly be seeing everything we do, everyone we meet, not through the tactical eyes of war, but through the eyes of love. We would see that there's no such thing as a blank canvas, an empty land or a new idea—but everywhere there is complex, ancient, fertile ground full of potential.

One of the biggest trappings of competition is how quickly it can twist love into fear and admiration into envy. We can start off friendly with the new colleagues who were brought in through a company merger. Then, at the first sign of them setting up shop in our territory, our competitive conditioning calls on us to square off against them because we believe there isn't enough room for everyone to succeed. We're rooting for our peers until they're promoted, and next thing we know our envy is off the charts because zero-sum thinking insists that when someone else receives something, we've lost everything. The most dangerous thing about all this is that the negative by-products of competition don't stay within the walls of our office buildings. They spill out into the rest of our lives and wreak havoc on them. Most of us know this only too well.

You're not alone in feeling this intense pressure to devote all your energy to your career so you won't "lose out." I worked with gender-equity expert and researcher Martha Burwell to survey more than a hundred women and nonbinary people about how competition affected their lives. A whopping 68 percent of respondents to our "uncompete" survey reported experiencing high pressure to compete in the workplace so they could advance, earn more, and protect their (and their family's) future. Most said either that competition was built into their workplace structures or they'd faced other women initiating competition because they felt threatened, intimidated, and/or jealous. Women of color often feel forced to battle it out with one another, especially when working in predominantly white organizations where upward mobility within the company appears to favor white employees.

TO UNCOMPETE AS WOMEN AND NONBINARY INDIVIDUALS

While I was writing this book, many people asked me if it was true that women naturally compete with other women more often than men compete with other men. First off, I want to acknowledge here that gender is on a spectrum and that reducing it to binaries is exclusionary. However, the available research on this subject, to date, does work in binaries. And the evidence about how competition affects men and women is mixed. There is some data to suggest that men are more competitive and other evidence to suggest that women are just as competitive as men. But what *is* definitively true is that men everywhere benefit from engaging in competition more than women do, especially in the workplace. For many women, being in work environments that are hypercompetitive, winner-take-all, and biased fosters highly competitive behaviors that are individualistic and even toxic to themselves and others. Think *The Devil Wears Prada*.

I've been researching and studying gender inequality in the workplace for more than a decade, so this isn't a surprise to me. Not only have I witnessed and experienced it; I've also participated in these competition-at-all-costs games. When workplace environments don't support women, the competition to get ahead can get particularly un-healthy.

Women and nonbinary people of every demographic, across in-dustries, across salary bands—*every* woman I know—has experienced vicious, winner-take-all competition with another woman. For women of color, the toxicity comes from white women as much as from other women of color. Competition in the workplace exacerbates entrenched gender and racial biases.

Journalist Olga Khazan makes a compelling case for why women compete at work while also acknowledging that narratives around women *not* helping other women can uphold and perpetuate gender inequity in the workplace. So I'll state it here plainly: Women can be hypercompetitive with each other in destructive ways, but it's not an individual failing, rather a structural one.

Khazan's article, "Why Do Women Bully Each Other at Work?," begins with the story of "Shannon," an ambitious, highly credentialed lawyer in a big corporate law firm who categorizes the women she works with into three categories of "bitches": "the aggressive bitch," "the passive-aggressive bitch," and "the tuned-out, indifferent bitch." There are almost no exceptions to where women fall in these catego-ries, according to "Shannon." The rest of the story sounds like a shock-ing violation of the human spirit, but it details to some extent the work environment of most women I've met over the course of my career: punishingly long hours, a nightmare for those who have or want to have children (where either they pay high prices for round-the-clock care or remain childless); little professional support; and, most of all, what the journalist describes as "wanton meanness" from other women, particularly senior women. At the end, Khazan concludes that women likely wouldn't bully other women at work if workplace cultures were healthier (and, I would add, anti-biased and antiracist).

There's an additional challenge for women when we navigate tokenism in male-dominated environments: Because there are so few women around and so few spots shown as available for advancement, women believe that they must operate like lone wolves to get ahead. In these situations, women will often align with men rather than help and collaborate with other women. UC Hastings law professor Joan C. Williams theorizes that this behavior is not a personal attack on women's behavior; instead, it's understanding that if men have all the power, then women would align themselves with whoever has the power—men over other women. Taking an intersectional approach, this theory also explains why some women of color often eschew same-racial-group relationships to build professional relationships with white women. I've often tried to forge work friendships with fellow South Asian women but faced dogged resistance. In the moment, it's painful and feels personal. But when I consider it from the lens of frameworks I propose in this book, it makes sense—if you've been conditioned to believe in scarcity and that individual, not collective, proximity to power is your only way to ascend, you're left in what feels like a no-win situation where you must compete to get ahead. Although it's an understandable impulse, it's also a troubling one. When we compete with the very people who we'd stand to benefit most from being in solidarity with, only the people with existing power win.

Our "uncompete" survey results seemed to suggest that for many women of color, there's additional pressure to keep proving ourselves, which can cause harm, most of all, to ourselves.

In one of her brilliant newsletters, Sahaj Kaur Kohli, author of *But*

What Will People Say?, characterizes an inner voice that many immigrants and children of immigrants contend with: "If you're not perfect/ the best, you will become obsolete. If you are not demonstrating your intelligence in a very specific way, you won't be considered smart. If you exhibit behaviors or norms outside of the White Supremacist culture, you are conditioned to believe you are wrong or bad. You must act quickly to ensure success or hold on to your sense of worthiness."

Sahaj's work, which focuses on mental health among immigrants and children of immigrants, resonates particularly with those from South Asian communities, and I can't capture the sentiments I grew up with better than the words she wrote. Often, the pressure to keep outdoing ourselves and each other is fueled by seeing our communities walk such a narrow tightrope of what's acceptable in a new country. For too many of us, being in competition with one another is the only way we feel like we can validate the sacrifices our families made to immigrate to a new country and navigate the challenges and racism they inevitably faced. I know this goes far beyond immigrant communities— the idea that if we don't constantly keep proving ourselves, we'll become obsolete. The hard truth is that the cost of constantly operating like this becomes too much to bear.

WHAT'S AT STAKE
IF WE DON'T UNCOMPETE

One of the truly detrimental impacts of the competition-everywhere-at-all-costs approach we see writ large in our world is that even when we get glimpses of how much it's failing us, we often feel powerless. So we continue on engaging rather than resisting, even if in our gut we know it isn't sustainable.

We looked at the impact of stress and burnout in our workplaces in the previous chapter. On a societal level, competition is also driving apart our communities and forcing us to go alone in various aspects of our lives that, for centuries, we've engaged in communally. In 2024 the US surgeon general sounded the alarm on how *parental* stress is a serious public health issue. Parents of all genders now work significantly more hours than in 1985 but also spend many more hours every week on childcare. As Murthy wrote in his health advisory, "Demands from both work and child caregiving have come at the cost of quality time with one's partner, sleep, and parental leisure time."

The report also cites how a "culture of comparison" around milestones, parenting, and achievements "has left many families feeling exhausted, burned out, and perpetually behind." Along with previous research on the loneliness epidemic in America, this advisory emphasizes how parents need societal support and connection to combat the isolation and stress of parenting. As someone who has often felt this pressure intimately and acutely and talked to other caregivers about this, I know for sure that our *choices, actions,* and *resistance of prevailing norms* can really make a difference in addressing this crisis.

Indeed, the competition/comparison pressure that parents feel can start early. If a family prioritizes their child's elite college education from birth, they'll be "wrapped up in the competition created by the education's instrumental value," argues Daniel Markovits in *The Atlantic.* The pitfalls of the competition required to get into an elite institution are clear: If it takes serious money to be able to attend—and in fact even to prepare to attend—then only people with privilege are guaranteed a lifetime's access to the education needed to win. I saw this firsthand when I attended elite institutions and even when I made inquiries at private schools for my son—the implicit message is often that financial donations supersede academic merit.

Competition even affects the very purpose of academic institutions. The same *Atlantic* article points out how the quality and purpose of education are eroded when college administrators are "perpetually insecure" about their college's rankings if they're not among the small handful of elite institutions—so much so, they often hire rankings consultants to tell them how to improve. This doesn't often serve any educational purpose. Then there's the fact that a competitive education frequently doesn't encourage or equip students with skills that serve in the public interest.

Students often study subjects that will bring them high salaries and prestige, careers that further private interests, not public ones. I think of this every time I hear of the financial woes faced by the various childcare professionals I've interacted with throughout my son's life—from day-care workers to elementary school teachers—who are often steps away from financial insecurity despite working long hours and putting in such hard work. Overall, competition in education erodes the purpose of education, moving it from learning to status seeking. The answer isn't to improve testing or ranking; the competitive hierarchy created and served by these mechanisms is the problem itself. We're trapped by a social and economic order that prizes and rewards "extravagantly" educated workers. As a result, so many high-achieving students are trapped in relentless competition to attain superiority, which is often meaningless to advancing humanity or our society.

Here's the quandary: I don't have a definitive answer on how to opt out. I'm not going to guide my child to forgo college or a lucrative career. I accept that both college and jobs that required diligence were necessary to my growth and sense of self. But my fervent hope is that competition doesn't overpower every facet of his life the way it did mine. I especially wish for him not to spend most of his early life believing he's powerless to choose a different way or that the measure of his self-worth is dictated by which college he gets into or how much money he makes, especially at the cost of his own happiness and relationships with others, which is par for the course in a competitive system.

This is the big picture of what's at stake when billions of individuals are taught to live this way: We begin to stop seeing one another through the lens of collective humanity.

Where I live in Seattle, Amazon's shiny headquarters in the South Lake Union area are hard to miss—complete with three giant spheres showcasing exotic plants, which are part of the company's $4 billion "urban campus." Although many of the white-collar employees who work in these buildings—including, admittedly, members of my family who are former employees—have earned much money from this technology behemoth, we're urged to ignore the plight of janitorial staff, delivery workers, and other non-white-collar workers who work for the same company but don't have access to the same benefits. There are reports of Amazon delivery workers who don't have enough time to use the bathroom lest they fall behind on delivering a customer's supply of hair gel on time. Yet most of us accept these inequities of modern corporations because we're conditioned to believe that those who struggle aren't working hard enough or are unfortunate to be collateral damage. We turn away, ignoring or even justifying the plight of other humans, resting on our beliefs in a zero-sum world. In this example and many others, competition deeply overlaps with entrenched inequality. The vast majority of these low-paid, overworked employees are people of color, while the senior leaders earning the highest salaries are overwhelmingly white.

The institutions we rely on every day—banking, education, government, and health care—are failing us by taking an individualistic, for-profit-at-all-costs approach. Take one example in health care. The United States has the highest rate of infant and maternal mortality among all other high-income countries despite spending the most on health care. One of the factors for this is the high rate of medically unnecessary C-sections. About a third of the ten thousand babies born each day in the United States are delivered via C-section, despite the World Health Organization's recommendation that this number be at 10 to 15 percent. Some experts say that the high number of C-sections that aren't medically necessary could be a result of doctors and hospitals being able to make more money than when babies are delivered vaginally.

In politics, the money pumped into winning competitions has reached astronomical levels. In the 2020 election, political spending was more than $14 billion, doubling the expenditure in the 2016 presidential election, making it the most expensive election cycle ever. When wealthy donors donate extensively to a political candidate's campaign, their issues are prioritized over the needs of the public, especially those who are most marginalized in our society. In 2024 CNN reported that the Foundation for Government Accountability, which is backed by conservative billionaires, "worked with legislators and elected officials to push for laws to deregulate child labor, stop Medicaid expansion and slash food stamps, among other initiatives." Since the 2020 presidential election, the same group has pushed to advance voting restrictions in order to benefit Republican candidates.

A similar thread binds these examples: When we make decisions solely motivated by money and individual or small-group wins, we most often do so at the expense of a larger community.

On a global scale, I'm afraid that the news isn't much better. Competition is inherently responsible for destabilizing regions, climate change, and a host of other devastating crises. An area I often think about is how close to the brink of climate destruction we are right now because of these same competition-at-all-costs, scarcity approaches that have characterized the colonization of most of the world. I feel this acutely, terrified about the planet my son will inhabit when he's older. It is impossible to explain to him why more leaders aren't collaborating on a solution.

One day, my son came home from school telling me about a quiz he had on the climate: "Mum, true or false, the island of garbage floating in the ocean is two times bigger than France." I answered *false* because I thought the island wouldn't be that big . . . but I'm sad that I was right. The answer is *false* not because the island is smaller than France but because it's closer to three times larger.

Despite large-scale global warnings from scientists since at least the 1970s about the impact of climate change, our competitive goals of outdoing the scale of production of other countries have led to irreversible damage to our planet. Humans are responsible for heating up the world faster now than at any point in history, with coal, oil, and gas accounting for more than 75 percent of global greenhouse-gas emissions and nearly 90 percent of all carbon-dioxide emissions. What's ironic is we actually do have a scarcity of climate resources now because of deforestation and consumption. Yet in this area where we should be preciously guarding what little we have left of the planet, modern humans continue to pillage the Earth as if there's an endless supply of it. And those who have the most power to work together to reduce climate change are its biggest pollutants. The richest 1 percent of the global population combined accounts for more greenhouse-gas emissions than the poorest 50 percent, according to the United Nations.

Climate change affects every single one of us. And even though many countries have "philosophically," or for good PR's sake, signed up to collaborate to reduce climate change, very few concrete steps have been taken to save our planet. The focus on competing with other nations at all costs to produce more, exploit more, and make more profit still supersedes the very real threat of climate-driven extinction. If there was ever a stronger case to be made for us to opt out of competition, this would be it. We are truly driving ourselves to the brink of extinction by choosing competition over collaboration.

Without a hefty wake-up call, I doubt we'd ever truly accept the notion that competition does more harm than good and dedicate ourselves to change. The despair that bubbles up when we're face-to-face with a grim reality like this one can be complicated and overwhelming. Dealing with these emotions is difficult because we've been taught to believe that nothing can be done. The competition-driven system that's in place at work and everywhere else we exist is too ingrained in Western society to be uprooted.

The good news is it's not too late to alter our course and embrace uncompete as a philosophy and strategy. We are not powerless, even if it's us choosing to uncompete as a group of individuals in the face of a society that doesn't make this choice. Because even if only a small group of individuals begins to uncompete, we'll be happier, healthier, and more prosperous for generations to come.

EXAMPLES OF UNCOMPETING AROUND US

When I was a surly thirteen-year-old, my mum took me to a small temple a few miles away from where we lived. "This is a gurdwara, where Sikhs come to pray. We're going there to pray, then eat lunch."

Eat at a temple? This wasn't customary in the Hindu temples we would frequent; there'd be a small offering of prashad, a (usually) sweet offering made for the gods, that we could have a small handful of after prayers. "We're here for langar," she said.

As I learned that day, langar was a communal kitchen where anyone, regardless of religion, race, or caste (it was set up in direct opposition to the Hindu customs, which forbade eating alongside people of different castes), could eat a free meal prepared by volunteers. This beautiful practice started with the birth of Sikhism in the fifteenth century and endures the world over. I highly recommend finding your closest gurdwara and experiencing the beauty of it yourself—usually on Sundays. Having volunteered in a soup kitchen attached to a Christian church in the past, I realized it's not the same concept as langar. At langar, everyone eats side by side, regardless of wealth. It isn't about charity, necessarily, but about community and the idea that everyone has a right to sit communally and enjoy the same food.

My jaded, angsty teenage self was duly humbled. And as I dug into that day's delicious langar, sitting at a large communal table with people from all walks of life in every direction—I can still smell the earthiness of the chole nearly twenty-five years later—I thought to myself: *What if more of us could see one another as a community? In competition-obsessed Singapore, where so many people in my community were about showing off their latest car or children's achievements or who-married-who, there was a tradition alive of making sure no person was denied food or dignity?* Wow. Suffice to say, that formative experience remains imprinted on my mind.

Now, of course, this is one among many non-Western traditions and approaches that remain obscured from the mainstream narrative. But even in corporate workplaces, I've seen the power of uncompete in action.

Years ago, I worked with an organization that was putting in place a "sponsorship" program that would match high-potential women and people of color with company leaders (who were largely white and male). The organization wanted to diversify its leadership team and address the issue of women and people of color lacking access to senior leaders.

After their CEO, John, announced the program with much fanfare, he returned to his office and found a long email addressed to him, his chief HR officer, and his chief legal officer with the title "Lowering the Bar with Reverse Discrimination?" A group of white male managers who weren't quite in high leadership positions expressed concerns that this sponsorship program would unfairly promote women and people of color who weren't the best candidates for the jobs, thereby lowering the high standards at the company. They were also worried it would disadvantage candidates who were the best qualified for leadership roles, like themselves, just because they were white and male.

John and his C-suite team realized that they hadn't communicated fully about *why* this program needed to exist—including outlining the systemic barriers to leadership that women and people of color had long faced at the organization. They also needed to communicate that their commitment to diversify their leadership teams wasn't going to come at the cost of letting current leaders go or having existing leaders compete with new candidates for existing roles. Their plan was always to add more new roles to the leadership teams *and* expand the table.

John and his team decided to hold an additional town hall to explain their strategy in detail. He also specifically talked about why the program needed to exist, including how employees from marginalized backgrounds often faced biases such as being erroneously considered "a diversity hire." He answered questions and challenges patiently, all while reiterating how important this program was to him personally and how deeply he believed in creating a diverse, equitable, and inclusive workplace for all.

Not everyone got it, and some managers resigned. But many did learn something new that day. And years later, because of successfully expanding and diversifying their leadership teams, the organization has found that workloads are more equitably distributed, which safeguards against burnout for all while also creating a more inclusive and welcoming culture for employees at *every* level. The sponsorship program created a diverse pipeline of leaders while also breaking down silos between all levels. In my DEI work, true change begins when people stop focusing on the zero-sum thinking that pits them against others and instead use their privilege to take responsibility for creating a more equitable workplace and world.

In every case, deliberate choice and action are necessary because the ubiquity of competition everywhere doesn't make it probable or easy to uncompete. It's still easier in every way to compete than to uncompete, but in choosing a different way, sea-level change is possible. Sikhism's langar tradition was born in direct opposition to the caste discrimination rampant in the Hindu traditions of that time (and still alive today). Sikhism is now the fifth-largest religion in the world. In corporations, when leaders like John stand up for DEI and reframe it not as an "us versus them" issue but one that would benefit all, they help people understand it isn't the norm, but it is a rising tide that lifts *all* boats, not just for marginalized employees.

Even in education, there can be another way. As I mentioned earlier, the competition I see among parents regarding their kids' education has been an area where even the most uncompetitive of the people I know harbor zero chill. The stakes feel so high that choosing to opt out of competition seems to mean sacrificing your child's chances of success in life. Many parents are caught in the pendulum between feeling burned out by the competitive approach rampant in education today and being fearful of choosing an alternative that could ruin their kids' chances later on.

Reading about the educational philosophy of Maria Montessori, who also happened to be the first female physician in Italy, provided an inspiring alternative to the rankings-based, competitive approach I've seen everywhere. Montessori was a badass feminist who opposed the fascist regime of 1930s Italy and set up a new method of eponymously named preschool education that focused on the principle that children should not be forced to conform to a scheduled, predetermined curriculum. Instead, she believed that young children should be able to move and act as they wished, play with what sparked their creativity and curiosity, with teachers acting as guides without direction or coercion. Montessori education also prioritizes collaboration, with classrooms set up to encompass children of different ages so that everyone can learn from one another. Most of all, there are no tests or grades, which also avoids competition. Since the introduction of Montessori schools more than a century ago, there's evidence that the unstructured time, allowing children to explore their interests, and collaborative principles have contributed to fostering the rise of people who later become technology innovators, artists, and political leaders. A caveat is that, especially in the United States, the Montessori education system has become largely expensive and exclusive, so even though its principles are beautiful and inclusive in theory, in a competitive world they've been co-opted to largely benefit a smaller elite. In a society where we uncompete, I envision that the "best" of everything wouldn't be guarded and monetized to benefit only the wealthy, but would be widely available to all.

Of course, as I read more about Native and Indigenous traditions the world over—ones that were woefully absent from any formal education I've received—I simultaneously feel deeply hopeful and heartbroken. Many precolonial Indigenous traditions throughout the world—dating back thousands of years—have considered conserving the Earth and making decisions based on preserving and cultivating biodiversity a necessity. In our Western, shareholder-value-driven culture, little thought is given to the long-term environmental impacts of clearing out ancient lands or wiping out biodiversity or building factories. Competition to grow, "innovate," and dominate beats out climate considerations. On the other hand, Indigenous communities treat respect for nature as foundational to livelihoods and creating belonging, in direct contrast to the Western, capitalistic, profit-at-all-costs approach. Indigenous-controlled lands are better conserved than even Western-controlled (stolen) national parks and forests, and studies find that their territories harbor more biodiversity than (Western) protected areas in Brazil, Australia, and Canada. Close to 36 percent of the world's remaining intact forest landscapes are contained within Indigenous territories. In fact, some Western (or formerly colonized) governments in different parts of the world are now trying to learn from these ancient traditions in an effort to reverse damage or at least to avoid any more. My hope is that, although this movement is very, very belated, it's not too late to learn from Indigenous land traditions and stewardship. Our planet depends on it. When communities view the Earth as sacred, not simply something that is necessary to exploit and destroy for competitive endeavors, everyone benefits.

TO UNCOMPETE IS A PERSONAL COMMITMENT

In 2016 I was sitting at my favorite neighborhood coffee shop on yet another gray Seattle day. My three-month-old son, Veer, was napping in his stroller next to me, his little eyelashes fluttering while he slept. As anyone who has been around an infant extensively will know, the days and nights stretch endlessly. But during quiet moments like this—when I could just stare and marvel at him—I couldn't believe how lucky I was.

This little excursion to the café was also the first time in weeks that I'd been out of the house and alone with my thoughts. I was eager to catch up on what was happening in my corner of the world. So with a delicious steaming cortado in one hand and my phone in the other, I logged onto Facebook. (This was 2016, friends!) I scrolled through the feeds of acquaintances, friends, and colleagues.

My friend from college had just posted a link to her recent TED Talk on how to be a successful, ambitious "girl boss" in a traditionally male-dominated field. It was creeping up to nearly a million views.

Another friend had shared a photo of herself at an award ceremony, where she was named one of the most inspirational women in her industry.

A former coworker had announced that a feature article she'd written for *The New York Times* was going viral.

It didn't take long for total panic to set in.

A few minutes before, I was a content (yet exhausted) mother on maternity leave who was enjoying her first peaceful afternoon coffee in weeks. But after seeing other people revel in their recent professional accomplishments and big leaps in their careers, I was feeling insecure, left behind, and unimportant. It didn't matter that I had impressive achievements of my own. The time off I was taking to connect with my child seemed like a huge mistake that I would later regret. I even considered going back to work early so I could close the distance between me and my peers. I just couldn't bear the thought of falling short of expectations—mine or anyone else's.

I was about to rush back home and log into my work email when Veer started to stir. I looked over at him, and he was smiling at me. I wish I could say that his precious face melted my heart and that all my worries vanished into thin air.

If anything, my thoughts spiraled even more.

Now that I'm a mother, what if I can't compete? What if my company fails? How will we survive?

It wasn't until I put Veer down for the night that I tried to unpack my emotions. I tried to blame my mini freakout on social media. But if I was honest with myself, this wasn't the first time I'd felt stressed out about falling behind. Whenever I went on vacation or was out sick or had to take a personal day, I would often feel this persistent uneasiness that I was falling behind. My mind was constantly contemplating how much ground I was going to lose and how much further a colleague or competitor might go while I was away. Even at the end of a regular business day, when my head hit my pillow, I was still concerned that someone, somewhere, was emailing me about something critical. And if I didn't answer it right now, I'd lose my client's trust, and they would move on.

Then it struck me. When I was working, I was thinking about getting ahead, being competitive, and achieving success. And when I wasn't working, I was thinking about the same damn things. It was bizarre how much time I spent worrying about my *life* interfering with my *work*, but I couldn't help myself. If I wasn't ambitious and didn't compete, I might not succeed.

And with a child to raise, the stakes were way too high.

This is all to say that my raison d'être for this book isn't to claim that I've magically stopped competing or that I automatically opt out of competition; on the contrary, I often struggle with defaulting to a competition mindset. But becoming aware of it has allowed me to press pause more often and ask myself where these ideas come from and whether they're true. At its core, uncompeting isn't about being perfect but about being intentional. As a woman, a person of color, an immigrant, and a mother, I know that to uncompete is a radical way I can create equity and change for myself and for others marginalized by our society.

I want to acknowledge that because competition is the only water most of us have been taught to swim in—the approach most easily available—the idea of choosing a different way feels so risky. The journey to uncompete takes deep reflection and commitment. Intentionality before action. Long before we choose to take any action or even resist the norms we've been conditioned to believe, to uncompete requires us to reframe long-held beliefs about the need for competition and ask ourselves why we may even want to choose a different way. Only once we begin to decolonize our minds can we make true change.

CHAPTER THREE

Reset Our Mindset

My mother—the most intelligent person I know—was prevented from pursuing a career outside the home after her arranged marriage at the age of twenty-one. So, when she had me at twenty-two, she devoted her life to being a mother. What inspired me as a child was how little she cared about the hierarchy and classism rampant in our society (and the South Asian diaspora) and how she actively railed against it in all the ways she could, given the pressures and oppressions she faced within a traditional society. I remember her looking everyone in the eyes and talking to each person with equal regard and respect. This was particularly noticeable in her treatment of people society typically overlooks, from janitors to elderly people to people with mental disabilities. Above all, she did everything she could to raise me and my two siblings with the idea that community—not competition—is the foundation of a healthy society. She also valued the joy and comfort that we experience in our relationships more than the temporary thrill we get from material things and status symbols. So it should come as no surprise to you that my mum always discouraged her children from competing with one another as well as with the kids at school.

I remember a time when I was fourteen and my family was invited to a gathering of fellow Singaporean Indians from our community. I already dreaded these events, knowing my taller-than-average, larger-than-acceptable body would be the subject of conversation. The Indian aunties had no trouble couching their cruel comments as "concern."

As we walked into this room of about seventy-five people, I could see one of the meanest aunties making a beeline for us. My heart pounded furiously, and I wished the ground would swallow me up. I could already see the comments about my adolescent weight gain churning in her mind. Her beady eyes were fixed on me.

"Seema!" she trilled as she saw my mother. "Wow! Look at Rashi!" She pointed and smiled at my eleven-year-old sister. "She's *so* slim and beautiful. Like a model!" Then she quickly turned her gaze to me, looked at me pointedly, her mouth about to form disparaging words of comparison about how I was the exact opposite of my sister.

My mother quickly jumped in. "Hi! Yes, thank you! I'm so proud of both my girls. Enjoy the party!" She then turned on her heel and walked away holding both our hands, choosing to ignore the auntie in question for the rest of the gathering. I can still remember every detail of that encounter, decades later. Sadly, this wasn't a one-off, not by a long shot. It's not an exaggeration to say that every time she made it known that comparison among us siblings—particularly between my sister and me, who were close in age and often subjected to impossible beauty standards common in our community—was unwelcome, I felt less likely to compare us even in our minds.

She carried her "together we rise" attitude everywhere she went. I remember that even when she'd hear gossip or disparaging comments about others—a quintessential part of the Indian society—she'd refuse to pass it on and would most often defend the person being disparaged. Did this make her less fun at parties in others' eyes? Possibly. But she became well-known among all who knew her for her generosity, kindness, and community-building approach.

She never saw any of her attempts to lift others up as sacrifices because her view was (and still is) that we live in a world of abundance. My mother's efforts to boost someone's confidence or give them a flying start when they couldn't take off on their own never came at her own expense. In her mind, there was plenty of room for all of us to be who we are, do what we love, and live in harmony.

I have to admit, when I look back on my childhood, I wonder how she developed these beliefs, given all the messages she received growing up. Her life's philosophy and actions flew in the face of the culture I often saw in Singapore, certainly the US culture I live in now, as well as the Indian immigrant diaspora, which are all deeply competitive. She was exposed to all the same propaganda and conditioning that her contemporaries encountered, but somehow, some way, she was able to escape from its clutches.

In writing this book, I realized that my mum isn't an outlier, although I imagine she has often felt like one. She's one of a litany of women around the globe, past and present, who have gone against the grain of outdated, exploitative social doctrines and helped themselves and their communities ascend from the ashes. From Sarojini Naidu and

Rosa Parks to Wangari Maathai and Michelle Obama, women have a long history of bringing people together and sparking a sea change that ripples out and touches everyone. Many in the public eye, like the ones I've named above. Some, like my mum, in quiet and unsuspecting but no less meaningful ways. Even though they came from different backgrounds, these women were all motivated by the same belief—that the success of a precious few means nothing if everyone else is suffering.

To follow the path of these brazen, courageous leaders, we sometimes need to pivot away from what we've been taught—in school by our educators, at home by our families, on the street by strangers—and adopt a new ideology. Change *is* possible, but importantly, we must believe that change starts with us and choose to take action.

All of that begins with a change in our mindset. We must do the challenging yet necessary internal work that will shift our perspective and raise our consciousness. Here's what the evolution could look like.

It starts by flipping the script from one of competition as a default to mindfully choosing to uncompete.

When we compete, we <u>submit</u> to:

- Accept, without question, our conditioning.
- Follow rules that help the few and harm the majority.
- Do what's expected, regardless of how it makes us feel or what we believe is right.

When we uncompete, we <u>decide</u> to:

- Examine and, where relevant, work to unlearn our conditioning.

- Write new rules that lift everyone up.

- Align our choices and actions with our values and live with integrity.

The biggest difference is that of making an active choice. A competition mindset is about submitting to, upholding, and perpetuating the status quo. When we uncompete, we consciously, intentionally, and mindfully choose to reject competition as an all-encompassing approach to life. The work begins by rewiring our minds: how we perceive the world and ourselves, what we believe to be true, what we focus our time and attention on, which in turn drive us to compete or uncompete in every situation.

WRITING NEW RULES
THAT LIFT EVERYONE UP

The idea here is to begin shifting our mindset so that we see and pay attention to the possibilities that uncompeting will bring into our lives. What this means is rewriting the narrative we've been conditioned to believe about competition and learning to critically evaluate whether it serves us and enriches us. In most cases, competition does not. Instead, we must begin to see that the beliefs we've upheld about competition as the water we swim in are actually like the sand in a mirage.

We can work toward rewriting the rules of competition by creating the **principles** by which we uncompete.

~~We're Hardwired to Compete~~
Competition Is a Choice; Collaboration
Is a Better One

Collaboration builds trust, but competition erodes it. Both are choices, not hardwired default settings. And although it's more socially acceptable in today's world to choose competition (even seemingly unconsciously), choosing collaboration leads to more opportunities. Collaboration creates safe spaces for us to share our opinions freely, while competition takes us into hostile territory where the flames of our fears are fanned. Collaboration is what happens in a community to make it stronger for all. Competition is what happens on a battleground to give the "winner" total control. To begin thinking differently about collaboration, we must start to believe that our happiness and success are not individual endeavors.

To reframe individualistic ideals isn't easy at all, especially for people in Western societies and workplaces. Despite growing up in a generally collectivistic culture in Singapore, the minute I set foot in my first Western corporate workplace, I immediately knew, in my bones, that what mattered most was my individual gains. It became crystal clear to me that to win, I had to see my peers as competition, not as part of my community. When I moved to the United States, this idea of individual success, no matter how much others were struggling around you, was cemented. The United States has the most individualist culture I've ever been in (and globally it's ranked as the most individualistic nation). Behavioral scientists see individualism as correlating with values like autonomy, self-expression, and personal goals instead of valuing and prioritizing group interests, like the family, community, country, or society.

But it's harming everyone, especially those already marginalized. Individualism is one of the fifteen tenets of white-supremacy culture named by Dr. Tema Okun, a DEI consultant in the 1990s who sought to identify some of the largest challenges to creating an inclusive culture. Over thirty years ago, Okun wrote how individualism in organizations shows up when "competition [is] more highly valued than cooperation and where cooperation is valued, little time or resources devoted to developing skills in how to cooperate."

To begin to undo the loneliness, parenting stress, and other mental health crises we see in our world today, we must begin to choose cooperation, collaboration, and connection as central, not as an afterthought in our lives.

Although many of our workplaces don't easily encourage collaboration (no matter the pithy marketing copy written on the company website), I believe it can be a key tool when we use it thoughtfully. Several professional women I interviewed for this book talked about collaborating and sharing resources even when it was actively discouraged—such as alerting their peers about salary numbers or tips to succeed when being put up for promotion. I've seen the power of identity-based employee resource groups at organizations, particularly in forming connections and banding together to create a more inclusive workplace for marginalized employees.

To be clear, this doesn't happen naturally: It takes intentionality, especially in working to dismantle the idea that competition is part of our DNA and that it's not personally beneficial to collaborate. One example is the way that the US women's soccer team banded together over five years to demand pay equality with players on the national men's team. The national women's soccer team came together to sue its employer, the US Soccer Federation, in the first gender-pay-inequality lawsuit of its kind in professional sports. What started in 2016 as a lawsuit by five female players turned into a class-action lawsuit in 2019 with all twenty-eight players participating, and later on, even the US men's soccer team showed solidarity by calling on fans to withdraw support from the federation's sponsors until equality was reached. The federation finally agreed to a landmark $24 million agreement that would award tens of millions of dollars in back pay owed to female players and now requires equal pay for all tournaments and the World Cup.

Despite playing at the highest levels of competition on the soccer field, the women's team knew that competition off the field, particularly with one another, doesn't work to build equality or justice. For that, collaboration is the answer.

One of the main goals of uncompete is to collectively pool our resources and work together to improve, grow, and lead the way for others so that they might do the same. Believing in the power of collaboration and actively choosing it are vital to changing an ingrained view that competition is a fixed point that we can never steer away from because our biological instincts won't let us. In the previous chapter, we also saw that collaboration has helped entire societies to flourish because they leveraged their collective assets. If we follow in their footsteps instead of holding on to the belief that only the fittest survive in this world, we'll be able to uncompete more easily.

~~Competition Brings Out the Best in Us and the World~~
Inclusion Is the Best Way to Build a Future for All

We believe that, like cream, the best ideas will rise to the top. That the playing field is level and through contests and competitions, innovation is assured. But as my life's work has shown, meritocracy is a myth, and competition often fortifies existing inequities in society. Instead, I see true inclusion as the antidote to this harmful and false narrative. When we are inclusive, we recognize that all voices aren't afforded an equal opportunity to succeed in our world today, and we all are responsible for bringing in the perspectives of those most marginalized. True inclusion requires us to seek out and understand the diverse and unique perspectives of different people and to make space to include all of them. This doesn't, as anyone in social justice and equity practice will tell you, come easily. In fact, true inclusion is filled with friction. Trying to make room for everyone to share their opinion and perspective and come to a consensus that benefits everyone is *really* challenging. But when we see the benefit of learning and understanding perspectives we may not have seen before—particularly from underestimated and historically excluded people—that challenge is worth it. Inclusion requires us to intentionally look for the voices that are most marginalized and left out, and to center them. It's pushing back against "in-group" dynamics, where we want only people like us to prosper, and instead believing that every voice in the group has value.

One powerful way I've seen inclusion built in workplace settings is having leaders who are committed to creating, supporting, and funding affinity groups. This requires us to reject the more prevalent norm of "my group loses out if your group advances." Supporting and propelling affinity groups and other belonging-focused initiatives can help create inclusion and community and weed out the competitive, zero-sum approaches so normalized in our workplaces. I believe that when more of us are committed to inclusion, we're able to see one another as humans who have shared humanity across identities and differences. It's only through fully understanding how many amazing people have been left out of innovation for decades because of systemic oppression and inequality that we can begin to undo the idea that competition brings out the best in all of us. In truth, as I've previously described, our current system too often privileges those with influence already, leaving marginalized groups out of the arena or left to fight over scraps. I know for sure that we could be building a better future for all if we all got a chance to have a say in it.

~~There's Only Limited Success to Go Around~~ *I Choose an Abundance Mindset*

An abundance mindset is the belief that there are enough resources for all of us, so there is no need to compete for them. A scarcity mindset drives us to compete, but an abundance mindset is foundational to uncompete. It can take hard work and intentionality to cultivate an abundance mindset. But when we do, this mindset translates to behaviors that show that even in situations where two or more parties have a common goal, there's a way for all parties to win. An abundance mindset guides us to uncompete because we are driven to be empathetic and work toward building and redistributing resources beyond just ourselves.

86

Reset Our Mindset

Psychotherapist Sahaj Kaur Kohli advises us to do this by noticing and becoming aware of our automatic thoughts. Noticing your thoughts, literally being mindful as they appear, allows you to question your beliefs, asking whether those thoughts are true or if they could perhaps be replaced with a different perspective. If a work colleague wants to join a project you're working on, an automatic thought might be that they might outshine you and take all the credit. But if you can notice the automatic thought and reframe it, believing instead that they want to collaborate and that there's enough room for both of you to work and succeed, then that is taking on an abundance mindset. An abundance mindset can help you see connections, broaden your perspective, solve problems, and make decisions that will benefit you in the long term—even when your resources are low.

An abundance mindset is also one where you open up yourself to the opportunity and possibility of what could be, Sahaj tells me. It can positively affect your mental health because you start to see yourself and the world differently when you have an abundance mindset. When Sahaj was in graduate school, she was asked to deliver a TED Talk. She really wanted to speak at TED because she thought that was the ultimate way to be successful in her career, and these limited opportunities are very hard to come by. But she was also really, really stretched with her school commitments and knew it wasn't a good time for her to commit to the talk. Upon reflection, she realized she was operating from a scarcity mindset—although it wasn't the right time for her to commit to such a big endeavor, she felt she couldn't turn it down for fear it wouldn't come back ever again. It took her weeks of agonizing over the decision, but eventually she declined the invitation. She described to me the fears she felt about declining—particularly, the worry that she had lost an important opportunity that might never again materialize in her career. But once she was able to sit with that fear, recognizing the place of scarcity it came from, she could recognize that it would cause her more stress than joy to achieve this career goal right now, and even if the same speaking opportunity didn't come back around when she had more time, others would.

I'm sure we can all think of times we've had the same fears creep up, and if you're like me, you've often stretched yourself way too thin by giving in to the scarcity mindset, especially when you're worried that an opportunity will disappear if you take a beat to think it over. But when we slow down the faster-than-the-speed-of-light thinking process, consider whether there's truly a scarcity situation (rarely), and believe that there's an abundance of opportunities out there for us when the time is right, we begin to make the switch from a scarcity to an abundance mindset.

An abundance mindset isn't a checklist of thoughts or behaviors but an approach that stems from the belief that you are worthy and that taking small steps to create a life you dream of, at your own pace and no one else's, is worth doing. It's particularly necessary to do the work internally first, to be self-aware, to reflect on essential questions: *What do abundance and scarcity look like in my life today? Where do I truly have scarcity, and where is there abundance? How can I create more of it?*

A DEEPER DIVE INTO A SCARCITY VERSUS ABUNDANCE MINDSET

SCARCITY MINDSET	ABUNDANCE MINDSET
"I'm miserable in my job, but I better just stay on; there aren't enough jobs out there, and I'm not good enough to get chosen."	"Perhaps I'm not in the right workplace, one that aligns with my values. What do I need to feel aligned with my values at work, and what can I do to seek that?"
"I'm overwhelmed, but if I don't take this project now, my rival will get it, so I'll overwork, no matter the consequences."	"I'm overwhelmed and I'll need to decline it so I can do a stellar job on my current project. I'm glad my peer can take it off my plate."
"I'm exhausted, but if I don't exercise today, I'll never reach my health goals."	"I'm exhausted today and am going to rest. Reaching my health goals includes resting when I need it."
"I'm not sure about this person I'm in a romantic relationship with, but if I don't suck it up and make it work, I'll be alone, unlike all my friends, who are in relationships."	"I deserve to be happy and don't want to ignore what my gut is telling me about my partner. If that means not being in a romantic relationship right now, it doesn't mean I won't find the right partner if that's important to me."

"My elderly neighbor is struggling with their groceries, but if I stop to help, I can't pick up my favorite drive-thru coffee before work. They'll figure it out."	"I'm going to text my manager to explain the situation, and I'm sure they'll understand. If they don't, maybe this isn't the right place for me to work in the long term."
"My friend is so attractive. I'll never be that good-looking."	"I'm happy for them that they turn heads. I know there's no one way to be attractive, and I'm comfortable in my skin."

As the table illustrates, we can approach situations that typically bring out envy, competition, or fear in a different way. Of course, it's easier said than done and requires practice. But as Chinese philosopher Lao Tzu is attributed as saying back in 500 BCE, "Watch your thoughts, they become your words; watch your words, they become your actions; watch your actions, they become your habits; watch your habits, they become your character; watch your character, it becomes your destiny."

A science-backed recommendation about how to build a long-term abundance mindset is practicing gratitude. Gratitude helps you become more aware of what you do have, moving your focus and fixation away from what you don't. I'm always deeply encouraged and feel the emotional rewards when I take time to write down, reflect, and become aware of everything and everyone in my life I'm grateful for. At the same time, I'm cautious about how gratitude is often weaponized against women, especially women of color, who are expected to accept bias, racism, and/or oppression and still show gratitude. Gratitude is a powerful personal practice that helps develop an abundance mindset. But when certain people are expected to "perform" gratitude publicly to be accepted, that's never OK.

~~When Someone Else Wins, I'm Losing by Comparison~~ Winning Requires Radical Generosity

When we buy into the tenets of competition—zero-sum thinking in particular—generosity is rarely something that factors into our thought processes. We're too preoccupied with what we're accumulating and storing away for ourselves. Giving our time, energy, and even our wealth to someone else in need feels like taking away from resources for ourselves. But approaching situations with an abundance mindset—the core belief that there's enough of everything to go around—can help us make the mental leap toward radical generosity. And understanding how privilege factors into opportunities we have—for example, keeping in mind that financial privilege means we're not thinking about where our next meal is coming from—can help us transform our relationship to this idea of winning and losing in binaries. Being generous opens our hearts and establishes connections with others instead of closing us off. Radical generosity—a concept that's still being defined but is gaining traction in leadership circles—means giving openly without the expectation of return. And the action can flow only when we change our mindset by believing that opportunities are not zero-sum. That by helping a peer negotiate her salary or giving her business advice, you're not somehow automatically lowering your chances at success. It's not a winner-take-all situation where being generous to someone else somehow means you're sabotaging your own success. And even as I write this, it sounds ridiculous, but it's how so many of us operate, including me.

This, too, is hard. We've all had at least some experience of being burned: in relationships, in friendships, and by our colleagues. It's hard to trust others, especially if we've been betrayed or let down by people we thought would be generous to us. In those moments, it's justifiable to fall prey to the thought "If I didn't get the help I needed, why should I help someone else?" But this is precisely why radical generosity is so important—if we choose the competitive, zero-sum, scarcity approaches we've seen, we're perpetuating the problem further.

True radical generosity creates goodwill instead of suspicion, fosters understanding instead of resentment, and welcomes instead of threatens. Studies have shown that acts of generosity can be contagious and cause a ripple effect, where people pass on an unexpected, random gift of kindness right after receiving one from someone else.

In our work lives, radical generosity could mean mindfully pushing back against tropes like "women leaders as Queen Bees" and helping rather than ignoring or, worse (especially if we've experienced it earlier in our careers), sabotaging junior women coming up behind us. It could mean encouraging a colleague when they feel self-doubt before a big presentation because we believe that *everyone* deserves to be championed and that the ten minutes we spend on a pep talk, rather than on a project, is time well spent. Radical generosity could be teaching our minds that we have a part to play in creating a more inclusive culture that advances women, people of color, and other marginalized employees.

Even in industries like philanthropy, faux generosity is often mistaken for radical generosity. One pervasive issue that my friends in the industry tell me about is how donors write big checks to nonprofits but often fund only nonprofits that are run by white leaders, not by leaders serving communities like their own, thus reinforcing white supremacy in society through (seemingly positive) philanthropy. This is faux generosity: operating within the confines of a system that hasn't revolutionized making change for marginalized groups. But true radical generosity often requires us to think outside the box and to use our privilege to give to and uplift people and communities most harmed by the system.

One example of radical generosity is billionaire philanthropist MacKenzie Scott's approach to giving. Since she began giving away billions of dollars in 2019, Scott and her team have researched and selected organizations that are making significant community impact and provided them with large, unrestricted donations. There is no application process. Out of the blue, Scott's team identifies a nonprofit and writes it a check without any restrictions on how those funds should be used. There's no big press announcement and no cumbersome application or reporting process (which too often excludes smaller community-led nonprofits from applying for or receiving grants). As of writing this in 2025, Scott has given away more than $19 billion to 2,450 nonprofits. I have heard firsthand from a few women-of-color beneficiaries that the process is truly a radical departure from how philanthropy has long been gate-kept by white, usually male donors.

Moreover, Scott's beneficiary organizations are small, run by leaders of color, and serve communities affected by racism. Without having any firsthand knowledge of Scott or her team's giving strategy, I imagine her approach was basically this: "The way the experts tell us to give money isn't really making a change. Let's shake things up radically." And the ensuing action flowed.

Radical generosity isn't a "soft skill." It is a mighty agent of change that can overturn the idea of the win-lose, zero-sum equation. When radical generosity is practiced at scale, it can be pretty damn, well, radical.

~~Competition Is Inevitable~~
Solidarity Is Necessary

Most of us—whether we know it or not—subscribe to the idea that "I don't need to get involved unless it affects me." To uncompete means that we must reframe our minds to believe that our collective success lies in advancing people who have been most marginalized in our society. Even if—*especially* if—we don't share the exact same grievances. Put simply, we should not want to create equality for parents only if we are parents, we shouldn't just engage in the fight for gender equality because we identify as women, and not only people of color need to work to create racial equality.

In their book *Solidarity: The Past, Present, and Future of a World-Changing Idea*, authors Leah Hunt-Hendrix and Astra Taylor define solidarity as "the recognition of our inherent interconnectedness and an attempt to create bonds of commonality across differences." They also go on to say that "solidarity depends on difference, on recogniz-

94

ing that we are all not exactly alike, but we can still come together and take collective action."

Solidarity can magnify itself beyond our immediate lives and even work to repair generational bias. In 1939 a Black couple, Gus and Emma Thompson, agreed to rent and eventually sell their home to the Dongs, a Chinese American family in Coronado, California. No one else in the neighborhood would rent or sell to Asian families because of racially restrictive laws that favored white buyers and families. But the Thompsons' solidarity with the Dongs changed the trajectory of their lives and all the generations that came after. In 2024 the Dongs announced they were donating $5 million to Black college students using proceeds from the sale of the house and the eight-unit apartment complex next door as a way to thank the Thompsons for helping them get established in American society. This is just one example of how solidarity can help us pay it forward for generations to come.

On the world's stage, solidarity has been the bedrock of political activism. In recent years we've seen communities of all stripes quickly organize to render aid on a global scale via social media. Thousands of miles away from the Middle East, I've seen antiwar protests shut down major US cities during Israel's war on Gaza. During the summer of 2020, after the tragic murder of George Floyd, among others, we saw protests against anti-Blackness and police brutality on a global scale. The actions of non-Black people vehemently standing up for Black rights and non-Palestinians protesting for the rights of innocent people in a faraway country were built on solidarity.

Global corporations have also aligned with and pledged funds in solidarity with social justice movements. In many cases, this is for branding purposes, mind you, but we can't discount the possibility of social change when powerful people speak up. In 2020 we saw multimillion-dollar pledges for racial justice from hundreds of large corporations around the United States. Although not all have materialized and some have even pulled back amid growing DEI backlash (zero-sum thinking strikes again!), we have seen some meaningful gains, including 94 percent of three hundred thousand new jobs in the S&P 100 going to people of color in 2021. I don't want to paint a rosy picture; many promises remain unfulfilled, and momentum has certainly been lost from the height of the 2020 reckoning. But when I started my DEI consultancy in 2017, companies overwhelmingly either didn't want me to address racism or preferred that I talked only about gender diversity without mentioning race. That has thankfully changed because more white people recognize and accept that racism affects diversity, equity, and inclusion in every way—and that societal progress for all of us depends on solidarity.

Solidarity is how we show up for our colleagues, friends, and families who need our support to gain access to benefits we've been given but they've been denied, to feel safe in places where we're secure and they're a target, and in a host of other dynamics where we might hold more privilege. I've seen this in meetings where men stop men who interrupt women by saying things like "Tom, you cut Ruchika off. I'd like to hear what she was saying." I've also noticed this among some of my cisgender students who have told me they use they/them pronouns to normalize these gender pronouns, especially so that all the burden wouldn't rest on their trans, nonbinary, and gender nonconforming peers. Solidarity can be practiced in small but meaningful ways, such as reminding someone not to say "guys" to include people of all genders or actively pushing back when a colleague makes a sexist or racist "joke" by saying something like "I don't think that's funny" or "We like to include everyone here."

Solidarity is also achievable when we're all on equal ground and join forces to seek justice and advocate for one another when our true worth isn't recognized. Former Indian national cricket team captain Rahul Dravid turned down nearly $300,000 that he was awarded as bonus prize money for coaching the national team to win the T20 Cricket World Cup in 2024. He opted instead to accept only what the other support staff on his team would be awarded. Solidarity can mean pushing back against a system that was designed to create a hierarchy among team members, as this example from Dravid highlights. We can take a similar approach when our manager praises us for work done by sharing credit with other teammates who supported us, rather than taking sole ownership. I know our corporate culture isn't set up this way, but this is where we can actively choose solidarity over the divide-and-conquer approach.

Only when we can push back against ingrained beliefs about success and operate with new principles can we begin aligning intention with action. When we uncompete, all of our choices—big or small—are made from a place of deeply understanding why the existing narrative that we've bought into and that we consciously or subconsciously uphold isn't working for most of us.

What we begin to create is a world where *re*written beliefs, the principles of uncompete—collaboration, inclusion, radical generosity, abundance, and solidarity—are prioritized and start to become the norm. Simultaneously, we *reject* the old competitive beliefs. If a situation requires us to engage in competitive behaviors, we need to be discerning about the cost versus benefit to our own physical and emotional well-being and to our community and society at large. This is extremely challenging because the system is designed for us to believe that competition and scarcity (and all the rules I've spent the last few chapters trying to rewrite) are just the way things are. You may even be treated with suspicion about an "ulterior motive" or be ostracized for choosing a different way. But there comes a point when you simply can't unsee the deleterious impact of competition and scarcity in your life and the lives of those around you.

And even when you feel powerless, defeated, and exhausted, I promise you that choosing to uncompete is worth it in the long run. At the end of the day, the rules of competition are so deeply programmed in us that most of us uphold them on autopilot. Meanwhile, to uncompete seems unnatural within the confines of society today. But as I live my life trying to operate with the uncompete principles—to approach situations intentionally choosing collaboration, inclusion, an abundance mindset, radical generosity, and solidarity—I've found an unexpected benefit.

I now have more agency over my "lizard brain" and a better grasp on understanding my emotions. This doesn't mean I don't compare myself to others or never feel envious (the next chapter will illustrate quite the opposite), but I've found that when I can name what's going through my mind—*This is scarcity thinking! Am I approaching this from a zero-sum lens? Did I just observe someone trying to divide and conquer us?*—I'm more likely to take a pause, reflect on a situation before taking immediate action or saying something I'll later regret, and use that space between stimulus and response to have a little more control over my mind and my ensuing actions. In that moment, I'm given a chance to align the two and live more authentically in my values.

In doing so, I'm reminded that I am my mother's daughter after all.

PART TWO
ACTION

CHAPTER FOUR

Reframe Comparison

I f your friend tells you they got promoted at work, what crosses your mind first? Do you immediately feel insecure about your job performance or resentful that you're not moving ahead fast enough? If you see one of your clients carrying an Hermès handbag to your business lunch, do you start looking at your trusty old unbranded purse differently? When your colleague shows off her extravagant engagement ring at your team meeting, do you feel *some type of way* that isn't delight?

If the answer to these questions is mostly yes, then you're likely in a face-off with competition's favorite emotion: envy. Envy is that feeling of discontentment or even resentment that comes from witnessing someone else's good fortune—whether it's their natural qualities they were born with, the things they have, or simply a bout of good luck. And it is often at the root of why we're always comparing ourselves with one another.

Social comparison is a fundamental element of being human and having a brain. By itself, it's not inherently negative; we are social creatures, and comparison can help us to understand (and navigate) our position within a social hierarchy and even make decisions on mate selection to move our gene pool forward. Comparisons come naturally to us, which is why it makes sense that people regularly and unconsciously make social comparisons even today. Approximately 10 percent of our daily thoughts are social comparisons, says psychiatrist Sue Varma.

The resulting *envy* we often feel when we compare ourselves is a common and universal cultural emotion. But envy is also a double-edged sword. It's both a by-product of competition and a source of fuel for it. Competition has us constantly comparing ourselves to others, and envy can be a painful emotion that knocks us down a peg. Then we get back up and compete some more until we get what we desire. We hope that achievement heals what's hurting us. But as most of us know, competing and comparing doesn't—and never will—make us feel better about ourselves because the goalpost for what we need to achieve to feel better keeps moving. This is also called the "hedonic treadmill," a theory for how we often pursue goal after goal, never truly feeling fulfilled no matter how much we achieve. It's a vicious cycle, to say the least.

And envy can get in the way of our ability to uncompete. When we covet a promotion or a possession that someone else has, we're more likely to reject wanting to build and collaborate with them. If we constantly feel left behind or not enough when we envy our colleagues' success, it's harder to cultivate an abundance mindset or practice radical generosity. Without understanding this powerful emotion and navigating it mindfully, we're unable to uncompete. The good news is, though, that we can learn to channel it effectively.

DISTINGUISHING BETWEEN MALICIOUS ENVY AND BENIGN ENVY

When I was about sixteen, my frenemy from school, Rachel, had gotten an expensive bracelet for her birthday. She was known for boasting about her expensive tastes and looking down on people who didn't have the kind of material wealth her family had. Her parents owned a beautiful bungalow off Orchard Road, which was (and still is) prime real estate in Singapore.

When I got home from school that day after oohing and aahing over Rachel's new bracelet, I talked about it pretty much nonstop with my mum. At every opportunity over the next few weeks, I complained about how Rachel's parents must love her so much for buying such a lavish birthday gift, unlike me. (Yes, I'm afraid that I was a rather bratty teenager!)

Rather than get angry, my mum just listened. Then, after weeks of my incessant complaining, she said, "It sounds like you envy her. But I want you to think—*really think* carefully—if an expensive bracelet would make you happy and, more importantly, whether it would show you I love you. If after a month of thinking it through, the answer is still yes, I'll buy you a (less expensive) bracelet."

Looking back, what I love about my mother's response is that she didn't judge me for being envious. In fact, many social scientists believe that feeling envy is not inherently "bad"; it's what makes us human. I spoke to several experts while writing this book, and Jens Lange, assistant professor of psychology at Universität Hamburg, made an interesting point about envy. Competitive behaviors are strongest when we're envious of something or someone who is highly relevant to us. I believe this is why we are both most competitive with people like us and stand to lose the most because of this. This idea makes a lot of sense in my situation with Rachel, who was the same age, gender, and race as me. So we are frequently going to compare ourselves with others like us, and that's par for the course as social beings. But we can choose how to channel envy to our benefit by understanding that it can be broadly distinguished into two categories: benign and malicious.

Benign envy motivates us to elevate our own status in the hopes that our feelings of inadequacy may fade away. For example, if we wish that our bodies were more athletic, like that of someone we admire, benign envy might motivate us to exercise more and eat healthier so that the voice inside our heads, telling us over and over again that we're inferior, might finally vanish. On the other hand, *malicious envy* can trigger our basest instincts to try to take away what others have. Instead of working on ourselves to attain what someone else has, the only thing we care about is bringing the other person down. So in the same example of envying, say, a celebrity's athletic body, malicious envy would show up as someone going online to make critical, mean-spirited comments about that celebrity's body or accuse them of using weight-loss drugs to "cheat." Social scientists say benign envy encourages us to strive to achieve excellence. Conversely, malicious envy can be associated with a fear of failure that motivates us to bring someone else down.

Both forms of envy *can* have negative consequences. Benign envy can often have us jumping through endless hoops as we try to improve ourselves to feel on par with or superior to someone else. With malicious envy, which is markedly inspired by vengeance, there's much more collateral damage. People are targeted and harassed. Humiliated and scorned.

So what are we to do? Regardless of which kind of envy we're dealing with, we can't just wish it away: It's an immovable part of the human emotional landscape.

Thankfully, Lange and other experts in the field have some recommendations for us to consider:

- **Feel where envy comes up in our bodies.** Is envy a persistent stomachache? A rapid heat flash across the chest? Tension in the jawline? Physical sensation is often the first indication that we're experiencing an uncomfortable emotion like envy. When we're aware of how envy manifests in us, we're more likely to recognize and rein it in quickly.

- **Notice the messages that our envy is trying to tell us.** Our feelings are messages to our innermost selves. When we take a beat to listen to them, it can change the trajectory of an emotional fallout caused by envy and other tough emotions. For instance, envy could be trying to signal that we desire or may even have dreams we haven't admitted to ourselves. Before I became an author, I would feel envious whenever my peers shared book news on social media. As I spent more time thinking through exactly what I felt and why, I was able to identify that deep inside, those were career goals that I had, too, and then I began working toward my own author journey step by step. As I began to realize what hard work it was (and is), it became easier for me to cheer on other authors rather than merely envy them.

- **Focus on leveling up.** Psychologists believe that highly self-aware people who are mindful of when and how envy comes up for them can access something called "leveling up" motivation. This means that someone can transform envy into a reason to look within and see opportunities to grow and evolve rather than try to improve to gain public approval or show themselves they're as good as or better than the person they envy. The key to becoming more self-aware is *naming* your feelings whenever you're experiencing them, whether that acknowledgment is in your head, written down in a journal, or told to a trusted friend or therapist. This process makes us more familiar with emotions and helps us act on them in a healthy, constructive way.

- **Give credit where credit is due.** Much of our envy stems from our perception of worthiness—of others and ourselves. But if we consciously make a point of acknowledging how someone else has deservingly earned their success, envy loses its grip on us. If we reflect on all the areas in our own lives where we've achieved "wins," we're much more likely to feel more pride and self-respect instead of envy.

Before we move on to tackling one of envy's biggest triggers today—social media—I want to double down on the advice to believe that others are worthy and deserving of their success.

A 2011 study had university students read about a high-achieving scientist, and the details of his success were shared separately with two groups. One group was conditioned to believe that the scientist's success was "incremental" and achieved through his persistent effort and overcoming obstacles. The other group was primed to have "entity" beliefs—that his success was a result of inherited intelligence and being in the right place at the right time. Priming is a concept used by psychologists to influence people to think a certain way without outrightly telling them to. For example, if you're exposed to different objects all with the number four written on them, subconsciously you're being primed to think of that number. So if someone later asks you to "randomly" choose a number, you're highly likely to choose . . . you guessed it, four. (Sorry, advertisers, I gave away one of your tricks!)

When the same students read about another high-achieving person—this time, a student like them—the students primed with "incremental" beliefs experienced benign envy and "leveled up" more than the other group. Basically, students who believed that success requires persistence were inspired and determined to work hard and improve their own success. They even indicated that they would put more effort into studying—not to surpass the student they read about but because they saw value in the process. The students who were primed to believe that success is a result of factors mostly out of our control (inherited intelligence and being in the right circumstances) were less likely to self-improve and change their behaviors.

Here's my takeaway: To uncompete is *proactive*, and competition is *reactive*. The students who saw their envious feelings as a chance to level up were open to trying something different and forging ahead. Reactiveness is a defensive posture. We fall into it when we compete because envy makes us believe that someone else's achievements are somehow an attack on us. This is why more of us must challenge environments that are set up to make us become obsessed with self-improvement or that try to make us knock others down a peg when we experience envy. The next section is all about one such ecosystem.

ENVY AND THE
SOCIAL MEDIA MACHINE

The average person spends 147 minutes a day on social media—or nearly 2.5 hours—according to consumer research company GWI. At its best, social media is a wonderful way to connect with and keep up with loved ones, especially those who are far away. It can help advance your career, too. Over the years, posting regularly on my social media channels has been extremely necessary for building and finding my audience. It wouldn't be a stretch to say that this book wouldn't be in your hands without the time I've spent online. Social media has helped activists from around the world assemble and organize, championing important global causes, raising the voices of marginalized people, and holding oppressive governments accountable through large protests.

However, although social media has its perks and can be an agent for good, it's one of the main drivers of envy in the modern age. That's according to behavioral scientists, mental health experts, and even some technologists. Most adults are intuitively aware of how our feeds are carefully curated highlight reels—not honest depictions—of others' lives. We all know that the photos are heavily filtered and that some of the videos are completely staged. But envy still threatens to consume and compel us to compete whenever we see others' lives compared to ours when we log into these apps.

Martha Burwell and I saw evidence of how social media impacted women's feelings of comparison and envy in our "uncompete" survey.

Women reported feeling high levels of envy because of comparisons on social media, especially with their colleagues' achievements and their physical appearance. Compared with white respondents, women of color felt more envy and pressure to change their looks at work based on their social media use.

In a different study, university students who used social media for more than three hours each school day suffered from poor sleep, poor academic performance, and much higher rates of depression, substance abuse, stress, and suicide. One of the reasons for this could be the constant comparison bred by social media platforms, concludes psychologist Nicholas Kardaras.

But completely disengaging from social media is not a viable option for most of us. Certainly not for many women of color, who often make invaluable work and community connections that aren't always accessible in real-life situations.

Undeniably, it's a privilege to be someone who can completely cut out social media and still be able to generate income and/or connect with your community. So rather than advocating for total abstinence from social media, I've curated some ways that experts recommend engaging more intentionally. In doing so, we have a better chance to create collaborations and cultivate an abundance mindset. I believe that it is possible to uncompete on social media if we do it mindfully.

Step I: Discern Who Really "Wins" on Social Media

Social media is designed to have us believe that our "worth" is based on how many followers we have and how much engagement there is with the content we post. Its algorithms rely on us comparing ourselves and competing with others on a regular basis. But when feelings of envy creep in, we can pause and remember that social media has become a powerful tool for companies to monetize our attention and benefit from our insecurities. We can reject the tactics of competition, start uncoupling our self-worth from the metaverse, and look within for validation. The best way to begin is by asking ourselves *why* we're using social media in that moment—"I'm on Instagram to post a photo I just took," "I want to see what my friends are up to," "I'm reading it for news"—rather than just mindlessly reaching for it. If we engage in social media with a purpose in mind, we have a higher chance of noticing when and how envy is showing up in our bodies. Then there's a greater possibility for us to log off and do an activity that grounds us, such as going for a walk outdoors or listening to our favorite music.

Step 2: Reframe Envy

The envy that comes from seeing people's highlights on social media, especially when we're struggling in our lives, can steal away every ounce of joy. The incessant comparison and the pressure to portray a perfect life and receive a comparable or greater amount of engagement than those we follow remain constant.

It's not easy, but being able to reframe some of those emotions and negative self-talk when we see others winning on social media could be useful in helping us navigate our feelings effectively. Here are some of the ways I've tried to reframe my envious feelings in my journey to uncompete online:

ENVIOUS THOUGHT AFTER SEEING A SOCIAL MEDIA POST	REFRAMED THOUGHT
"My friend just got promoted at work. It makes me feel so bad about my dead-end job and myself."	"She must have worked really hard for it and deserved it. What are my envious feelings trying to tell me about my job? Is it time for a new challenge?"
"My friend just went on an amazing vacation. I'm broke. I deserve it so much more than her; it's unfair."	"I bet she saved up for it! Are there ways I could find joyful activities on my budget?"
"My friend keeps posting videos of her body in a bikini. It makes me so frustrated about my own body."	"They also often post photos of them working out. They've worked hard on their physique. What are my feelings trying to tell me—do I subconsciously have aspirations of changing my physique, and what can I do to achieve them?"
"This celebrity I follow always posts photos and videos of herself on a private jet. It reminds me how little money I have. #NepoBaby."	"Let me reflect on why I followed this celebrity in the first place. Could I reduce interactions with her profile if she's not posting the content I originally followed her for?"

Step 3: Take Meaningful Breaks from Social Media

It's no secret that social media algorithms are designed to reward us for posting more and spending more time on the apps. Our phones also activate the parts of our brains that produce dopamine, and this is why it's so difficult for us to put them down. Taking a break from social media is a great way to reset our internal thoughts, which often turn negative and self-hating the more time we spend on it. Experts recommend setting planned breaks from social media—such as during weekends, evenings, or even one day per week. I've also benefited from setting timers that log me out of social media after I've spent a certain amount on it.

Step 4: Follow, Support, and Boost Those Who Are Using Social Media Thoughtfully

Following creators and websites that do not immediately stoke feelings of competition is a great way to combat envy and strengthen our resolve to uncompete. There are so many creators out there who are sharing more realistic looks at their lives. For example, Zoe Blaskey and Motherkind, Mom Life Comics, and the Not Safe for Mom Group are Instagram accounts that offer honest approaches to motherhood and how hard it is. Brown Girl Therapy by Sahaj Kohli, Lizzo, and Alex Light promote body confidence. POC in Tech and Decolonize Myself provide antiracist content.

We can also use our own social media to practice radical generosity and solidarity by supporting and boosting other creators, especially businesses or channels owned or run by women of color. Every July, I turn over all my social platforms to amplify creators who applied to be amplified (via an online form). My social team then shares each applicant's content once every weekday of July, so by the end of the month, we amplify more than twenty individuals, spreading the word on books, podcasts, businesses, nonprofits, art, and other amazing projects that people had shared. A few people asked me why I had turned over my platforms for the *whole month*—after all, don't I have my own books, consulting, and speaking services to amplify? Why a month, why not just a day every week? What if I lost followers? People were choosing to follow me for, well, me?

Obviously, I understood the concerns, and it was a "risk" in terms of pure growth and engagement numbers. But Amplify July is a huge hit for me every year. I don't lose followers. I get to learn about interesting people around the globe who also uncompete and create a better online community and world. More than anything, I seem to "trick" the algorithms away from suggesting creators who seem to live "perfect" lives of travel, luxury, and beauty and toward recommending other accounts that are built on community and collaboration. Win-win!

Step 5: Advocate for Less Addictive, Safer Social Media Algorithms

To uncompete at scale, we need social media companies to acknowledge that social comparison and competition are harmful. As consumers and humans, we need them to radically rewrite their business models so their profits are not directly tied to their users' feelings of envy. This is literally how their algorithms work: They're trained to understand and incite our deepest insecurities! For instance, on days we've been feeling vulnerable about our appearance, we get a stream of content suggestions on platforms like Instagram specifically showing us photos and videos of conventionally attractive women as well as suggestions of expensive products to buy. One of the ways I've tried to stay informed is by supporting organizations advocating for better social media platforms. A short list includes the Center for Humane Technology, the Organization for Social Media Safety, and the National Cybersecurity Alliance.

I'm not trying to tell people how to "break up with their phone." All I want is for us to believe—really believe—that we have an active choice in how we spend our time online and to demand that companies act responsibly in turn.

UNDERSTANDING FOMO— ENVY'S CLOSEST ALLY

In Singapore, there's a slang term for the selfish attitudes and behaviors that stem from the fear of missing out: *kiasu*. Growing up, we were taught that being kiasu was the only way to succeed. You stood in long queues to buy the latest gadget lest it run out. You would hover around the table of a family eating lunch so you could swoop in on their territory to reserve your spot at the hawker center the second they were finished, no matter how awkward it was for all involved. Your elementary-school kids were enrolled in multiple enrichment classes so they someday would be able to outcompete your friends' kids on college applications. Being conditioned to be kiasu, which is part of my national identity as a Singaporean, has affected me even as an adult. Until I began my journey to uncompete, I was often in perpetual fear that someone, somewhere out there had it better than me or that I wasn't doing enough to get ahead.

Some years ago, a Western term that captured a less intense version of the kiasu sentiment started taking flight. Introduced in 2004, the term "fear of missing out" (FOMO) has become ubiquitous in just over two decades to describe the perception of missing out on activities or opportunities that others are engaging in. British psychologists define it as "pervasive apprehension that others might be having rewarding experiences from which one is absent." Psychologists link the rise in FOMO to . . . you guessed it . . . social media usage.

According to Mayank Gupta and Aditya Sharma, "Today, more than ever, people are exposed to a lot of details about what others are doing; and people are faced with the continuous uncertainty about whether they are doing enough or if they are where they should be in terms of their life. FOMO includes two processes; firstly, perception of missing out, followed up with a compulsive behavior to maintain these social connections." They say that FOMO, just like social comparisons, is a natural outcome of the way humans are hardwired with the need to belong and form strong relationships with others. But FOMO can also foster a problematic attachment to social media that is "associated with a range of negative life experiences and feelings, such as a lack of sleep, reduced life competency, emotional tension, negative effects on physical well-being, anxiety and a lack of emotional control; with intimate connections possibly being seen as a way to counter social rejection."

The acronym is credited to Harvard Business School student Patrick McGinnis, now a venture capitalist who also hosts a podcast aptly called *FOMO Sapiens.* Patrick's use of the acronym was to describe the in-person environment at Harvard (*not* social media), where, as he writes on his website, there was "a pervasive fear of being left out of the action going on around you, especially if it could end up being bigger, better, and brighter than what you were doing at the moment.

Even if you didn't have a name for such feelings, and my classmates and I didn't yet have one, you constantly struggled with them." So one of the hardest-to-get-into universities was structured to make students believe there was always someone better than them out there and that they had to prove their worth at every turn or run the risk of missing out? Fascinating!

Whether we see FOMO as a phenomenon driven by social media, as many psychologists do, or the result of being in any competitive environment, a scarcity mindset underpins this fear. The worry that there isn't enough time, opportunities, parties, or "coolness" to go around is pervasive. When we're bombarded with images of others living a fabulous life while we're doing the dishes, cleaning up dog poop, or, let's be real, sitting on the toilet, it's easy to lose perspective and feel like our life is much less fabulous and we're missing out. Symptoms of FOMO include obsessively checking social media to see what others are doing, experiencing negative feelings when comparing oneself to others, and feeling mentally exhausted, according to a 2021 report in *Technological Forecasting and Social Change*. Psychologists I've talked to add that overscheduling ourselves as a result of FOMO—trying to be everywhere all at once so we can compete with how others are showing up on social media—is also a common issue.

"Our digital habits, which include constantly checking messages, emails, and social media timelines, have become so entrenched, it is nearly impossible to simply enjoy the moment, along with the people with whom we are sharing these moments," writes Kristen Fuller. How does this relate to trying to uncompete? A scarcity mentality, the fear that others are winning by comparison, the push to *do more* even if we don't want to, and envy are all at the core of the competitive behaviors that FOMO creates. What are some possible solutions that lead us toward uncompeting?

One of the antidotes to FOMO is the cutely named "joy of missing out" (JOMO). "JOMO is the emotionally intelligent antidote to FOMO and is essentially about being present and being content with where you are at in life," writes Fuller. In essence, we do not need to compare our lives to others' and instead must learn to tune out "shoulds" and "wants" and let go of worrying that we're doing something wrong. "JOMO allows us to live life in the slow lane, to appreciate human connections, to be intentional with our time," she writes. JOMO makes it OK to practice saying no, to give ourselves breaks from technology use and the permission to acknowledge where we are, and to feel emotions.

The competitive and anxious space in our brain taken up by FOMO can be freed up by JOMO because it adds spaciousness to ask ourselves if we are being motivated to do something by our own free will or ruled by a competition and scarcity mindset. JOMO is central to uncompeting—it allows us to prioritize collaboration, inclusion, an abundance mindset, radical generosity, and solidarity.

When we aren't rushing to cram our calendars with every event under the sun, we're more likely to have the space to reflect on what *really* matters to us and how to allocate our time toward that. JOMO can create opportunities to collaborate and spend time with people who inspire and fulfill our lives rather than deplete our energy. It also allows us to build solidarity, particularly among like-minded individuals, as well as gives us the space to intentionally show up for others in need. When we're mindlessly rushing from one thing to another because we don't want to miss out, we can't fully engage wherever we find ourselves or connect with people we could build deeper bonds with. We also then lack the energy to learn about other communities' struggles or thoughtfully engage in activities that build solidarity—like mindfully attending a community event where we learn about perspectives different from our own.

JOMO helps us live our lives with an abundance mindset. When you believe you have enough time and opportunity to network/party/travel/work or whatever would motivate your FOMO, then "missing out" is reframed as "missing out for right now but not forever." Rather than refreshing our social media feeds and feeling anxious about missing yet another gathering, an abundance mindset guides us to check out of social media when it's not serving us and engage with it again when it is. The spaciousness of JOMO gives us the bandwidth to practice radical generosity and mindfully include others because we can see who is being excluded and bring them in. We take actions with intention rather than run on autopilot.

Given the overwhelm of modern lives for most people today, particularly women, JOMO feels like a welcome solution yet one that can be very hard to actually put into practice. Years of conditioned guilt of "letting others down," worries about "falling behind," and stress about competing with others have made it so much more difficult to decline opportunities. Yet that is precisely what we need to do to live present, whole lives where we can invest in ourselves and our communities. As far as pithy internet quotes go, one of my favorites will always be "No is a complete sentence."

HOW WE CAN PRACTICE JOMO IN OUR JOURNEY TO UNCOMPETE

I. Someone Else's Success Doesn't Reflect Our Failure

JOMO guides us to reframe the negative feelings we may have that someone is living a fabulous life and it's unfair that we aren't to the belief that their success doesn't automatically mean we're a failure. Moreover, to believe that they deserve achievement or enjoyment. If we believe that others are living a great life and we've been unfairly dealt a bad hand in comparison, that resentment can drive FOMO. Instead, try to feel joy that others are getting or experiencing what they deserve while telling yourself, "I'll also have what I want when the time is right for me." When we have an abundance mindset about opportunities, the negative feelings we have about others "achieving" while we're "losing" can be dealt with more effectively. Believing that others are deserving of their successes and joy is also a tool to manage envy effectively, as you read earlier.

This sounds easier said than done, and it is. But as a developing field of research, neuroplasticity shows us that it's possible to rewire our brains to think differently. Our neurons *can* modify the strength of existing synapses (such as our go-to thoughts that it's so unfair that everyone else is living a great life except us) and form new synaptic connections (believing that others are deserving of their great lives and your life has positivity and possibilities, too!). This is precisely why I believe in the power of learning to uncompete. Most of us haven't been conditioned to opt out of competition or even shown how to, but with intentionality, practice, and action, we can train our brains to think differently and take action accordingly.

2. Become Mindful About How You're Spending Your Time

FOMO produces the anxious behaviors I described above, such as overscheduling or an addiction to checking in on what others are up to on social media. Unfortunately, these anxious actions create a vicious cycle where the more you engage, the more FOMO is created. To cultivate JOMO, reflect deeply on which activities are most meaningful to you.

For example, a close friend of mine, Mia, loves to socialize but often finds her social life competing with her overworking tendencies. In her FOMO phase, she would often try to constantly squeeze in both (and feel exhausted) or haphazardly choose one and feel regretful she wasn't doing the other. She would feel especially bad about herself when she would see friends gathering (when she was at work) or see or hear about her colleagues working a longer day than her when she chose to socialize.

Eventually, Mia had to sit down and intentionally carve out how she was spending her time. She set goals for what a reasonable work schedule would look like and had a plan in place to decline invitations that wouldn't allow her to fulfill her work goals. She even engaged friends to help her keep her commitments to her work goals—they would either remind her that she had the option to decline social engagements or reschedule them to accommodate her work schedule. And, of course, focusing on how she was able to prioritize her work and then go home early to rest when she *wasn't* invited to a party her friends were at became even more important to cultivating JOMO. The more she stuck to her plans and chose how to spend her time intentionally, the more JOMO she felt: She was exercising agency over her time.

3. Say No More Often

It may sound counterintuitive, but the more we intentionally decline opportunities we can't make time for, the more we'll find that "better" opportunities (more aligned with our goals, financially lucrative, more enjoyable) come our way. It's not easy for most of us to say no—I feel this acutely as an Asian woman—but we must *learn* to get a lot more comfortable with declining opportunities. In developing a more abundant mindset, try to remind yourself that the opportunity you're declining today isn't the only one you will ever have. Have faith that there are more where they came from! I promise that with practice, saying no gets easier. One powerful by-product of saying no is creating opportunities for others. By saying no to an opportunity, perhaps you could recommend someone amazing in your place who does have the bandwidth to attend? Perhaps that could help them in their lives and their careers? Additionally, we need to truly believe that saying no doesn't mean you won't ever be tapped again.

The truth is, most of us weren't taught how to manage emotions like "envy" or the fears of falling behind or missing out. We were told that our emotions were bad and should be avoided. Or we faced the larger societal message that we're "less than" and others are doing better. This can become a very destructive situation. Turning away from or denying these emotions doesn't serve us, but identifying, understanding, and accepting them can be powerful in shaping how we react.

By the way, if you've read to the end of this chapter and are wondering whether I ever got a bracelet after my envy of and obsession with the bracelet of my tenth-grade frenemy, Rachel, the answer is no. I never ended up asking for the bracelet after all. A month spent reflecting on whether an expensive bracelet would bring me happiness or proof of my mother's love was a solid lesson early in my life. Envying others' shiny objects (in person or online) without figuring out *why* we want them, what they represent, or if we even need them can cause unnecessary competition, comparison, and anxiety. It's a lesson I come back to often.

CHAPTER FIVE

Choose Joy

When I think of the word "joy," it's full, ripe, and juicy, like the middle-of-summer peaches from my favorite farmer's corner stand at Pike Place Market. Hands full, juice dripping down my chin, eyes closed with abandon, heart and belly full. Every single person deserves to enjoy something that makes them feel this way.

If we are playing by the standard rules of competition and capitalism, then we're deserving of pleasure only *after* we achieve something. It must be earned. Happiness is something we have to work hard for, and the amount of joy we experience is directly proportional to our effort. The only people who get a pass are the powerful 1 percent who have inherited their "happiness" through generational wealth.

But the rules of uncompete are built upon the belief that joy is our *birthright*, no matter who we are and where we come from. We are worthy of joy simply because we are human, no special achievements or "earning it" necessary. And this, dear readers, is 100 percent nonnegotiable. We've all been taught that a strong society is founded upon hard work, so this might be the part of our journey that's hardest for us to wrap our minds around. Honestly, the idea that we are entitled to joy—just because we exist, not as a reward for achieving something—is one that the immigrant (and child of immigrants) in me has deeply resisted. After all, immigrants are taught and shown in every way that their right to exist within a society is entirely dependent on how much they produce. In fact, many visas are granted based only on the work you do, and millions of immigrants the world over would instantaneously lose their right to live in a country the moment they lose their job.

But I've come to realize that if we accept that joy is always available to all of us—regardless of our accomplishments—we can buck the competitive system we were born into. If we begin the work toward radical self-worth, which underpins whether we believe we are deserving of joy, we are able to subscribe to a whole new life perspective that gives us permission to pursue joy freely without stopping to think, "Have I earned the right?"

Our joy is deeply dependent on how worthy we feel. No doubt, for those of us who have intersecting underestimated identities, we may be looking at undoing a lifelong conditioning that we are "less than" when compared with men, white people, nondisabled people. Doing the work to deprogram competition beliefs to instead believe that we have infinite value *no matter* our identities is highly radical. The status quo, as we've seen, isn't working. Engaging in competition erodes any measure of self-worth because we are chronically judging, comparing, and doubting. Here's how I imagine what letting go of that and choosing ourselves instead could look like.

WHAT HAPPENS WHEN
WE CHOOSE OURSELVES

In the summer of 2021, a bright twenty-four-year-old athlete felt the weight of the world on her shoulders. She was representing her country at the highest level of competition, and all eyes were on her. As she sprinted down the eighty-two-foot runway, then jumped on a springboard to propel herself onto the vault, something didn't feel quite right.

As she catapulted into the air, she felt like her mind and body had separated. If she tried to do the two and a half twists required by the move she was about to perform—the Amanar vault—she could dangerously hurt herself. So she twisted one and a half times and landed in a deep squat, dazed and disoriented, barely able to stay on her feet.

Shortly after, the famous Olympian withdrew from almost the entire competition to focus on her mental well-being. Critics rushed in, cruelly calling her "weak," "selfish," and a "national embarrassment" for choosing herself over her sport. Three years later, after taking a much-needed break and focusing on her physical and mental health, she trained relentlessly for another grueling set of Olympic games, where she won three gold medals and a silver in Paris, becoming the most decorated American gymnast of all time.

That Olympian is, of course, Simone Biles.

The three years between the 2021 Tokyo Olympics and the 2024

Paris Olympics must have been the hardest ever for her. To exit the biggest competition in the world while millions of people were watching her was courageous beyond belief. We know women, women of color—particularly Black women—aren't allowed to be anything but strong, no matter what.

But Biles chose herself that day because of her strong sense of self-worth. She knew that being a gymnast wasn't the only thing that defined her worth and that her health and happiness mattered way more than pushing through pain and disorientation to prove herself. She's chosen herself again and again, on and off the Olympic podium, and the joy she radiates is completely undeniable. So much so that in my eyes, her return to the sport after a break only to dominate it in the 2024 Olympics was almost a sidebar. The real story is how courageously, unapologetically, and unflinchingly she modeled what it means to put yourself first. And how from that brave choice, everything else flowed. She now often wears a necklace with a diamond-encrusted goat pendant—a clever nod to her Greatest of All Time status.

I believe we all can learn from Biles's level of self-worth to cultivate joy on our own terms. Showing up for ourselves and our communities depends on our ability to uncompete.

SETTING UP THE RIGHT FOUNDATION TO ACCESS JOY

For many of us, high self-worth—described by mental health therapists as a positive self-evaluation focused on *internal* beliefs versus relying on the outside environment and achievements—is elusive. Even confident and successful people have a hard time believing that they're deserving of love, respect, and consideration.

Most psychologists say having a healthy childhood is one of the surest ways of developing high self-worth, particularly when children are shown by adults around them that they are safe, loved, and worth spending time with, regardless of external achievements. But for a lot of us, that ship has sailed. In fact, nearly half of US children experience childhood trauma. Experiencing childhood trauma can seriously affect one's quality of life in adulthood and, unsurprisingly, contribute to low self-worth. The choices we make as we grow can help us navigate that, which is why for many, like me, the road ahead may be longer, but we can cultivate a stronger sense of self-worth with practice.

If I step back and take a broader view of all the scarcity, zero-sum, and winner-take-all thinking (and action) I see many of us defaulting to, it's clear how much of it stems from insecurity and a lack of self-worth. Of course, for most of us, that insecurity and the feelings of unworthiness come from experiencing subtle or overt marginalization in society. When you're constantly reminded that you don't belong, that your way of saying, doing, and being is "less than," it makes complete sense why so many of us go through our lives without finding or believing in our own unconditional self-worth.

And this is also precisely why I feel that our access to joy lies in rejecting expectations placed on us to try to define our worth. Ultimately, every overachiever will tell you—particularly those of us who aren't accepted regardless of the degrees, experience, titles, or wealth we amass—achievements have very little to do with self-worth.

And certainly nothing to do with "unconditional" self-worth. So what does it take to develop it?

I've learned so much from the groundbreaking work of clinical psychologist and author Adia Gooden. In her TED Talk, Gooden candidly shares her struggles about never quite fitting in with her Black friends *or* white friends. Struggling to belong in childhood can create coping mechanisms that eat away at your self-worth: perfectionism, constantly seeking accolades (and never being satisfied because there's always a new goal to reach), self-criticism, shame, and unhealthy behaviors.

Gooden makes a critical distinction in an article on TED.com:

> We can bolster our self-esteem by improving our skills or performance, and our self-esteem goes up and down depending on how we're doing in various aspects of our lives. In contrast, unconditional self-worth is distinct from our abilities and accomplishments. It's not about comparing ourselves to others; it's not something that we can have more or less of. Unconditional self-worth is the sense that you deserve to be alive, to be loved and cared for. To take up space.

Wow. The idea that any woman can and should take up space is counter to everything many of us were taught about being "good" girls and women.

In my Indian community, I was taught that although I would be rewarded for achieving, I should never become too proud or confident about myself. That good girls should achieve, but never outshine the boys. Having a strong sense of self-worth, self-esteem, or self-confidence makes women too arrogant. I've seen this reinforced more in various Asian and immigrant cultures, but friends socialized as femme the world over have told me they've grown up with similar messages.

The idea that a woman deserves to be joyous and have a strong sense of self-worth is so antithetical to the way we've been socialized to be. And yet. This is the deepest, most profound work we can do in learning to uncompete. This is radical and necessary, even though it's so counter to our narrative and conditioning. To move our focus away from producing, achieving, and doing to *being* and knowing we are whole and worthy just as we are.

Even after achieving the highest highs of my career, I have felt the crushing anxiety of "What's next?" Most of us are addicted to reaching a high bar, only to meet it and immediately focus on an even loftier goal. Low self-worth can lead to health conditions like depression, anxiety, and substance abuse, according to Gooden. The antidote to this is cultivating unconditional self-worth as an ongoing practice.

As I wrote this book, many people I trust rightly cautioned me not to make this book about shaming women, people of color, and other marginalized folks to "be nicer" and trust others more. In truth, so many of us are generous and trusting and compassionate, only to be burned, exploited, and condescended to while being told that to be self-sacrificing is better than taking care of ourselves.

So I'll say it here and throughout the book—to uncompete is *never* about being taken for a ride or being too trusting and vulnerable with people who your instincts or past experiences have signaled to you aren't trustworthy. Yes, one of the principles of uncompete is to practice radical generosity, which starts with practicing radical generosity with yourself and honoring your instincts. In tandem, it does not mean practicing radical generosity with someone who has constantly let you and others down. In a world that tells women, especially, to ignore our instincts or, worse, just to "forgive and forget" even egregious harm done to us, unconditional self-worth is an approach and practice that we can cultivate not only to learn to trust ourselves but also to discern who else is worthy of our trust. Many of us—myself squarely included—did not learn how to cultivate unconditional self-worth in our lives. As such, I've often ignored my own instincts and experiences, even dishonoring what felt right to me in service of others, to the detriment of my health, peace, and joy. That is why it is so necessary to start by treating yourself with the principles of uncompete first, then spreading that outward into the world. To do that, we must learn to develop unconditional self-worth.

Gooden makes four recommendations on how to cultivate this: Forgive yourself, practice self-acceptance, be there for yourself, and connect to supportive people. Let's explore each one.

Forgive Yourself

When people ruminate over failure and find it hard to forgive themselves, it can lead to a vicious cycle of linking all positive emotions only to achievement. "Forgiveness involves acknowledging and accepting what has happened. Acceptance releases us from blaming ourselves and others and allows us to move forward," writes Gooden. "To forgive yourself, reflect on the circumstances that led to past mistakes, acknowledge the pain you experienced and identify what you learned from the situation. Then say to yourself 'I forgive you'—in an honest and kind way." Learning to cultivate self-worth by forgiving ourselves is so important, particularly for those of us who have seen our self-confidence and self-esteem tied up in external validation.

Practice Self-Acceptance

We receive so many messages from society and even from those close to us that we're not enough or that we would be more worthy if we only changed _____. If we focus only on what we're lacking, an extension of the scarcity mindset, then we'll never feel truly worthy. Instead, Gooden's perspective is to focus on the things about you that you *do* like. Bonus points if they're not what society tells you to embrace—quirks like your bushy eyebrows, belly laughs, or out-of-the-box way of thinking.

When we accept ourselves just the way we are, we believe we're worthy of love and joy in this moment, not in a future moment after we've achieved something or changed ourselves to be considered worthy. This is a simple idea that's so profoundly hard to do in the context of our society today, particularly in a consumerist society that tells us that only by altering ourselves are we worthy. But, of course, the irony is that the more you achieve or change, the further back the goalpost moves. In trying to change to become worthy, the less achievable that sense of self-worth becomes.

Be There for Yourself

When things are rough, we're often hardest on ourselves. Research shows we often talk to ourselves in ways we wouldn't even to our worst enemies! We don't think often about being there for ourselves, nor are most of us taught this skill or even encouraged to cultivate it. But if you think back to difficult moments in your life, wouldn't it have been transformative to hear, "I see you. I'm there for you. If you're in pain, you're not alone."

In a competition-driven society, we expect others—a spouse, a friend, a family member—to step up and validate us. When we uncompete, we recognize that a strong relationship with ourselves can help us navigate hard times in tandem with, or even in the absence of, community support. "The next time you experience emotional pain, acknowledge how you were feeling and offer yourself some comfort. Place your hand on your chest, give yourself a hug or say something kind and soothing to yourself," advises Gooden.

Connect to Supportive People

When we're low on self-worth, we may pull away from our community and feel isolated. Unfortunately, loneliness can reinforce feelings of unworthiness. One of the strongest ways to deal with this is to connect with supportive people, even if we fear being vulnerable and exposed. Knowing we are loved and cared for even when the chips are down can help us recognize that a tough situation doesn't mean we are unworthy of love and support.

I've experienced how self-worth can be cultivated, even later in life, by having the right community around me. I often turned to the strong messages of love, respect, and support I received from my mother—these were an antidote to those ideas that I heard from my father and other adult family members when I was growing up. I now believe that championing others and embracing others' joy can only happen when we feel worthy of being championed and experiencing joy ourselves. I know for sure that I wouldn't be on a lifelong journey to uncompete if I hadn't had the seeds of self-worth planted in me by my mum. One parent watered those seeds, and the other actively starved them of sunlight, but ultimately I saw modeled in my mother what nurturing self-worth can do to bolster courage in those of us who are marginalized. For people like us, we need to look to ourselves in harmful situations and in societies that teach us we're unworthy of joy in many ways large and small. In a world that tells most of us that we aren't enough, imagine what we could do, believe, and let go of if we genuinely saw ourselves as worthy of love, respect, and joy, no matter what.

FINDING JOY IN OTHERS' JOY

We must also learn to simultaneously embrace wholehearted, deep-in-your-bones joy when someone *else* succeeds—the type of true joy that doesn't immediately have us jumping to the (more common than not) narrative that "their success means I'm a failure." As we've established in previous chapters, we're all intentionally programmed to see others' achievements as our failures. But there are small steps and actions we can learn and take to feel joy for others while intentionally disrupting the harmful patterns of competition and comparison.

Approaching this idea with an abundance mindset (as reframed Belief 3 of uncompete guides me to) has led me to embrace a line of thinking that's gaining momentum among social scientists: "freudenfreude," or finding pleasure in another person's good fortune. It's a word made up of the repetition of *Freude*, the German word for joy. It also happens to be the opposite of *Schadenfreude*, an actual German word that means taking pleasure in another person's misfortune (literal translation: "harm-joy"). In today's world, freudenfreude might seem like a philosophical unicorn—theoretically beautiful and practically impossible. Yet I think if more of us could commit to it at scale, taking joy in other people's happiness would bring about a future where uncompete would be our default setting.

Freudenfreude is like a social glue that makes relationships "more intimate and enjoyable," psychology professor Catherine Chambliss said in a *New York Times* interview. Social intelligence is a vital part of many of the foundations of how we uncompete—by building community, establishing solidarity, and practicing radical generosity. We have better relationships when we can suppress our competitive reactions and learn to be supportive and joyful of our peers' good news. Here's how to cultivate it.

BE GENUINELY INTERESTED IN OTHERS' SUCCESSES

After being burned out by the racism and sexism I encountered in the tech industry, I realized that in my pursuit of financial and "title" success, I'd invested little time in building community in Seattle despite living there for two years. Of course, so much of it was systemic. Between a stressful job, a long commute, and time on weekends dedicated to chores or exercise, I literally didn't have a spare moment. The older I get and the further away from the version of myself who believed my worth was intrinsically tied to my professional title or the amount of money I made, the more I see that among the biggest societal impacts of late-stage capitalism is that so many of us are left with little time to invest in building our communities outside of work. When I left tech, I was undeniably lonely, but I was also craving the type of friendships that I had enjoyed in my "pre-career" life, where not every conversation revolved around how to advance at work.

In 2015 I learned about a casual group of professional women in the nonprofit industry who would gather monthly for a happy hour. I reached out to the organizers and asked if I could help with organizing these gatherings and open it up to women beyond the nonprofit sector. I'm so grateful that Jamie, Alessandra, and Madeline said yes, and for a number of years after, we'd bring women together monthly in different areas of Seattle. There was no fee to attend and no expectation that anyone attending needed to buy anything at the venue. And there wasn't ever a formal agenda.

But there was one activity we would always engage in, which many attendees later told us was the part they most enjoyed. We would stand in a circle, introduce ourselves one by one, and typically answer a question like "What's a win you want to share?" or "What's something you're excited about?"

Engaging in hearing other women—many of them strangers— unabashedly share their joys helped me stretch my own ability to celebrate others' successes without it immediately causing me to reflect on what I didn't have. This was a solidarity-building practice on a most practical level, with everyday stakes, and it worked. Becoming genuinely interested in a wide variety of other people's successes helped more of us connect beyond surface-level interactions. I do think that asking people "What's bringing you joy right now?" more often could help many of us get comfortable with hearing it. After a while, it became easy to attend these events expecting that there would be people who would be sharing "wins" that would induce envy in other contexts. I had conditioned myself to expect hearing about them and, as a result, usually felt joyous when I heard about them, not envious or self-flagellating.

Being primed to hear about (and to vocally celebrate) others' successes in these happy hours often made it so that meeting people outside this context sharing joyous news would also bring me joy instead of self-comparison. To me, learning to uncompete means finding ways to immerse ourselves in others' joys as a practice, whether that's sharing our wins with a group of trusted friends or with strangers.

Chambliss also encourages us to engage in "shoy," described as "intentionally sharing the joy of someone relating a success story by showing interest and asking follow-up questions." What's important here is not just to sort of nod and move along, but to stop, take stock of, and genuinely engage when someone else is sharing a joyous moment or success story.

Many of us probably find this harder to do because of social media, where we're often made to feel like everyone else is always winning all the time. In general, social media networks aren't all that encouraging about sharing joy genuinely. Adding a "like" distractedly on someone's joyous social post isn't the same as truly engaging, listening, or asking follow-up questions like "How will you celebrate?" or "How can I celebrate you?"

But in smaller groups, this practice can be meaningfully cultivated. When many university classes shifted fully online at the start of the COVID-19 pandemic, I, like other professors, would often begin my classes by asking each student to share a recent "win." My hope was that even in such unpredictable and painful times, we could find little joys in our own lives and that celebrating others' joy would help us find solace, too. Later that year, students often made note in my teaching evaluations that naming their own wins and celebrating their peers' successes became one of the moments in my class they most looked forward to. Although this practice may feel uncomfortable at the start, it gets easier and more natural, especially when paired with the next prompt.

VIEW INDIVIDUAL SUCCESSES AS COMMUNITY WINS

We often see magazine covers dedicated to lone-wolf business geniuses (most often white and male) without assessing how nothing worth building or truly useful could be built without communal effort. Yet we are geared to see individual success as individual effort, particularly in the United States. Unfortunately, when we don't prioritize collaboration and inclusion—two important foundations of uncompete—it becomes our default to see wins and losses as individualistic. Instead, the practice of embracing others' joy requires us to reframe it as a *community* achievement. I think we inherently know this, but we don't quite have a model in society that truly celebrates success communally.

When a colleague wins an award, it's more common to view their success as their individual win, but what if we could reflect on how their success makes our entire team or organization look good? That the halo effect of their win benefits more than just one person? We have deviated so far away from the practice of "someone in our lives has succeeded and we all had a part to play in that success" that it feels more normalized to compare ourselves with each other than to take joy in their success, too, and see it as a reflection of our own community's wins.

Several psychologists, including Marisa Franco, author of *Platonic: How the Science of Attachment Can Help You Make—and Keep—Friends*, say that when we feel happy for others, their joy can become our joy, and we can benefit positively from those feelings. I want to acknowledge that our culture doesn't normalize this in any way. In fact, it would be viewed as selfish if we tried to insert ourselves into taking any credit or responsibility for a friend's child's successful first year of life. But changing the narrative from an individual to communal success is precisely how to start. A small but meaningful way could be through vocally thanking others for your success and acknowledging how their contributions led to it, as detailed below.

GIVE OTHERS THEIR FLOWERS FOR YOUR SUCCESSES

Related to the earlier point, prevailing competitive norms tell us to view our success as coming only from our individual effort, hard work, and sacrifice. But we can take real action to disrupt this flawed narrative by crediting and sharing credit with others for our successes. I'm acknowledging again that this isn't the regular playbook in society and especially in the individualistic cultural norms we see in the United States. Yet when we recognize how much we've lost in our competitive landscape, it's clear that approaching our wins with the spirit of collaboration and radical generosity can help us build community joy.

When we express gratitude after someone else's success or support leads to our own success, it's called "bragitude," and it is another way to cultivate freudenfreude. To engage in bragitude, share your win, then express gratitude by telling the other person how they contributed to that win. If you won an award and your friend helped you prepare your acceptance speech, tell your friend that you appreciate their help in getting you ready for your big day.

I really love this practice because it helps us see how we're all interconnected and that joy isn't something to be hoarded or jealously squirreled away, but shared openly. Of course, it must be genuine and relevant to the moment, but once we start appreciating (first by thinking of it, then vocally saying it) how others have supported us, an achievement that may have caused envy in the other person becomes a shared celebration. We can create a culture where malicious envy isn't the default when someone else succeeds.

I'd also like to see more families credit their children's successes to other caregivers: babysitters, nannies, and schoolteachers. I genuinely see my career and well-being achievements as a direct result of their support and nurture for my son. When I meet any of them and am asked about my professional successes, I'll be sure to mention how grateful I am for their support and the big role they unknowingly play (or have played) in any of my achievements. Bragitude can be so powerful that it has been known to alleviate depressive symptoms, according to mental health experts like Chambliss.

"Practicing bragitude is like sharing dessert: Both parties enjoy the sweetness of the moment, which enhances freudenfreude for them both," concludes the same *New York Times* article.

BE A COACH

If we think of coaching as a skill where, through feedback and genuine interest, we help someone improve their life, I believe we can all coach those around us, to some degree. Of course, there's a huge distinction between a professional coach—whether in sports or business—and coaching someone informally. Professional coaching skills are different and (rightly so) somewhat regulated. But even in our day-to-day lives, I've seen how much we can create communal joy when more of us take responsibility for cheering one another on and helping others get back on their feet when they fall.

For many people from marginalized communities, particularly those of us who have been underestimated our whole lives, even informal coaches are out of reach. When I and my coauthor Jodi-Ann Burey wrote about imposter syndrome in a viral *Harvard Business Review* article, we questioned whether women's imposter syndrome was a result of internal confidence issues or the compounding impact of being underestimated and facing bias in the workplace. If women were validated and championed in the workplace as often and as enthusiastically as our white male counterparts, it's likely that most of us wouldn't be burdened with second-guessing ourselves. One of the antidotes to an exclusionary, imposter syndrome–ridden culture, and a way to create an inclusive workplace culture, is to champion women—to set them up for roles they're eminently qualified for but often overlooked for, and then cheer them on, using language like "I believe in you" when they express self-doubt.

We can experience true joy in the success of others if we take time to invest in it. When children from underserved communities heard from teachers that they were rooting for them, it played a critical role in their feelings of belonging and staying on in school, writes Stanford professor Geoffrey L. Cohen in *Belonging: The Science of Creating Connection and Bridging Divides*. We often underestimate the power of our words of encouragement to spur someone to do better or how practical feedback delivered kindly could change the trajectory of their career. Yet when you read the biographies of remarkable individuals, from athletes to business leaders, the vast majority of them talk about how having someone recognize their abilities and cheer them on was intrinsic to their achievements.

To be more inclusive, when mentoring young people and professionals who are women of color, focus on being extra encouraging and supportive. All too often, we receive little external validation in our homes and among our own communities, which is further reinforced by being dismissed and overlooked when we're out in the world, particularly in Western environments.

One powerful antidote to this is when we understand and engage in microvalidations—small, positive words and actions that affirm the people you work with, particularly those who have experienced exclusion and bias. Like microaggressions (exclusionary behaviors like mispronouncing someone's name or stereotyping them), microvalidations "are equally subtle but powerful actions or language that demonstrate affirmation, encouragement, and belief in a person's potential. They can include gestures as simple as acknowledging and affirming someone's experience of a microaggression or giving encouraging feedback and sincere compliments," researcher Laura Morgan Roberts and her team write.

Microvalidations require us to *intentionally* choose to act with radical generosity, especially toward people who are least likely to be treated with generosity and affirmation because of societal bias. We engage in this practice not as a strategy to advance in our careers but because we are motivated by the belief that everyone deserves validation and joy. That in being more intentional in celebrating people who aren't always given their flowers, we take personal action and accountability for creating a just society and workplace.

The more we receive validation early in our lives, the more we are able to nurture the self-worth that's necessary for us to live healthy lives, to access joy, and, in turn, to pay it forward to our communities. In a culture that doesn't normalize us cheering others on unless we're paid to do it formally, this is a powerful act and a practice that truly grows the more you do it.

In my wildest imagination, I dream of what the world would look like if we could cultivate joy at scale! Can you imagine being able to fully, deeply, in the very fibers of your being feel joy when others succeed? To celebrate their successes as your own? To view our own joy as interconnected and interdependent on the support and help and championing of others, and tell them, so that the joy could be shared? Perhaps it could be a powerful antidote to even some of life's most painful experiences.

As my friend Dr. Tanmeet Sethi writes in her groundbreaking book, *Joy Is My Justice: Reclaim What Is Yours*, "Every footstep you take toward Joy, even while still living with fear or rage, is a radical act of Justice that defies the oppressive weight of your pain and creates a powerful change in your biochemistry. Joy is here for you. Joy is your birthright."

Tanmeet's approach to joy as justice is truly radical, especially because life has unarguably handed her pain no mother should have to endure. Her beautiful son, Zubin, was diagnosed with a fatal disease at age three. Yet she has found that in intentionally seeking joy, we can transcend grief and find meaning even when things feel devastating. I truly believe more of us can find joy, or at least remember that it is available to us, even when it feels impossible.

Fortunately, we are able to access more examples of communal joy in the world if we look for them.

As the 2024 women's gymnastics competition in the Paris Olympics came to a close, the world witnessed a remarkable sight. Rebeca Andrade, the Brazilian gymnast who won gold in the floor competition, was bowed down to during the medal ceremony by silver medalist Simone Biles and bronze medalist Jordan Chiles, both from the US gymnastics team. The all-Black-women podium was a sight to behold as it is. Then to see the reverence and respect from two competitors to the winner who was from another country—it was a master class in what it means to uncompete. Despite being pitted against one another in competition, the gymnasts could take joy and inspiration in all of their remarkable, gravity-defying achievements and cheer one another on as human beings, not competitors.

When they later received criticism for bowing to their rival, Simone responded: "We're always going to keep a good face and support our competitors because they've worked just as hard as we have for that moment. So you have to give them their flowers. She deserved it."

As I watched those bows that reverberated around the world—without a word—my heart felt overcome with joy.

CHAPTER SIX

Create an Abundant Community

I n October 2021, I opened an unassuming email with the subject "podcast request." When I saw that it was from the executive assistant of a *really famous person*, my heart leaped into my throat. As I read it, I couldn't believe my eyes. I was being invited to appear on a podcast dearly loved by millions. Former guests included President Barack Obama, Beto O'Rourke, Abby Wambach, and America Ferrera.

I had a feeling this would be a career-defining moment for me, and I wasn't wrong. After I was interviewed on the podcast about my book (which the host had underlined, dog-eared, and wholeheartedly endorsed!), *Inclusion on Purpose* sold out across multiple stores and was back-ordered for weeks. This kind of attention is an author's dream.

I'm grateful to the host and their podcast team for the great conversation and for elevating my book, but it was never lost on me that the person who helped make this crowning moment possible was my friend Aiko Bethea, founder of RARE Coaching & Consulting and author of *Anchored, Aligned, Accountable*.

Unbeknownst to me, Aiko had recommended my name to the host and their podcast team when she saw that my book was releasing. *Inclusion on Purpose* had already found a modest audience, but without Aiko's championing I know for sure that I wouldn't have landed on the celebrity host's radar. Reflecting on the way that Aiko elevated me—and how she does the same for countless other women of color—two words come to my mind: *abundance* and *community*.

Aiko and I would be competitors in a traditional workplace context. We both run DEI practices that pitch similar clients (one year, we literally pitched for the same consulting project, and Aiko ultimately got it—YAY!), we're both public speakers (we've been keynote speakers at the same events, different years), and we're both authors. She's extremely established and has been doing this work for far longer than I have, but even so, the prevailing Queen Bee narrative would tell us to see each other as rivals.

But when Aiko and I were first introduced to each other—I can't even remember when—we looked across the table and in silent acknowledgment our eyes communicated this: "You're my community, not my competition." When I reflect on this profound connection, I think we both understood that the way we regarded each other was intimately tied to the type of change we deeply imagine for the world—more belonging, more justice, more inclusion. That these big, lofty, seemingly impossible goals couldn't be achieved in individual silos. That we had to trust each other to advance in these risky endeavors of advocating for anti-Blackness and equity in rooms full of people who are often uncomfortable at best and strongly resistant at worst. We had to trust that we had each other's backs.

True community is built on this very foundation of trust. The belief that we are stronger, more impactful, and more successful when we advance each other. The outcome of mine and Aiko's trust? Close to a decade of friendship, mutual admiration, and celebration. I know that what I have with Aiko is precious and rare; we're so busy in our respective lives parenting boys while building our businesses that sometimes a whole year will go by before we talk. Even so, if I needed to text someone *any time* of night or day for advice on a big hairy work problem, Aiko's name would be in the top five.

That kind of trust is extremely rare to find today, and I don't take it for granted. Competitive systems erode trust between individuals and communities, and also benefit from this trust erosion. The breakdown of trust among people who should be aligned and collaborate is central to a divide-and-conquer strategy that's as old as our civilization. To get ahead in many organizations today, we are required to act strategically and politically; we're meant to connect only with people who can help us reach our goals and not bother building relationships otherwise. In our winner-take-all society, it's more than OK to turn on someone if they stop being "useful" to you in advancing your goals. We've seen a drop in public trust in institutions like the government and the media. Research shows we've also become increasingly distrustful of people in our lives: coworkers, employers, and leaders within our workplaces. When you add systems of oppression—racism, misogyny, poverty, ableism—the divisions between groups further diminish opportunities for trust. I understand why it's hard—if not impossible— to create a community that's anchored in trust. The water we swim in doesn't encourage it. In fact, the same research shows that more Americans now have less willingness to deal fairly and honestly with coworkers and workplace leaders.

Yet *communities* benefit from a society and workplace built on trust; trust at work leads to better performance. Employees in high-trust organizations are more productive, have more energy at work, collaborate better with their colleagues, and stay with their employers longer than people working at low-trust companies. They also suffer less chronic stress and are happier with their lives, and these factors fuel stronger performance, according to neuroscientist Paul Zak, who has spent decades researching trust at work. Trust leads to higher citizen engagement in a well-functioning democracy. We're more likely to invest in our communities and participate in them if we believe that they're built on trust, integrity, and accountability. Building a community to reframe the competition mindset we've all been brought up to believe requires us to first operate with integrity and trust. We can't bemoan the lack of it in society without taking personal accountability. When I say, "It's hard to trust anyone these days," I have to ask myself—uncomfortably—who do I really mean? And do I always operate with integrity and think of ways to earn trust in others? Of course, I don't mean that I act in bad faith or maliciously hurt or harm other people. But without consciously, intentionally building trust with others by practicing radical generosity and abundance, I'm often just creating surface-level connections, not community. People may not be harmed by me in those encounters, they may even like me, but do they feel like I have their backs? Probably not.

Building a community founded on trust is not a transactional endeavor. It requires a long-term approach and long-term commitment, which directly challenges many white and Western ways of working and living. Too many books about success in the workplace *literally* guide us to approach every interaction with this strategy: "What can you do for me?" You can even see it at workplace events when you introduce yourself to someone new: Their eyes start searching for others to talk to if they assess you're not senior enough or "useful" to their career at that moment.

Instead, when we uncompete to create and build our community, we never approach it with "I scratch your back; you scratch mine." Life is rarely ever that linear. It is extremely hard to discern upon meeting most people that if you collaborate with or help them, that there'll be an equal reward waiting for you. That's why instead of seeing people as rivals immediately, there's more value in seeing them as colleagues. Our mindset must be *I'm helping you succeed here because I'm actively making a choice to uncompete. I believe your voice must be elevated, and I have the privilege to do that, so I will. That helps me create a community of trustworthy citizens who trust one another.*

I've found that this approach will create a knock-on effect of someone else doing that for you, even if it's not the same person you were generous to. It requires us to be relational, not transactional. It will normalize an approach that rewards community and trust building. At work, it can create and boost a culture of collaboration and solidarity. It includes more marginalized people when we intentionally choose this over quid pro quo, which in Latin literally means "something for something." To uncompete invites more of us to choose, instead, pro bono publico, "for the public good." In other words, for the good of our community.

SPONSORSHIP: THE BEDROCK OF ACTION FOR OUR COMMUNITY

We all know that *who* we know is *how* we level up. And if we have influence in our own careers, particularly if we've advanced to a leadership role, we have a responsibility to advance others. You may have heard of this as being a mentor—taking a person under our wing and giving them advice on how to succeed. We share our tips and tricks for doing a job exceptionally well. We advise on everything from how to handle office politics and ask management for better compensation to developing expertise in a certain area and knowing when to look for a new gig. And yes, mentorship is one way to build trust in our workplaces and communities. But mentorship can only go so far and is more likely to be directed and led by the mentee, who typically bears the responsibility to reach out when advice is needed. Plus, it's typically a one-to-one relationship and therefore rarely as effective in building a broader, trusting community.

Sponsorship, though, is a lever that has far-reaching potential. Sponsorship is using your influence and privilege to advance another person. Like mentorship, it can be especially meaningful in the workplace. But unlike mentorship, it's external facing and proactive; it means using your access to speak someone's name in rooms they wouldn't otherwise have access to. It requires us to advocate loudly, vocally, and regularly for other deserving people in our life to receive opportunities they wouldn't have otherwise. It means willingly sharing our contacts and making introductions to people of influence. It could involve recommending someone for a job they might have been overlooked for or being a glowing reference for them. Outside of our career, sponsorship can look like connecting a person who is new in town to your trusted group of friends or going out of your way to put a good word in for someone applying for, say, a team or club you're part of.

Aiko's action to recommend my name to a career-changing and life-changing podcast is a perfect example of sponsorship. She leveraged her social capital to elevate mine without me even asking or knowing that the opportunity was on the line. And she did so without expectation for a return favor. Each of us has an opportunity to do that for at least one other person, ideally many more, in our lives. Sponsorship negates any divide-and-conquer tactics that may be in play while planting the seeds of abundance and solidarity among those who need them the most. It requires us to think and act radically, with generosity always, even if we weren't shown generosity in the same way. Most importantly, sponsorship aids us in building a strong, inclusive network of people who want to band together for the greater good instead of tearing each other down so only one of us can come out on top.

For centuries, members of the dominant culture (largely white men) have been using sponsorship as a method of achieving upward social mobility. Because we live in a competitive world, they've shared the fruits of their efforts mostly with one another and have kept opportunities close to the vest rather than sharing contacts and influence outwardly. Many have historically not seen it as their duty to help people outside their inner circle to succeed, a pattern that creates more of a closed circle than an open-ended, ever-broadening community. When sponsorship happens within a closed circle, there can frequently be a quid pro quo quality to that sponsorship, keeping influence trading among a smaller and tight-knit community. Nonetheless, the impact of sharing power and influence is something we all can learn from—and when done within the context of uncompeting, sponsorship extends beyond whatever group we identify with. Sponsoring people from historically marginalized identities is how we actively undo the systems of competition and oppression we've been conditioned to believe in. When my white peers have vouched for me and introduced me to other white families at the community playground near my house, or at the day care or schools my son has attended, I've noticed how those families are then more willing to include me or my son in the community. I wish it didn't have to be that way, but I know that because of systemic racism, bias, and the conditioning to only see others like us as part of our community (even in places like "liberal" Seattle), this type of sponsorship can truly alter how welcome a person of color feels. Sponsorship is how we shape an inclusive community where more of us support one another, especially those who are and have been marginalized throughout history. In fact, the more that white people in particular use their racial privilege to make calls, write letters, and recommend people of color for great opportunities, the higher the chance we'll be able to create a more antiracist society. In doing so, our community becomes stronger.

HOW CAN WE BECOME GOOD SPONSORS?

Rosalind Chow, a Carnegie Mellon Business School professor whose book, *The Doors You Can Open*, is about how we can all be reliable and trustworthy sponsors, suggests thinking of sponsorship as being *some-*

one else's brand manager. I love this analogy because it truly speaks to our modern sensibilities and to how living in a social media society has us conceptualizing our identities as "brands." We've been conditioned to focus only on expanding our own brand or controlling our own narrative. But in the realm of uncompete, we're all responsible for elevating other people's brands, not just our own.

One of the ways we can sponsor others is through *amplification*: bragging about someone else publicly so that others have a positive impression of them. Amplification was popularized by the female staffers in the Obama administration. When a woman made a point in a meeting, other women would repeat it enthusiastically and credit the author. This would safeguard against a common phenomenon most women and people of color are all too familiar with—where our ideas are either ignored or remain uncredited, compared with our white and male peers. At its core, amplification ensures that women and other people with underestimated identities are heard, validated, and appreciated in the workplace. In turn, a community steeped in trust and solidarity is also formed.

And although it's not my first goal in mind, the knock-on effect is that amplification benefits the amplifier, too. In chapter 4 I wrote about the Amplify July campaign I run annually on my social media to highlight other women of color. One of the most inspiring people we featured was Antionette Carroll, founder of the Creative Reaction Lab. Antionette was a resident of Ferguson, Missouri, in 2014, the year Michael Brown, an unarmed Black teenager, was shot and killed by Darren Wilson, a white police officer. The city (and country) rose up in protest against racism and police brutality, and Antionette was on the front lines of advocating for social change.

155

Using her passion for social entrepreneurship and design, Antionette established a community by founding Creative Reaction Lab, an organization that trains Black and Latinx youth to design healthy and racially equitable communities by tackling some of the biggest social challenges of our time, from youth voter apathy to inequitable access to education. Central to all the work done at Creative Reaction Lab is the belief that systems of oppression, inequality, and inequity are by design; therefore, they can and must be redesigned. In the process, the lab has engaged thousands of youths of color and deployed hundreds of thousands of dollars to them directly.

When her team applied for Amplify July, the choice to feature her was a no-brainer. I shouldn't be applauded or celebrated for Amplify July, and yet after the month was done, my social media team told me that our engagement across all platforms was the highest it had ever been. Antionette's story and important work reached thousands of people as a result.

Research shows that sponsoring others (through tools like amplification) makes us better leaders at work because it can help us boost our brand and legacy and build our leadership capability. In fact, senior executives who sponsor rising talent are 53 percent more likely to be promoted than those who don't, according to research by economist Sylvia Ann Hewlett. Most important, sponsorship can also be leveraged for societal change and empowerment for everyone. Currently, there's such a lack of it that it's heartbreaking. In the workplace, women were less likely than men to say that a senior leader they worked under directly helped them get a promotion or a stretch assignment. That's even though women were more likely to have a formal mentor assigned. For women of color, it was even harder: Most who were surveyed said they rarely (if ever) had bosses who promoted their work contributions to others, navigated workplace politics, or connected them to informal networks that would advance them, according to a 2016 Lean In/McKinsey report. Sadly, only 5 percent of high-potential Black employees have sponsors, compared with 20 percent of their white peers. Just 5 percent of high-earning Latino professionals in large companies said they had sponsors.

Not all sponsors need to be *executives*, though—much of the gap between white employees and employees of color comes from not having other team members at any level advocate for, elevate, or advance us in ways that help build our standing in the organization. Anyone, at any level, can choose to amplify a deserving teammate. But if you're reading this, then, like me, you have some level of privilege that can be leveraged to advance others.

For all of us to become sponsors, we must ask ourselves some serious questions about our privilege and influence and think critically about how to maximize them. This can sometimes be uncomfortable—but it can also be empowering. And it can help us get to work. Even without a big job, title, or budget, it's necessary to recognize that we all have our spheres of influence and levers to pull. As we know, more often than not, big change comes from the accumulation of small actions. Ask yourself the following questions:

1. **Where do I have influence?** With a competitive mindset, we more often focus on the gap between where we are and where we want to go than on the ways we already have influence and how that can be used to affect others. Flip this narrative: Where do I have influence—in the workplace, socially among friends, in my community, and beyond that? If I offer my boss an idea or a recommendation, does she listen to it? If I offer feedback or

advice to my friends, do they take it seriously? If I post an issue to social media, do I hear from my circle that they appreciate my perspective or even act on it? Does anyone in my life come to me for advice or with questions?

2. **Where will my privilege enable me to speak up and amplify someone else?** When men repeat an idea that a woman said earlier in the meeting, people are more likely to listen and think it's a great idea. This phenomenon is called "he-peating" and is also relevant to when white people validate a person of color's idea when they repeat it. Is there an opportunity to "he-peat" my colleague's idea *and* ensure she gets credit for it? Something to consider: Are there opportunities for you to speak someone's name in a setting where you know you will be heard but where they've often been overlooked or even denied access?

3. **Who can I think of that doesn't have access to the same groups as me because they're of a different race, gender, or socioeconomic status?** If we don't intentionally seek to create communities where everyone has equal access, we often maintain and perpetuate existing structures where only a dominant majority leads. Reflecting on who is left out is the first step to creating a different way.

4. **How can I use my privilege to change who might be excluded from this group? To actively change whose voices are included and invited into this group?** Only once we take stock of who is being excluded can we intentionally include and build a wider table for all. This reminds me of the saying that many of us advocating for a fairer world come back to: Talent is evenly distributed in society; opportunities are not.

5. **Are there people who I might feel competitive with right now or in the future, but could still sponsor to succeed?** We're conditioned to advance others only if we feel we've already "scaled that mountain." But what would it take for us to reject that idea and work toward "scaling the mountain together"? Would it be possible to see it as a stepping stone to building a trusting community that's based on relationships, not transactions?

Sponsorship may seem like a one-to-one action that affects only you and your protégé. But I believe we can practice sponsorship in so many ways, big and small, by building trust and solidarity with a wide range of people and regularly asking ourselves, "Where do I have the influence to help someone else succeed?" Sponsorship within a community signals that this kind of action and accountability is not only possible but also necessary. It is a powerful antidote to the oppression and scarcity we still see in every facet of our lives.

NOT HALF-HEARTED SPONSORSHIP: SKIN IN THE GAME

There are times when we can sponsor someone without really sponsoring them wholeheartedly because we still have a competition mindset. A few years ago, I was invited to be part of a big conference where many peers told me that I, as a woman of color, should feel grateful to attend. As many of us have been conditioned to feel, I was grateful to be invited, although in hindsight I was eminently qualified to be there.

Once I arrived, I thanked several people who had advocated for me to be there. The sessions during the day went well, and each night I stopped by a local café to pick up dinner on my way back to my room. On the third night, I bumped into one of my peers, a white woman I'd seen earlier at the conference, looking dressed up. She sheepishly admitted that some of the other attendees had been invited to dinners paid for by the organizers, where they could continue networking with one another. As many of us know, that is where the greatest opportunities to really build relationships occur, not during planned conference sessions.

I realized that many of the people who had advocated for me to attend thought they'd "done me a favor" just by inviting me but wouldn't consider sharing other more exclusive opportunities, like those dinner invitations. To uncompete, our sponsorship can't be half-hearted and can't involve only the easy opportunities to turn over, because then we're still operating from a competition mindset.

I can admit that I've done this too and have had to mentally check myself many times. As I've ascended in my career, I've tried to pay it forward in ways that still prioritize my interests and comfort. I've recommended women of color for positions and prizes and grants that I've gotten before (so the sponsorship isn't a direct "threat" to my success). But sponsorship when you're uncompeting requires you to take a broader approach. It needs you to put skin in the game, which means that maybe the people you sponsor become more successful or win more awards or "win" in ways you didn't.

This is why the mindset of uncompete precedes action. Change happens when we sponsor others for opportunities they'd be great for, even ones that we may well want for ourselves. It means focusing on the larger prize: *I want you to win, too, without strings attached, because it benefits our community and creates a culture of goodwill beyond just my individual gains.*

According to Rosalind Chow, other ways to practice sponsorship beyond **amplification** include **boosting** (such as writing letters of recommendation or making referrals), **connecting** (for example, a sponsor might invite a protégé to an exclusive event or meeting to increase their visibility to important individuals who might advance their careers), and **defending** (when we attempt to change others' perceptions of a person from negative to positive). She emphasizes that defending is the most important but is rarely done for people of color in the workplace.

In all my work on practicing allyship with marginalized groups, when I'm asked why more people with privilege don't actively "stand up" against racism, sexism, or other forms of bias, my answer is that many don't see the need to personally defend or take responsibility for standing up to it. Or they're too scared. Most of us aren't taught to defend others, especially if they're not directly related to us. But we have to make it our business; we must push back hard against bias and, most of all, defend those who have been directly harmed by bias and oppression.

One such example is how a senior partner defended Kenneth Frazier (former CEO of pharmaceutical giant Merck) earlier in his career. Frazier shared a story in the media about a time when he worked for a law firm in Philadelphia. One of the firm's clients asked that he be removed from a case because he is Black. Frazier's senior partner took a stand, telling the client, "You may take your business elsewhere, but we believe in him and we're not going to replace him."

Defending someone requires us to vocally stand up against bias and even risk losing face with the perpetrator. It is one of the most important antidotes to the bias we see in our world today. Imagine what could happen if more of us took the responsibility—and I acknowledge how much courage it takes—to go against the tide and say something like "I don't agree with the way you called our colleague aggressive in a performance review. I've never seen her behave in any way that indicates that. Could her race and gender have you making up a story about her that isn't true?" I know for sure when white women have backed me up publicly or privately in the face of bias, I've felt a connection of trust and community that is more meaningful to me than any other form of sponsorship.

BUILDING COMMUNITY REQUIRES PERSONAL ACCOUNTABILITY

The traditional competition mindset tells us to help others *so that* they can be available to help you win when it's your turn to ask for it. Moving away from the quid pro quo motivation to help others is hard, especially because we've been conditioned to believe this is a fundamental rule of success. One of the ways I've attempted to let go of this approach is to try not to expect favors for me from people I've previously sponsored, amplified, or helped in some way. I'll admit that I've not had a perfect track record in this regard; it is a work in progress. Instead, I am intentional about calling in favors when it comes to elevating *other people* in my network. So if I helped someone, I'd rather reach out to ask them to use that goodwill to help *someone else in* my network than to ask for a favor that would benefit me directly.

This is a deliberate mindset shift that helps me pay it forward into the general universe and into my hope to create an unlimited flywheel of good, leading to a larger culture of uncompeting rather than getting caught up in the details of ruminating over why someone I previously helped didn't help me. I'll admit that I spent a lot of time doing that in my past. I'd keep track and score. I'd stew in anger and hurt whenever someone whom I had previously gone to bat for declined to support me. In the end, it didn't feel good and didn't foster a sense of community.

I want us to move away from the belief that we are owed a favor because we helped someone win previously. But even here, I acknowledge that privilege and power play a huge part. The more we have of both, the less we have to ask for favors or keep score. In my journalist days, I'd interview so many white male CEOs who said they were "just tapped on the shoulder for the top job and never even asked for it" that I've lost track. In contrast, women of color have had to fight doggedly for opportunities, use every connection and resource, and call in every favor to make it half as far. I still know that the rules of success as we know it are rigged mainly in favor of those who demand, cajole, and intimidate to get ahead. Even so, I've learned the hard way that winning transactionally but having no relationships or community to celebrate your wins isn't worth the pain. More of us, particularly immigrants, women of color, and others who are the "firsts" and "onlys" to reach the pinnacle of success in societal terms, find that the cost of loneliness is just too high to bear.

To uncompete asks us to be intentional: *What's more important to me: helping someone so they can help me in the future or building a community beyond transactions? How will my approach serve my life's goals in the short term versus the long term?*

A powerful and inspiring example of intentionality to sponsor and elevate a whole community comes from a British scientist. In 2017 a twenty-nine-year-old physicist, Jess Wade, was surprised to learn that American climate scientist Kim Cobb did not have a Wikipedia page, despite making huge contributions to the field. So she spent time creating a Wikipedia page for Cobb and figured it was a one-off endeavor. Cobb wasn't a friend or someone she personally knew.

But when she began searching on Wikipedia for other women and people of color in STEM fields who had inspired her career, Wade kept encountering a glaring lack of entries. Soon, she had taken it upon herself to write one new entry of an overlooked female scientist per day, spending upward of two hours per entry, despite having a very busy job as a *physicist* in a top lab. But Wade just couldn't sit idle while so many living scientists deserving of recognition—and so many past scientists who would be forgotten by history—continued to remain obscure in the eyes of the general public. So, as she sheepishly admits, while watching real-estate shows on Netflix every evening, she continues to create new entries for incredible scientists and recently even for people in non-STEM fields, according to a profile in *The Guardian.* At last count, Wade has created more than two thousand Wikipedia entries of women scientists and scientists of color.

When asked whether her incredible work was motivated by the sexism she faced in her career, she's quick to quell that narrative. In fact, it's precisely the privilege of growing up financially comfortable and supported as a white woman that led to her action, when it became clear to her that progress in science, like every other field, had more to do with your gender, race, and financial background than your scientific prowess. Wade was brought up with the view that it was intelligence and hard work, not privilege, that dictated progress in science, but she now actively works to resist that idea.

In her spare time Wade *also* nominates women and people of color for science grants, awards, and prizes. Many of these people are more than deserving but have never been tapped to apply because . . . sexism and racism again. If that's not enough, she also regularly speaks to girls in school about pursuing scientific careers and co-led a crowdfunding campaign to have Angela Saini's book, *Inferior,* which is about the shoddy science that's been used to oppress women in society, available in every state school in the United Kingdom. And she *does* have a Wikipedia page, written by others, but hasn't read it, according to interviews with her. She's too busy promoting others.

Whew. As I typed that out, I was thinking how much more *I* could do personally to ensure that women and people of color continue to win. Wade is a remarkable (and remarkably humble) human being who demonstrates what it means to uncompete by creating a community built on trust and solidarity. My biggest inspiration from her action is that she clearly operates from this belief: "I'm responsible for helping you win."

SHARED SISTERHOOD: PERSONAL ACCOUNTABILITY TO BUILD AN ANTIRACIST COMMUNITY

Creating an abundant community and solidarity with other groups who don't share your identities requires trust. If we have privilege, we also have the responsibility to earn others' trust by demonstrating that we genuinely have their success in mind. That we actually want others to win in ways that are meaningful to them. That we won't be throwing them under the proverbial bus when things get tough. And this trust feels particularly hard to cultivate across races when we've all been harmed by white supremacy.

Women of color report having long been dismissed, manipulated, or even sabotaged by white women at work. Our distrust is justified; white feminism has long excluded or even sabotaged women of color while advocating for gender rights. From the white suffragettes who gathered in Seneca Falls, New York, in July 1848 to advocate for the right of only *white* women to vote to how white women have made gains in society while perpetuating inequities that keep women of color in lower-paid and unsafe jobs, trust between white women and women from communities of color is a big gap to bridge right now.

This is particularly why building the kind of trust that knits together a community relies on developing a deep solidarity, which needs those of us with privilege (particularly racial and socioeconomic) to actively push back against racism and bias.

I often turn to the Shared Sisterhood framework, which was designed by two academics to build solidarity among white and Black women, to guide me. The authors, Tina Opie, who is Black, and Beth Livingston, who is white, realized that there was a glaring lack of collaboration between white women and Black women at work.

Over the course of her career, Tina, a well-regarded keynote speaker, author, and professor at Babson College, was particularly harmed by the lack of solidarity. It was clear to her that white women largely weren't advancing Black women like her in the way that they amplified and sponsored other white women. Recognizing a dire need for there to be more collective accountability to advance Black women, Tina collaborated with Beth to develop the three-step Shared Sisterhood framework with the aim to bolster the fairness, equity, and, most of all, trust needed for community building across racial lines. The framework challenges people, particularly white people and those with status and privilege in the workplace, to reckon with their assumptions and stereotypes about other people's identities. Both authors emphasize that the Shared Sisterhood framework can be adopted by people of any gender or race—not just women and not just Black or white people.

As I shared with Tina, I found it applicable to nonwhite women with privilege, like me, to build solidarity with my Black women peers, too.

The framework requires us first to *dig*—essentially, to reflect on questions such as *When did you learn that you were Black or white? How do you feel about your Blackness or your whiteness? Where did those beliefs come from? How did those beliefs affect how you see the world? How do you see other people? How do you navigate the workplace?*

Entrenched racism, combined with the way competition distracts and exhausts us, makes it so that we rarely, if ever, dive deeper to ask ourselves these questions. We continue to largely build community on autopilot, usually only among people who share our same identities and often passing over or rejecting those who don't. When we dig, we're able to interrogate not only our own biases but systems of power as well.

From there, we *bridge* to connect with people on the shared value of equity, people who have a different identity than us. Simply put, as an Asian woman, I can seek to connect with a Black woman because we both believe in the importance of justice in society and in the workplace. We can form an authentic interpersonal connection based on empathy, trust, risk-taking, and vulnerability. Without developing a connection based on these four factors, we can't have a true relationship in which we believe that the other person has our back. Lastly, the

Shared Sisterhood framework guides us to *advance*, which requires us to work together to dismantle systems of inequity and prioritize collective action toward equity, rather than focusing on individual successes. One of the tools they recommend to accomplish this is one we're already familiar with: *amplification*.

WIN WITH BLACK WOMEN

I believe we have so much to learn from Black women about personal accountability, trust, and building an abundant community. It is crystal clear that Black women show up for one another because it's a survival mechanism and a practice of radical joy in an anti-Black world.

A number of Black women I interviewed for my last book, *Inclusion on Purpose*, and for this one told me that investing in, sponsoring, amplifying, and being part of a community of Black women has been essential to their survival. I've also seen many Black women I've had the honor of connecting with operate from a space of generosity and abundance that is truly inspiring, and they show it toward other non-Black women, too.

In my own life, from Aiko, whom you met at the start of the chapter, to Tina, to many of the trailblazers throughout this book, Black women have modeled and led this work for centuries. I've benefited from this effort personally, and I'd be remiss if I didn't explicitly name it.

It's remarkable to see how Black women leaders from Oprah Winfrey to Michelle Obama (and so many others who aren't household names) guide us to realizing that true success comes from taking care of one another and by rising together. It is diametrically opposed to the "winner-take-all, sharp-elbows-out" approach I've seen deified in white-dominated professional workplaces and Western societies. It is what I hope more of us non-Black women learn about uncompeting: Our collective liberation isn't happening if we don't help *one another* win, if we don't take the personal initiative to actually show up, sponsor, amplify, and practice shared solidarity.

I was heartened to see tangible progress toward Shared Sisterhood when Kamala Harris made a bid to run for president in July 2024. It started with "Win with Black Women," the swift collective action of a group of Black women who, within hours of the announcement, mobilized 44,000 Black women to support Harris's bid through an online call, nearly broke Zoom, and raised $1.4 million in an hour. Within a few weeks, at least 140 other grassroots groups kicked off their own virtual calls in support, which were vast and varied: White Dudes for Harris, Win with Black Men, Comics for Kamala, White Women for Kamala, Republicans for Harris, Latino Men for Kamala, and several others, raising millions of dollars and also attracting celebrity endorsements.

Like others, I was absolutely energized by the level of engagement, knowing I was witnessing a stunning alternative to the long history we have in this country of downplaying (or outright denying) how much our identities influence the privilege or oppression we experience. The solidarity calls showed me what could happen when we gather intentionally within groups where we have influence during a historic campaign for the country's first Black and South Asian female presidential candidate.

"By coming together as white people who recognize that the

United States has given them very different experiences than it offers Americans of color, they are pinpointing precisely why joining a broad coalition matters," wrote Koritha Mitchell, author of *From Slave Cabins to the White House* and *Living with Lynching*, about the identity-based groups mobilizing for Harris. "Coalition requires acknowledging that there are very real differences, but that those differences matter less than working together to make gains that benefit people far beyond one's family and friends. Groups that operate in solidarity with groups that are undeniably different are taking steps that run counter to what American culture encourages and are operating in ways that will ultimately make the United States less hostile for more people."

Personal responsibility remains the key ingredient in making collective change. Too often, we get caught up in (and immobilized by) the scale of the challenge. Systemic bias is no small thing to take down! Knowing how much the system is geared toward overworking us to not have a single spare moment to invest in community, I realize that this is really hard. But creating an abundant community that has each other's back is so important to dismantling competition and creating a different path—in small ways at first, then in larger ways, as we can. Equality and liberation don't lie in only *one* of us winning the prize or getting ahead. We have to show up consistently and loudly to demonstrate that our win alone isn't a win if more of us aren't advancing as a community.

I often reach for this statement by Toni Morrison to guide me in this endeavor: "When you get these jobs that you have been so brilliantly trained for, just remember that your real job is that if you are free, you need to free somebody else. If you have some power, then your job is to empower somebody else."

Indeed, to uncompete requires us to believe that the real work—and our purpose on Earth—wasn't just to extract every last drop for ourselves and people like us. Our life's purpose and the real reason we were put here was to free others, particularly those from whom so much has already been unjustly extracted. It requires us to build trust, solidarity, and abundance by showing up for one another consistently. Only when our community expands abundantly do we as well.

CHAPTER SEVEN

Build Collective Power

We all deserve power. We all deserve wealth.

This idea might appear counter to the premise of uncompete I've been going on about so far. But the best way to build power focuses on community, abundance, solidarity, inclusion, *and* radical generosity. That means building collective power and building communal wealth. But not power and wealth the way you might be used to thinking about. The power I envision as fundamental to uncompete is not the individualistic, winner-take-all kind. It is not the power hoarding and wealth hoarding that come from exploiting our communities and planet for a small elite to rise. And it's not the kind that is typically amassed in a single lifetime or awarded to a single person or small group. The power fundamental to uncompete is meant to create the opportunity for as many people as possible to benefit, thrive, and win. It is a collective power that can help build generational wealth for many, and with a broad impact. This type of group power expands intentionally and over the long term.

I acknowledge that this is nearly impossible to do in our current paradigm. I also accept that it is well and good for me, a cis, straight South Asian woman who has never experienced poverty or true financial insecurity, to write this. But I have experienced how systems of oppression force so many of us to compete over scraps by denying us access to building wealth by systematically underpaying and excluding us. I know what it's like to be systematically underpaid for the same work as my white peers, to feel so broken by bias that I literally couldn't go on working at lucrative but soul-crushing jobs and not have generational wealth to fall back on. I've also experienced the both/and of simultaneous proximity to and distance from the centers of power at different times of my life—as a woman, as a person of color, as an immigrant, as an Ivy League graduate, in different jobs, as a mother. I have seen firsthand what happens when power is easily meted out to some and quickly denied to so many others, contingent upon their race, gender, ability, and bank account. I've seen powerful people lauded for their "hard work" or "winning the competition of life" instead of honest acknowledgment of how much their exploiting of existing power structures has played a role in amassing their good fortune.

Nowhere more than around power—and by extension, wealth—are scarcity beliefs more corrosive. We come to believe we must fight off, dominate, and win against others for any illusion of power, and this process especially harms people of color and other marginalized groups. Our ability to build generational wealth for so many of us has been stolen from us because of racism, colonialism, and exploitation.

So we turn on one another. When we elbow others like us out of the way because of an entrenched competition mindset, we reinforce existing inequalities in accessing power. That's why even when one oppressed group advances, it sometimes tears another down instead of expanding the table.

In June 2023 the US Supreme Court announced a stunning reversal of a nearly fifty-year policy on affirmative action, or race-based considerations, in college admissions. The suit to challenge affirmative action was brought forward by a conservative white man, Edward Blum, but devastatingly, it also divided Asian American communities. Some Asian American activists spoke up in support of the suit, saying affirmative action unfairly took away spots from Asian American students in favor of Black and Latinx students. But, as predicted, competing over the already-minimal spots taken by Black and Latinx students instead of looking to fix advantages for white applicants—from legacy admissions to sports-based advantages—would only harm enrollment for students of color. Indeed, a year after the affirmative action ban, Black and Latinx admissions declined, and in some colleges, like Yale University, so did Asian American enrollment. In many colleges, white enrollment went up or wasn't significantly affected by the ban. We know that in our current system, access to an elite college can lead to building power and wealth, and this option has been seriously curtailed by yet another tactic to fragment us in a bid to disempower and disrupt that pathway to building more power among marginalized groups. It's a modern example of how white supremacy successfully divided and conquered these groups in their bid for individual group gains, even though, in the long run, these groups could have amassed more power if they'd collectively pushed back.

This is precisely why I believe that the old playbook of "focus on individual gains while pushing others out of the way to build power" is in direct opposition to opportunities and liberation for those who are most disenfranchised. In fact, building wealth and power alone hasn't ever fully worked for those of us who are already marginalized in society. Oprah Winfrey is a badass billionaire who has changed lives all over the world, but in a racist society built on disempowering Black women, she still faces discrimination. In 2013 a salesperson in Switzerland refused to let her look at a handbag because they considered it to be "too expensive" for her to purchase. At last count, Ms. Winfrey is worth $3 billion. In the same year, Hollywood actor Forest Whitaker was wrongfully accused of shoplifting in a New York deli. Research shows that close to 50 percent of Black and Latinx scientists report having been mistaken for janitorial and administrative staff. As someone who got all the right education and knows how to code switch in Western environments and how to dress above my station in life, I've still experienced bias and discrimination because of my skin color.

I've learned that individual gains—a handful of people of color ascending to the wealthiest and most powerful level alone—can't overturn the anti-Blackness, bias, and general racism that are widespread in society. For that, we need to build power and wealth collectively, to challenge entrenched stereotypes in society, and to normalize our influence.

So can we redefine power? I believe we can. It requires us to be more intentional about what it means to build power, how to build it, and who deserves it. We can start by thinking of power not as something that *must be* concentrated among a small number of people but as communal influence, communal wealth, and the ability to take care of one another. Power and wealth may almost always go together—true—but the end purpose of building power does not have to mean enriching only individuals. I think it would liberate us if we could un-learn the common scarcity narrative that "people who work hard de-serve wealth and are therefore justified in hoarding it" to the idea that everyone, everywhere is worthy of power. Most of all, I'd like us to stop operating with our colonized minds that tell us that a wealthy person can get away with anything, no matter how harmful, just be-cause there's some special waiver for the powerful.

CONTEXTUALIZING POWER

We've been obsessed with the idea of power from (at least) the birth of our civilization. Underscored by ideals of hierarchy, authority, and domination, much of even modern theory has made power seem dis-tinctly masculine and relevant only when one holds power *over others.* Let's acknowledge that this definition of power is extremely Western and is associated with the military. Particularly in comparison to how, in many collectivistic communities, especially Indigenous traditions, power has long been seen as universal, constantly evolving and contin-ually redefined.

In the Western world, management theorist Mary Parker Follett provided the first true distinction between definitions of power in or-ganizations during the 1930s. Follett described two separate ways to understand power: power-over and power-with. She wrote, "So far as my observation has gone, it seems to me that whereas power usually means power-over, the power of some person or group over some other person or group, it is possible to develop the conception of power-with." In essence, power-with is about the power we gain from working together, not working against one another.

Philosopher Hannah Arendt took this a step further in the 1970s, essentially calling the power-over approach "violence," and her definition of power corresponded with power-with. In 1978 Audre Lorde wrote that "eventually institutional racism becomes a question of power and privilege rather than merely color, which then serves as a subterfuge." What a profound statement, which explains how all oppression has long been used to maintain privilege and power, using arbitrary measures (color in her example) to divide us!

I'm not advocating for one group to replace another, simply putting the power-over into new hands. That's a paradigm I've spent most of my career pushing back against: The advice given to women to be more assertive, be more dominant, show less emotion, be "like men" to get ahead in the workplace literally makes me feel nauseated. Similarly, I don't want more women, people of color, and others of us to amass power and influence only to replicate the very harmful, dominant systems we've already experienced. We can—and must—choose something different.

Uncompete views power as unlimited, expansive, and sustainable precisely *because* it is shared. Power and the ability to influence do not exist to serve individual gains but to make change for those around us. We don't hoard power or exploit others to dominate them or make them fear us; instead, we earn trust and work collaboratively to benefit more than just ourselves.

JASS, a key contemporary leader in this thinking, has long guided me. JASS is a feminist movement support organization anchored outside Western countries that's focused on strengthening the collective power of women. "Power is the capacity of individuals or groups to determine who gets what, who does what, who decides what, and who sets the agenda," writes Srilatha Batliwala on JASS's website, quoting and expanding on the definition by Aruna Rao and David Kelleher. Their work guides us to see power as neither intrinsically good nor bad. They go on to define different types of power: Whereas coercive power is often "oppressive, violent and unequal, transforming power can make deep changes for the better."

What if when we thought of power, the idea that first came to mind was that of transformational power? What if instead of power being in lockstep with domination, we always associate it first and foremost with responsibility? This is, once again, a mental shift that expands out in incredibly tangible ways. If power's main definition is "power-with," then the influence that comes with power is the ability to be a responsible steward, to enrich our communities, and to create possibilities for future generations that previously seemed unthinkable. When we define power this way, it moves away from being unequal and exploitative and toward something that's full of promise and possibilities. I often reach for this response from Stacey Abrams when she was asked if she someday wanted to run for president: "Do I hold it as an ambition? Absolutely. And even more importantly, when someone asks me if that's my ambition, I have a responsibility to say yes, for every young woman, every person of color, every young person of color, who sees me and decides what they're capable of based on what I think I am capable of."

The ambition—or bid for power—that Abrams is talking about isn't a selfish, exploitative "me as the individual who is all-powerful seeking to oppress others" but a demonstration of a growing number of leaders, most from marginalized backgrounds, who believe that responsibly wielding power means opening doors for those coming behind them—this is the ultimate goal.

There's usually an inextricable link between power and wealth in our world today. And as someone who is ambitious *and* likes nice things, I don't want us to forgo wealth but rather to build both power and wealth with a communal approach.

THE NEXUS OF POWER AND WEALTH

Arlan Hamilton is a queer Black female venture capitalist with a multimillion-dollar investment firm focused on elevating underestimated entrepreneurs. Her firm, Backstage Capital, is backed by Mark Cuban and other well-known investors, and it exemplifies the idea of collective wealth and power building. Arlan is incredible in how she's shaken up traditional VC investing (which is overwhelmingly pale and male), and her mantra—even while she slept in airports—is "I came for the cake, not the crumbs."

Her words aren't a toxic-positivity version of a "you can mindset your way out of structural and generational poverty" slogan. They're a vision board for her life that helped her align her choices and build power and wealth *while ensuring others like her also had access.* Her best-selling memoir, aptly named *It's About Damn Time: How to Turn Being Underestimated into Your Greatest Advantage,* is illuminating, and what stands out to me the most is how Arlan believed—even when others didn't—that her lack of wealth said virtually nothing about her as a person. Her circumstances were not an indictment of her character. Being broke didn't mean that she was undeserving or that wealth would never be attainable. Imagine being able to have this conviction in a society that reinforces in so many ways that a lack of power and wealth is a personal failing!

Over time, she doggedly built an empire around her beliefs by intentionally calling in and empowering people who had long been left out of the VC industry: entrepreneurs of color—particularly Black entrepreneurs—and a pool of first-time investors, many who were also people of color. She started Backstage Capital in 2015 by accepting small checks from accredited investors, which is how I became accredited and made my first investment. Most VC funds require hundreds of thousands of dollars to get a buy-in—making them completely out of reach for the vast majority of us, particularly those who don't come from elite backgrounds. But rather than just reaching out to rich investors to get richer by investing in companies founded by white men (how business is generally done in the VC industry), Arlan wanted to ensure that even those who didn't have a lot to invest could still get their foot in the door. She believed that there was money to be made and power to be built by giving entrepreneurs and investors who were otherwise firmly shut out from accessing venture capital access to . . . you guessed it: venture capital. One such company is PopCom, a company founded by serial entrepreneur Dawn Dickson, a Black woman whose robotic pop-up shops are found in multiple US airports. Given that Black women entrepreneurs receive statistically 0 percent of venture funding—with mounting legal challenges against investors that specifically fund Black women founders—it's not a stretch to say that tens, if not hundreds, of companies wouldn't exist without Backstage Capital's help.

While Arlan's fund continues to face ups and downs (par for the course in such a risky industry), she has built her power by determinedly demonstrating that there *is* space for so many more people than the narrow archetypes we've seen dominate the headlines. In my mind, her influence is infinite.

Power (especially when you define it as "power-with") feels compatible with the ideas of uncompete, but can we make the same argument for building wealth? Is it even possible to build wealth without having some level of scarcity thinking? If I shared my $100 with you, then isn't that less for me in absolute numbers? The answer is yes. And giving up some of that excess is worth it. Hear me out.

When we think about wealth, our minds instantly conjure an extravagant lifestyle for ourselves. Jetting off to far-flung places on a private jet. Vacationing at one of multiple summer homes. A sky-high bank balance. No need unmet. No desire unfulfilled. Wealth is about having a swath of resources and the ability to use them at every whim. We live in a capitalistic society, after all! And the ultimate lie is that the harder we work, the more money we'll make. The American Dream! Recent data from the Federal Reserve states that the average American's net worth is a little more than $192,000. Not enough for that private jet, but not too terrible either, right?

However, as we know, many of us aren't living the American Dream. When you disaggregate that same net-worth data by race, the numbers are deeply concerning. What skews the data, as an example, is that the median net worth of white Americans is more than $284,000, which is six times higher than that of Black Americans ($44,000) and almost five times higher than that of Hispanic Americans ($62,000). The median net worth of Americans with college degrees is more than $400,000, while Americans with a high school diploma have a median net worth of just over $100,000. Americans between the ages of sixty-four and seventy-five generally have a median net worth of $410,000, which is eleven times higher than the average of Americans under the age of thirty-five. We see wealth disparities by race across every single conceivable metric: homeownership and average worth of homes owned, access to retirement savings (68 percent of white families have access to an employer-sponsored retirement plan, such as a 401(k), but only 56 percent of Black families and 43 percent of Latinx families have this benefit), liquidity of money, and even business revenues. Black-owned businesses account for just 1 percent of all business revenues, compared with the 89 percent of all revenues that come from white-owned businesses.

This uneven distribution of income and wealth has exacerbated inequities for generations. What's worse is how a competition mindset falsely asserts that the only reason these disparities exist is that only the most honorable, hardworking people succeed. If someone is struggling financially, has failed to make a payment, has filed for bankruptcy, or is loaded with debt, it's because *they* made bad choices and weren't smart or determined enough to avoid it. It's insulting when you reconcile this narrative with how high the cards are stacked against so many communities. For those who have been dealt a great hand—because of something as arbitrary as our race, our gender, or how much money our ancestors amassed—we've been told to never acknowledge the winning hand (our privilege). Oh, and to retain whatever winnings we further amass for ourselves. Not only that, we're often taught to keep up the ruse.

In a previous job, when I negotiated hard for a higher salary than was advertised, my white male boss told me it was a "one-off" and not to let my colleagues know that an exception had been made. But guess what I did? I called the next woman who applied for a similar job in my department and said, "They'll tell you there's no room for negotiation, but there is. Also, they desperately need someone in this role, and you'll be great, so ask for more!" She did. And when they denied it, she said she'd reconsidered the job offer. So they paid her more.

I don't want a prize or award for sharing the information. I want it to be so ubiquitous that it's expected of us—heck, that it's not a dirty secret! And I want to acknowledge that I had the privilege to share my numbers because if I was fired for talking about my salary to a peer, I knew I'd survive, with savings and a high-earning spouse. Yet many of us who can take these risks don't, out of fear of scarcity. Even for so many of us who do have the privilege to choose another path, we've been so deeply conditioned by scarcity to believe that building wealth is a solo endeavor and that it's not our responsibility to also create wealth for others. As unfair as our current system is, to uncompete we can (and must) still begin by maneuvering within it—and closing these divides. The problem wasn't created by us, but we cannot afford to stand by waiting for others to solve it. When everyone is on stronger footing, no single person suffers because there's more than enough to sustain all of us.

One of the reasons I see such promise in building wealth intentionally is because I've seen how communities are transformed when wealth is shared. Even though sharing my $100 means less for me in actual numbers, it's worth it. Simply put, from a community approach, wealth building is investing not only in the now but also in a future we cocreate, with intention. We've got to think differently, then act differently.

In Seattle's Central District, which I now call home, gentrification over the past decades has meant that a neighborhood that was 80 percent Black is now under 10 percent Black. Families and businesses were uprooted, and so much of the richness that made this neighborhood special was scattered—from generations-old restaurants to multigenerational families that were priced out. Fortunately, initiatives to bring Black-owned businesses and build Black economic power in the area have finally begun to bear fruit. It takes intention to do this. For example, real-estate developer Lake Union Partners not only bought a parcel of land to develop into a mixed-rate development with affordable housing and Black-owned businesses on its ground floor, but in an almost unheard-of deal in real estate, it also sold portions of the development to Black community members who rented spaces. Rather than being motivated by monetary profit, Lake Union Partners was motivated by *value*—it was looking to create opportunities for Black wealth, mobility, and culture for generations to come, working in partnership with Africatown Community Land Trust. It is worth noting that as of this writing, no one at Lake Union Partners is Black, yet they were able to understand how urgent it was to preserve Black culture and create opportunities for Black generational wealth.

And as a larger community, we are all benefiting from the value creation, both as consumers and from the broader economic gain in the community. Some of my favorite restaurants, ones I feel most welcome in as a person of color in Seattle, are within this neighborhood (special shout-out to Black-owned Communion!). Built without the exclusive (exclusionary) approach of many upscale neighborhoods around Seattle and the world, the Central District is rich with murals and street musicians, and it welcomes people from all backgrounds.

Of course, not all of us are working with the same levers as a real-estate developer. But intentionally choosing to spend our money and financially support the people, institutions, and causes we hold dear allows us to leverage whatever privilege we might have. It creates a profound impact on a small and large scale, too. Even if we don't have the type of wealth that allows us to make huge investments and donations, we can still make a difference by intentionally choosing a person-of-color-owned coffee shop to buy our daily cup of coffee from instead of a big-box retailer. We can choose an LGBTQ-owned sandwich shop and buy clothes from a small business whose owner happens to be disabled. Although the competition-and-scarcity narrative has us thinking we couldn't possibly make a difference until we reach some towering economic status, the truth is that the daily choices we make on how to spend our money add up to empower others. That's what I mean about sharing the $100 versus hoarding all of it for personal gain. For those of us who can make more intentional spending choices, it's *still* easy to fall prey to the "let me always find the best deal" mentality. This, of course, is scarcity talking—and it continues to fuel the systems that proliferate inequality. When we choose to buy fast fashion instead of ethically made garments (which are, in general, far more expensive), we're voting with our dollars to let the industry keep exploiting lower-income laborers and polluting our planet. Yes, we get to keep $80 of our $100 from choosing the low-cost option, but in the long term we've enabled continued cycles of harm.

This will look different for all of us and is, of course, always a function of the levers—of both wealth and power—that we have available to us. But we still often have choices. In my business, I've made it a practice not to bargain down fees and pricing unless it's absolutely untenable for me, and even then, I come up with future profit-sharing agreements. I'm continually inspired by the businesses that engage in salary transparency. One such example is the social media app Buffer, which openly publishes employees' salaries on its website (unless someone opts out because of privacy concerns)—including that of its CEO.

On the other hand, I've talked to so many women in lower-paid jobs (overwhelmingly women of color) who have experienced scarcity thinking from their rich employers, from housekeepers having pay docked for eating a snack from an employer's pantry after a long day to nannies who live in poverty despite raising the children of multi-millionaires. As wealth experts like Rachel Rodgers will tell you, an abundance of money doesn't automatically change scarcity thinking. In fact, many wealthy people believe that it's their frugality that got them rich in the first place. It takes intentionality to change our mindset around wealth and to not use wealth as a tool to wield our power over others.

Choosing how to spend our wealth is not about short-term gains; it's a long-term strategy. If I pick the big-box retailer for my coffee because it's cheap, my choice and the choices of others like me over time will drive out locally owned small businesses. But if I recognize that spending a little more to support an immigrant-owned business today could result in keeping small businesses in my neighborhood for years to come, perhaps it would mean that my son, or even his kids, could come back there for their cup of joe in future decades.

If we focus only on lining our pockets, we're forgoing the opportunity to create a diverse, abundant community that prospers or to make an impact that lasts beyond our lifetime. But if we focus on building wealth intentionally, with community, uplifting others as well, then we have a chance to make real change.

Another important way to expand our concept of wealth is to view it as a means of safety against harm and violence. For many in the world—and especially women and girls—a lack of financial security means being compelled to stay in unhealthy and even dangerous situations. I feel this acutely, coming from an Indian background where none of the women I knew growing up were financially independent. Even for the women I knew who were born into comfortable (or even rich) families, they did not feel they could ask for financial help from their families of origin if they wanted to leave a bad marriage. Every Indian woman I got to know was financially dependent on her husband, and whether she was in a happy marriage or not, there was an implicit belief that there was no way out, financially or otherwise: It was her fate.

Seeing this as a child made me determined to never be financially dependent on a partner (which could only be a man, of course, as I was taught growing up). Even though I've personally built wealth through my work and business, I see it as incomplete if other women of color don't experience the same agency in their lives. Building wealth in community means creating the type of network where if one of us has wealth, others don't feel shame for tapping into it when things are rough.

At its core, obtaining economic freedom is how we get to a place where we can be independent, build and distribute our wealth with intentionality, support one another, and move the needle of influence over the long term.

BUILDING A COMMUNITY OF POWER

Mandi Woodruff-Santos met Tiffany Aliche in 2014 at a conference for financial bloggers. The spark was instant between these two Black women who were deeply passionate about helping other women of color build wealth and live a rich life. They quickly exchanged contact details, and within a few months they launched a podcast called *Brown Ambition*, where the duo openly talks about money, budgeting, ambition, and even dating in a way that is predictably absent in the media to date.

Their podcast makes it sound like they were the best of friends, but Mandi was hiding a secret.

"I would have competitive thoughts about Tiffany," she admitted to me during an interview. Her cohost had already established a large online presence, was getting invited to share her expertise as a personal-finance expert on television, and was fast becoming a public figure. Mandi was still working a corporate job and building her name as an independent finance expert. So when Tiffany would innocuously ask her about her day, or mention that she just had a stint on *Good Morning America*, Mandi would feel pangs of envy. After a few years of feeling envious, Mandi realized it wasn't helping—not her relationship with her cohost, whom she wanted to build a successful and meaningful podcast with; not the popularity of the show; and most of all, not her peace of mind.

"Somewhere around 2016, when the show had been around for a few years, I told myself, 'When Tiffany wins, *we* win.'"

It wasn't an immediate shift but a gradual one that required Mandi to cultivate an abundance mindset. She had to tap into her rational (and experienced) brain and commit this fact to memory—no opportunity was one-and-done. If Tiffany got quoted in an article or had a media appearance or won an award, it didn't mean that an opportunity wouldn't come up for Mandi in the future. Tiffany being an absolute badass would elevate their podcast and Mandi's public presence, too. And it absolutely did. Their podcast now has over eight million downloads.

These powerhouse women exemplify a type of collective power often lacking in traditional white male definitions of it: plurality. Unfortunately, most of us still fall prey to approaching power as an individualist endeavor. But when we uncompete, we stay open and curious to those who current culture would tell us to compete with. When we meet people who spark in us competitive feelings, what if instead we reframed that, figuring out how to get inspired by, learn from, and feel energized by them? What if our proximity to them could help us (ideally, many of us) build power?

Since I interviewed Mandi for this book, Tiffany left the show at the end of 2024. The episodes where the cohosts talked about their "breakup" got the highest engagement of the year! In one episode, they invited Dr. Joy Harden Bradford from Therapy for Black Girls to help them talk through Tiffany leaving and what no longer being cohosts and business partners meant for their relationship. "I'm so proud of how we prioritized our friendship above all and ended up in a really good place," Mandi told me. I'm deeply inspired by how these ambitious women modeled the importance of friendship and community over finances—unlike some famous cofounders whose conflicts have been reported in the media. One example: None of the original founders of Facebook (now Meta) talk to each other, embattled in lawsuits. When we uncompete, we believe that cultivating relationships with amazing people is far more important than competing with and outshining one another.

Aminatou Sow and Ann Friedman, best friends and coauthors of *Big Friendship: How We Keep Each Other Close*, describe this as "shine theory," which is a conscious decision and long-term investment in a partnership where both people are dedicated to collaborating and to bettering each other's lives. They believe in approaching others with the belief of *I don't shine if you don't shine.* Shine theory is the act of putting our envy and egos aside and making more room for fulfilling relationships that expand our horizons in a variety of ways, including building wealth. When we meet someone shiny, sparkly, and amazing, we literally benefit from admiring and befriending them because we believe that our lives would be enriched by being in community with them.

We all know what it feels like when we're around spectacular women who inspire and lift us up. But years of comparing ourselves and being compared take their toll. And instead of nurturing those relationships, we often push them away because of deep-seated insecurity. As a result, we miss out on the power-building (and in many cases, relatedly, wealth-building) opportunities that collaborating with others can bring us. Because when power and wealth are built in community, they compound faster than we might imagine. In fact, I've experienced this personally.

WHAT I LEARNED ABOUT POWER IN PARTNERSHIPS

In 2021 I was introduced to La'Kita Williams, my business coach and a remarkable leader in the professional world. She was the first person who specifically and consistently guided me to shape my business with the approach that "my wins aren't mine alone." When we started working together, my consulting business, Candour, was barely breaking even, and I couldn't pay myself a salary. As a solo entrepreneur, I was doing everything—from making sales calls to writing copy to sending out invoices to bookkeeping.

Before we connected, I was convinced that I had to do it all on my own. On one of our first coaching calls, I told La'Kita I wasn't sure I could afford to get an assistant and bookkeeper, let alone bring in any take-home pay. La'Kita's response was to quote rapper YG: "Scared money don't make no money!" She pointed me back to how I had clearly stated (and written down) that my career and life goal was to help other women of color win. If that was my primary metric of success, I'd have to reframe my idea of business success and wealth creation and be intentional about how I used my financial resources.

Together, we figured out where to cut expenses and where to invest money boldly. We uncovered that by trying to do it all when I clearly needed support, I wasn't being efficient or making enough money for myself, let alone staying true to my ultimate goal of elevating other women of color around me. The payoffs of moving from a scarcity approach to one of abundance were huge. By trimming areas that weren't serving my business and financial goals while ramping up and focusing on ones that did, I was able to grow my business. Eventually, I made enough to hire Vanessa, now my chief of staff, without whom I couldn't now imagine growing or running my business.

All this led to new business deals and partnerships with numerous entrepreneurs who also happened to hold various nondominant identities: women of color, nonbinary, LGBTQ+, and disabled people. In some cases, this meant paying people a higher rate than they quoted me, knowing how underpaid and undervalued marginalized entrepreneurs are. With La'Kita's guidance, I learned to see this not as money taken away from my business but as investments made into the type of entrepreneurial ecosystem that aligned with my values. These collaborative relationships also helped these entrepreneurs to grow their businesses and use *their* collective wealth to pour resources back into our local communities. When I couldn't take on a client, I had an excellent referral network and tried, as intentionally as I could, to ensure I was sending clients to as many people as possible. Competitive thinking tells me that anyone in a similar business is my competition. So even if I couldn't take on a project, it wouldn't be savvy to refer business on to "competitors." But when I thought about how to uncompete, I realized that I had much more to win by building a powerful community of people like me who were rising in solidarity. Many of us are taught that the only way is to automatically see others as rivals, but in working to decolonize my thinking around this, I realized that there was more benefit in building a powerful referral community of people in the same business, rather than going the isolationist way that a competition mindset recommends.

In three years of working with La'Kita, my business revenues have doubled annually, and La'Kita has received more clients through my referrals. Today, I am proud to be directly responsible for the paychecks of at least ten women of color. La'Kita continues to share her wisdom and strategies with more leaders, who in turn have profited from and used what they gained to strengthen other relationships and organizations—many whom you would recognize or likely use services from. I deeply believe in the ripple effect of how abundance begets abundance. It's a remarkable thing to behold.

The idea of building out whole communities to build wealth and power might sound intimidating, but it can start small. Like compounding investments, our efforts to build relationships, when done with intention, can increase exponentially. Here are five lessons I've turned to in my efforts to build powerful communities and communal wealth:

1. **Reach out to someone who inspires you.** It can be a peer who works in the same industry or a person who is making strides in a field that you are trying to break into. What we're looking for is someone who reflects our values and who shines brightly. In the traditional narrative, they'd be your rival. But when you un-compete, they're squarely who you want to build power with. Genuinely compliment them, highlighting exactly *what* about them you admire—and that's it! Praising someone for some-thing awesome about them, without an accompanied ask, is so rare. I often get "I love your book" letters followed immediately by laborious requests for unpaid mentorship or ways to elevate someone else's career. But when someone genuinely reaches out just to say, "Good work, keep going, no reciprocity needed," I feel a genuine connection with them and have often come back to further that relationship.

2. **Display genuine curiosity.** When you meet someone you en-vision being part of your community, nurture that relationship. As I get closer to someone new, here are some questions I often like to ask: *What is the purpose of your life? How do you define suc-cess? What kind of impact are you hoping to make? What does collabora-tion mean to you?* If their answers tell me they're approaching life with an abundance mindset and an approach to uncompete, I know I want to strengthen that connection going forward. In most cases, I'll make an offer, a connection to someone or an opportunity that I believe could be helpful for them. (If their responses instead make me feel cautious and apprehensive, then that's my cue to politely table the discussion.) The key here is to stay open—curiosity is fuel for true connection, and being in true community with others makes our own world big-ger, too.

3. **Once you've built trust, talk numbers.** I believe that any real relationship of trust requires us to talk openly about money. And of course, this is a difficult task because we've been condi-tioned to fear those conversations in a competitive system. But transparency about wealth—what we're making, what an op-portunity is worth, what you want your friend to ask for when

she's pushing for a big role—is one of the strongest ways to build collective power. The only way to do this is by practicing. I've made it a habit to never share an opportunity without the numbers I have at hand: "Would you be interested in this speaking gig/this consulting project/talking to a recruiter for a job? Here are the numbers they've shared with me." Negotiations expert and Columbia Law School professor Alexandra Carter told me that we can't build collective power or wealth until women start talking openly about money with each other. Because unlike what the dudes tell us, a good negotiation is never zero-sum, she says. Both parties should ideally benefit.

4. **Take stock of the relationship.** Checking in with ourselves and noticing how this relationship makes us feel over time is very necessary, especially when it comes to protecting our mental health. Are we feeling secure and supported or diminished and intimidated? Do we feel seen and validated or taken advantage of? Many of us have work to do in rejecting the competition mindset we've been conditioned with, and without dismantling it, some people can do more harm than good. I've worked to build strong partnerships with people who say the right things about collaboration and abundance but then follow up with actions that don't align with those words. To uncompete is never about being mistreated or being taken advantage of because then we're operating within existing structures of power and oppression. It's about finding people who share these values and who act according to them with integrity. If your intuition says that someone is unhealed, it's not only personally necessary but even for the greater good that you move away from them. People who cause us cynicism and bitterness make it that much harder for us to practice uncompeting with others in our community.

5. **Identify others to join in the community.** To uncompete means believing that growth and generosity go hand in hand. That's why we should always be keeping a lookout for others to share our resources with and build community together. The

bigger our inner circle gets, the more wealth and influence we can generate. This doesn't mean that everyone becomes a best friend or you engage with each person the same way. Life is busy, and I'd never ask anyone to stretch themselves too thin (the next chapter precisely shares the opposite). But where a competition and scarcity mindset tell us to keep our circle small and close to the vest, I'm of the opinion that we have the power to expand and contract our circle based on our bandwidth. Some relationships can be built on trust and mutual admiration just over email or an annual interaction. Helping another person reach their goal doesn't have to be a daily, time-consuming endeavor. I've recommended people for roles, filled out a reference form, written an online review, or bought someone's book without spending copious amounts of time. For those of us who get many requests, I've found it helpful to carve out twenty or thirty minutes a few times a week to work through these requests, knowing that spending my time this way further enriches the community I'm aiming to build. I know that others have generously done the same for me.

As I was writing this book, many people asked me, "So are you saying we shouldn't aim to be millionaires or even billionaires?" Not at all. In fact, all I want is for historically excluded people to be able to live comfortably and never worry about paying the bills. Rachel Rodgers, author of *We Should All Be Millionaires*, joins a chorus of women of color telling us we are worthy of achieving all our financial dreams, and I've long held this ambition, too. Personally, I love luxury, and when I set revenue goals for my business or family income goals with Paras, my husband, I aim high so I can live the life I've always dreamed of. But—as the principles of uncompete guide us—we must do this with intention and self-awareness. Questions I like to ask myself include: *What is the number that's enough for me? And in trying to make that amount, am*

I competing with others for it? Am I operating with a scarcity mindset to achieve it? Am I exploiting others in my quest for it? Is my purpose to build this wealth for individual gain (my singular family unit) or for community gain? As a woman of color, I know I'm treated better, frustrating as it is, when I wear more expensive clothes, drive a nice car, and live in a better neighborhood. I know I'm seen as more powerful because of the wealth I've been able to build. The last thing I'd want to do is tell other women of color not to do the same. When we uncompete, the number matters less than our approach to building our power, the people we are taking along with us, and ensuring that we don't have a competition and scarcity mindset.

THE MARK OF TRUE WEALTH

Power building doesn't always mean aligning only with people like us. It's equally important to assess where we can provide a strong foothold to people who are just starting out and send the ladder back down, so to speak.

Two of the world's biggest superstars could teach a master class on this. Personally, I love how Beyoncé (or Queen Bey to me and all my fellow worshippers) constantly elevates other women of color in her orbit so that they can shine brighter and build influence and wealth. For instance, she hires mainly Black musicians to perform at her concerts, which inspired an iconic tweet that (rightfully) reminds us: "Beyoncé can find 24 black trombone players, but your company can't find a single black intern, associate, or board member?" Beyoncé has taught us time and again what it means to elevate other Black creatives in her own ascent, from refusing to work with an advertising agency because of its lack of Black representation to pushing the boundaries of music by becoming the first Black female artist to dominate the Billboard country music charts while also elevating other Black artists already in the genre. She's steadfastly demonstrated what it means to spread your power liberally for community benefit rather than hoard it.

Taylor Swift reportedly gave out a total of more than $55 million in bonuses to the members of her massive 2023 Eras concert tour. She saw how much of their lives they were giving to support her on tour and gave them a big portion of the dividends—not just as a token of appreciation, but to send a message to the world about who she values and what their partnership is worth to her over and above what was expected of her. Over the years, Taylor has put up-and-coming artists (like Sabrina Carpenter) in front of her fervent fans, which has super-charged their careers.

And the way Bey and Tay each showed up for the other's film premiere in the fall of 2023 is what it looks like to uncompete out in the world, particularly in a music industry built on competition and tearing others down for media mentions. I know they're billionaires because they're supremely talented and put in extraordinary effort, and these two are on the extreme end of examples of wealth and power. But that's exactly my point—both these women have made it a point to build power and wealth in a community-driven, intentional fashion, yet it hasn't made their stars any smaller. In fact, I'm willing to wager that generosity has a lot to do with their bombastic bank balances. Ultimately, I believe we are each deserving of the power that comes from intentionally building an influential community and creating and spreading the wealth that allows us to live the life of our dreams.

In March 2023, I gathered twenty-five incredible women in Seattle, all of whom had played a part in my professional and personal growth over the decade that I had lived there, and hosted a dinner to celebrate them. This was not a client-appreciation dinner (as corporations have made ubiquitous) where I was angling for someone to renew a contract with me or buy my books. It was simply my way of appreciating how much these diverse-in-every-way-imaginable women had lifted me up when things were down.

Their generosity included picking up my son from school when I couldn't, writing the foreword for my last book, being a shoulder to cry on when I was navigating grief, and advising me (informally, but as experts) on how to best invest and grow my income. Once we'd made it through the appetizers, I stopped the dinner midway. I then went around the room and vocally thanked each woman for the outsize role she had played in my life and for always approaching me with abundance. Their presence in my life made me believe that not only was a community without competition possible, but it was also absolutely transformative in building collective power.

Everyone there had demonstrated to me exactly what creating power and wealth in community is about. Together, the women in that room had spurred me to negotiate for more money, take on career-making challenges, find grace for myself as a mother, be more confident about my body, and set better boundaries. My hope is I had done the same in some small way. In introducing this amazing group of women to one another, I was sure that more such friendships would spark—and they have.

I also know with absolute certainty that the financial wealth I've been able to build in the past few years through multiple new consulting contracts, speaking engagements, and book sales would not have been achieved without this circle of shiny women, all from different walks of life but each showing up so generously for me.

No competition, no envy, no shade. Simply the transformative power of women who all uncompete.

PART THREE

RESISTANCE

CHAPTER EIGHT

Liberate Our Bodies

I n previous jobs, I'd hear coworkers brag about pulling all-nighters and never taking a sick day, no matter how unwell they were. Comparison and competition over who worked longer hours and sacrificed more rest were ubiquitous. Despite the fact that I left my last corporate job more than a decade ago, the hustle-always narrative related to career success remains omnipresent. When we read a profile of a "successful" person, nowhere is there mention of rest or pauses in their career-growth story. Typically, the more well-known (popular and rich) a person is, the more their success is attributed to self-sacrifice—"they slept under their desk at the office," "didn't take a vacation in years," or "worked nonstop."

We've all been conditioned to believe that success and rest are like two fish swimming in opposite directions. To be successful, rest must be sacrificed. If rest is mentioned at all in our workplace narrative, we learn that it can be *earned* only after burning the candle at both ends. Many of us are taught to brag about being too busy to eat, sleep, or rest but never about taking time to eat, sleep, or rest. As an entrepreneur, I've grappled with the shame and stress of taking time off—for sickness, for vacation, for childcare, or even just to rest—because of the overarching concern that it would affect the success of my company and my dreams.

But to uncompete, we need to prioritize deep rest and radically reframe the idea that resting makes us less worthy or less ambitious. It's become undeniable that operating from a place of embodiment—literally, being present in our bodies—and spaciousness is central to our individual, workplace, and collective well-being. This means doing away with drifting from work to home to life to work as if in an endless loop in favor of being truly connected to our bodies (which include our minds) wherever we are.

Nothing and almost *no one* in the working world makes this easy for any of us. It takes courage and commitment to constantly and deliberately listen to and choose our bodies, especially because there's no road map, no award, no playbook for living a life where you can consciously live in your body and rest when you need to. I'd urge people with power and privilege to deliberately and loudly choose embodiment over overwork—whether that's forgoing hustle culture in favor of rest or explicitly taking time for caregiving duties instead of putting in more hours at the office. When people who *can* take a rest do so—those who are not in situations where overwork is the only way to afford necessities—it affects the message that we all receive about our bodies. Simply put, if more of us who didn't have to hustle nonstop stopped hustling, we'd have more empathy to support others who don't have that same luxury in forgoing constant grinding. Everyone benefits from this.

I envision us liberating our bodies to uncompete in three ways:

1. By resisting the false equation between success and overwork.
2. By learning to listen to and honor our bodies.
3. By prioritizing embodiment at work and in life.

HOW TO RETHINK THAT SUCCESS CAN BE ACHIEVED ONLY WITH OVERWORK

In November 2022, after a whirlwind seven months of traveling to promote my last book, working through multiple illnesses and insomnia, weary and worn, I checked into a hotel room in Philadelphia. The next day, I was due to give the keynote address at a health-care conference with more than eight hundred attendees. A friend had given me a copy of *Rest Is Resistance* by Tricia Hersey.

I am not exaggerating to say that for the next three days, I spent every spare moment devouring Tricia's book. Rather than network or use the time I had on the road to be productive, I lay curled up in bed or sat in parks (Philly, your parks are amazing!) reading this book, often with a highlighter in my hand and tears in my eyes.

Tricia opened her book with the powerful ritual of afternoon naps that her mother and grandmother would take to rest their weary souls, built from the ancestral trauma and grief of coming from a lineage of formerly enslaved Black women. I realized that this ritual of rest (and thereby, resistance) united so many Black and brown women the world over—my own ancestors were born in British-colonized India—and how so many found these little pockets of time for themselves even when every outside force told them their bodies did not belong to them and were tools to be worked and exploited. Always urgent, always on.

This particular passage of Tricia's rocked me to my core:

> There was time now to just be. Before experiencing this revelation, I believed that I had to figure out everything in my internal and external life that was causing me harm and correct it immediately with the information I had in front of me. Things were always urgent and rushed. A feeling of anxiety of what needed to be done was always hovering over me. I was never taught that I had a wealth of healing information and guidance waiting for me in a slowed-down state of a DreamSpace.
>
> **I was told the opposite: that you had to always be doing labor to fix.** I didn't see my body as a place of infinite wisdom but instead saw it as a tool to be used to push, create, figure out, and do. Most of us surviving the demands of grind culture are here. I know this by how so many react when they first hear of our work and they begin to sink into the idea that it's about way more than actual naps. Daydreaming is a form of rest and feels like the opening of your heart doing what it's supposed to do.

Tricia's incredible book outlines a wisdom I've now found deeply rooted in Black and brown communities, that making time to *be* in our bodies is inextricably connected to the principles of uncompete. When we choose to honor our bodies, when we take time to rest or day-dream, for example, we resist one of the most pernicious and enduring myths of competition: that our bodies are worthy only when in direct, immediate service to capitalism. And when we prioritize being embod-ied or connected to our bodies, we are reclaiming ownership of ourselves.

Competition as the default has done our bodies a great deal of harm. Modern life keeps us in fight-or-flight mode. We regularly ex-perience physiological reactions that past humans activated only when they perceived a threat or danger to their survival. Now we feel it ev-erywhere: when we're worried that our peers will outcompete us if we don't make a work deadline or when we say yes to every task coming our way, which, as we've learned in previous chapters, causes chronic stress and disease.

This is just one of many reasons we must intentionally, consis-tently, and even controversially choose to honor our body and listen to what it needs. Those needs could be as vast and varied as inten-tional rest, nourishment, meditation, movement, or restorative prac-tices. When we can be regularly present in our bodies, it makes it that much more possible to opt out of a competition mindset that often stems from being overwhelmed or fearful and on autopilot. Basically, we must go from doing what's expected and pushing past pain to doing what feels good and healthy for us. Let me also clarify that although there is a clear connection between rest, productivity, and creativity, that isn't entirely the point of resting to uncompete. When we uncom-pete, we opt out of the notion that taking rest now can be justified by better productivity later. Instead, we choose our bodies first simply because it's what we need.

We're conditioned to think that work is our sole source of value.

By extension, we learn at an early age that our body was put on this Earth to produce. We're taught that a human who doesn't perform daily, hourly, and even every minute inherently has no worth. Americans have the distinction of balking at taking vacations—more than four in ten US workers don't take all their paid time off. In fact, the higher up the income ladder Americans go, the *less* paid time they take off. The reasons? People say they don't need more time off, are worried about falling behind, or feel bad about coworkers having to pick up the slack if they take time off. Add to this the statistic that one in four US mothers go back to work ten days after giving birth. The United States is the only industrialized country in the world that doesn't guarantee paid maternity leave, and this fact tracks with why we are so conditioned to feel ashamed of or even disassociated from our bodies that we don't fully believe we need embodiment or rest. Many women, particularly women of color, feel this acutely; in the face of bias and racism in the workplace, we feel we must outwork and outperform our male and white peers to be considered competent. This is why we have higher levels of workplace burnout, work-related injuries, and chronic stress than our white peers. Obviously, a culture of overwork is oppressive for *literally* everyone with a body, but it is particularly harmful to disabled people, people with chronic illnesses, people with mental health issues, and people at every intersection of marginalization by race, gender, sexual orientation, and immigration status, who don't get the luxury of a second opportunity if we're facing biased notions of laziness.

The fallout of this hustle-till-we-grind approach cannot be overstated: We lose touch with ourselves, and in the best case, we're able to simply accept this and cope on autopilot. Access to good health care helps *some* people figure out how to just "make it work" on poor sleep, lack of rest, nonexistent time off, stress, anxiety that they'll fall behind if they're not always grinding, and little space to make mindful decisions about what their bodies need. Newer research shows that these people are—you guessed it—mostly male (men get fewer autoimmune diseases than women, for example), white (a Harvard health study literally kicks off with the statement "Being a person of color in America is bad for your health"), and rich. For those of us who don't occupy some or all of these intersections, the toll on our bodies and spirits from always competing and ignoring our somatic needs is a cost too high to bear.

UNDOING THE COMPETITION WE HAVE WITH OURSELVES

I'll admit that this chapter has been one of the hardest to write for me, as even I haven't fully let go of the underlying belief that I'm unworthy of being unless I'm working. I can typically get behind this idea when I apply it to other people, particularly those I admire and love, but my self-compassion is still sorely lacking. This is precisely why I've personally found it necessary to learn to honor my body and listen to what it is telling me.

In our "uncompete" survey, Martha Burwell and I discovered that several of the hundred-plus respondents wrote that the biggest competition they felt was with themselves. Initially, I was puzzled. Then I realized that I, too, felt this way in that I constantly think of myself as a project to improve. The impulse to push (and punish) myself to keep working through hardship is, of course, conditioning—to be better than, more successful, more worthy. For years I believed that competing with myself would result in self-improvement but had nothing to do with how I treated and valued others: I could have empathy for others when they experienced illness, overwhelm, or pain, but could not do that for myself. Except that wasn't true. Not really. Even if I could have more empathy for others than for myself around work boundaries, the truth is, of course, I was co-opted by a system that assigns worth based on a person's immediate efficiency and ability to be constantly available.

By constantly devaluing what my body was telling me—whether I needed time off or the space to be a mother, partner, daughter, or sister . . . or even just time to myself—I was subconsciously judging others who had better work boundaries and honored their bodies as being "less ambitious." It's taken me a lot of deprogramming to question this. How could I push back against the larger, more influential, external forces everywhere that said a body not producing has no inherent value, when I didn't believe it? I've only just begun to process the messages my body tries to tell me on a daily, if not hourly, basis—whether it's crying out for rest, nourishment, movement, or leave from paid work. We—all of us who have explicitly and implicitly received the message that our bodies are too big, too dark, too hairy, too unworthy—are often conditioned to tune out any messages our bodies are trying to tell us in order to survive in a competitive, sexist, racist world.

I'm proposing that we begin learning to *honor*—not *love*—our bodies. That's because I don't think it's truly possible to fully deprogram the harmful messages we've received about how whiteness, thinness, ableism, Eurocentric body ideals, and so on are "worth" so much more in our society and, often as a result, are more worthy than embodiment and rest. I also worry about toxic body positivity—a topic for another book, perhaps. It is why, if I'm radically honest, I've internalized the idea that as a larger-bodied woman, I don't *deserve* to rest, that my only worth is in production. I've had this conversation with many women of color, which is why I believe that this reframing must be done in community.

In working to reframe this message for myself, I now believe that true liberation can come only from us choosing to honor our bodies, exactly as they are outwardly, with a deep connection to how we feel inside.

I've detailed some ideas on how to do this:

1. **Reflect on your relationship with your body, your relationship with rest, your relationship with disability, and the intersection of these three.** How do you generally feel about your body size, structure, shape, and weight? Do you feel positive, negative, or neutral? If you do not have a disability (physical, mental, invisible, or visible), what are the messages you have learned about people who are disabled? How would you apply that messaging to yourself if you acquired a disability in the future? How does the idea of resting make you feel— positive, negative, or neutral? Do you feel like you need to earn rest or be punished for taking it? How do you feel about people with larger bodies taking rest? How do you feel about disabled people taking rest? How has your conditioning made you feel about the relationship between body size, rest, and disability— both for you and in your relations to others around you?

2. **Read books and consume media that widen your aperture.** It's only by reading across a diversity of authors, experiences, and disciplines that we embark on the journey of decolonizing

our minds from toxic ideas such as these: *Lazy people rest, rest is unproductive, only when you produce is your body worthy, only thin people are healthy, fat people are lazy, rest should be earned, disabled people should be pitied, only people with disabilities need to rest but then it's justified that they earn less than nondisabled people....* I've cited reading *Rest Is Resistance* as a watershed moment in sparking my new relationship to rest (and going back to the wisdom of traditions in my own culture on rest). I also recommend Sonya Renee Taylor's brilliant book *The Body Is Not an Apology.* It can be life-changing for so many of us, particularly women, who often spend more time in their lives apologizing for their bodies than not. As such, there are several fantastic ways to widen your lens (and mind) around these topics that will ultimately help dismantle the competition mindset we've had with ourselves and others around our bodies. We can find communities to help us heal, learn from the social media accounts of leaders with larger bodies, visit fashion websites that elevate a diversity of bodies as stylish, and admire leaders with chronic illnesses and disabilities who share self-directed narratives about their lives and bodies.

3. **Inform yourself about what's scientific and what's not.** In hypercompetitive Western societies, myths and pseudoscience around all these topics have played an outsize part in our understanding of our bodies. I've fallen prey to the false belief that exercise and "eating right" would solve all the challenges I've had with my weight in competition with myself and others. I have since learned that so much of what I held as scientific truth was false. One simple example is how much we underestimate the role of racism and equity—access to fresh, healthy food, outdoor spaces, and leisure time—on body size. Again, competition and capitalism condition us to believe that people could easily change themselves if they chose to. As we begin to educate ourselves further about the impact of racism on medicine and science, we should be outraged by how many people of color are navigating preventable (or more manageable if diagnosed earlier) chronic illnesses. It's heartbreaking to see ableism in every facet of our society, particularly in the exclusion of

disabled people from our workplaces and our communities. By sifting out pseudoscience from science, it's only now that scientists and health experts are realizing that adults need more sleep than we were forced to believe and that cisgender women can—and should—lift weights to build muscle endurance as we age. Many women are taught that they should be "feminine" and that lifting weights would make them too "bulky"—a harmful belief that literally affects women's health and quality of life as they age. Most of all, we must learn that we don't need to "earn" rest only after we've worked our bodies to illness—and that this narrative goes against actual science. You can't "make up" forgone sleep or overcome chronic burnout with a one-off massage.

4. **Intentionally curate diverse, body-reflective communities.** Being in community with a plethora of people from a diversity of racial and ethnic backgrounds, people of various body sizes and types, people with chronic illness, disabled people, neurodivergent people, and more has truly provided the healing I have deeply needed. It is not an exaggeration to say that being at war with my body robbed my mind of peace and joy for years. I have seen how my disabled friends derive joy in an ableist society that constantly tells them they don't deserve any. I've seen how in a community that is representative of the diversity of bodies we see in the world, I've been able to undo the competition with others and myself to constantly "improve" my body to be more palatable—and to ask, "Palatable to whom?" But if we surround ourselves only with people who conform to a narrow definition of a worthy body, we will forever be in competition to reach an ideal that will always be out of reach.

I know for certain that narrow definitions of worth—based on the size, color, ability, and strength of our bodies, based on racist, unscientific, and frankly arbitrary measures—have created comparison, competition, and trauma to keep us in our places and be permanently distracted. To make it so that we're never "enough" and always in pursuit of a goal that we can never reach. To not have enough pause to question and resist the systems of oppression that have kept us feeling like we're always in deficit. What a simple, powerful revolution could be achieved with the words "If you have a body, rest must be abundant."

BEGIN TO BELIEVE YOU DON'T HAVE TO SACRIFICE YOUR BODY

For anyone reading this who identifies as the first, the few, the only, or the different (or "FOD," as coined by brilliant filmmaker Shonda Rhimes, the first woman to create three hit television shows with more than a hundred episodes each), there can often be a true cognitive dissonance between achievement and deserving rest, precisely because we've overcome so much to get to where we are.

Let me explain. I'm the first woman in my whole family to be able to complete a four-year college degree and get a master's degree, to do paid work outside my home, to have control over my finances, to have a career, and to have agency over my body and be able to choose whether to have children and how many. The goal of honoring my ancestors' wildest dreams—particularly my mum's—is at the back of my mind every single day. The responsibility of achieving goals for all my female ancestors lit a fire in me, especially through the hardest moments of applying to colleges, completing multiple exams, and raising my hand for the most challenging projects at work. Making my mum proud has been such a mainstay of my life. So much so that I'm not sure what my identity would be without it.

Most of my closest friends—women of color, particularly—don't take this ambition lightly; whether to push past low expectations they've had placed on them by other people, to seek justice (subconsciously) for all the opportunities denied to their ancestors because of systemic racism and sexism, or to be unapologetically ambitious in cultures that expect then penalize women for being so, I know that so many of us carry this weight of *doing more*. So many FODs are fueled by the responsibility of carrying on and pushing past physical and mental pain (reminder: the mind is part of the body!) to ensure that we don't take all the diversity out of the room the moment we leave.

But many tell me about the impossible task of reconciling those slivers of joy and purpose with the bone-deep exhaustion of being the first, the only, the different, or one of the few.

I know this only too well. I have left for the airport in the dead of night in the middle of winter, four weeks in a row, telling myself, "You're the first Indian woman keynote speaker they've ever had, so just carry on," only to feel unwell for months afterward. And when I speak to my women-of-color peers who have chronic illnesses or who are single parents or who are juggling their career ambitions with caregiving duties, I've heard indescribable challenges and pain, punctuated with "But it's worth it in the end, right? I can't squander this opportunity, because if not me, then who?"

And so, as in other parts of this book—this feels like hard advice to give, let alone follow—we must let that scarcity thinking go. We may have struggled hard to get here, but that struggle doesn't have to define the rest of our lives. We simply cannot continue sacrificing our beautiful, brilliant bodies in this way. As scholars like Tricia remind us, rest does not have to be earned or justified. It is more than OK to rest *just because*.

And I know why it's so hard to rest. I remember seeing white male peers show up to classes late, get poor grades, and still be in leadership positions a decade later. I'd never hear this type of hunger to *persevere no matter what* from upper- and middle-class white women who frequently had role models for career success who looked like them and would still go on to line the upper echelons of organizations and win awards. My last book was *literally* on how women of color must be at least twice as good and work four times harder to be considered half as good. I understand the hunger to prove—and to keep proving once you've achieved—and I feel it deep in my bones. But even though the scarcity thinking of "no rest until I'm dead" comes from a valid place, to uncompete requires us to intentionally choose rest. Especially in those moments when we're hustling on autopilot.

Can ambition and rest ever be compatible? I turned to La'Kita Williams, whom you met in the last chapter, for an answer. Apart from being a badass leader and leadership coach, La'Kita is also a Black woman who was diagnosed with multiple sclerosis (MS) in 2020. La'Kita is among the women of color who I've seen actively practice a life of abundance (one of her highest beliefs) and demonstrate what it means to uncompete. For someone who was ambitious and dreamed of financial abundance from a young age, being diagnosed with a chronic illness initially devastated her, but it eventually helped her understand that honoring her body was a key component of sustainable ambition. Her body literally gave her no other choice.

Unfortunately, competition and late-stage capitalism have us believe that rest is for the lazy, unambitious, and unsuccessful, a stereotype even more harmful for women of color, especially Black women. But as many leaders, particularly those in the disability and social justice community, have taught me—and helped me to decolonize my mind—this is a toxic and unhealthy narrative that helps no one. What does? Thinking of rest as a "wraparound service" that enables your life's ambitions.

La'Kita's background in social service guides her to reflect on the wraparound services we need to fulfill our life's goals. One way to do this is to reflect on every single *system* that affects us and ensure that we have support across all systems, La'Kita tells me over Zoom from her virtual office, a dream catcher waving in the background next to a print of Hokusai's *The Great Wave*. While dreaming and planning for any goal, we must always be assessing: *What supports do we need physically, emotionally, mentally?* Our competitive system tells us we "just need to work hard," but for more trailblazing leadership experts like La'Kita, the right question is "How do we manage our energy so we can rest when we need, and push hard when we need?" When we intentionally work toward our goals and ambitions, free of the competitive, comparative "shoulds," we set ourselves up for success by factoring in not just what we achieve but also how to plan for the natural human depletion of energy that goes into achieving a goal.

Questions to reflect on: *What's going to support my development? What is going to support my motivation, my productivity, my inspiration?* Then build with intention all the things that would support you in all those areas, not just the goal achievement, she says. Start with placing yourself in the center of a circle, then assess what "circles" need to wrap around you to achieve the life of your dreams. Think about mental health, physical health, emotional health, community, financial well-being, physical safety . . . all those things that wrap around you as an individual. If you are always at the center of that and you're building a plan to support yourself that includes those elements, then you start to become more in control of your life instead of feeling controlled by it, says La'Kita.

La'Kita believed in the importance of rest and somatic practices for several years before she got diagnosed with MS, but she admits to ignoring or not elevating rest to the levels she does now, where every decision is made based on what her body needs. Practically, this means setting humanistic time frames (not rushing to deliver something in four weeks that, when including rest, could be delivered in eight weeks) and being intentional about the *why* behind pursuing a goal or ambition. La'Kita and I have talked extensively about the number of goals we reached for (and even achieved) because it was someone else's plan for us or even finding ourselves in competition and comparison with others.

"Now when I look at others' achievements, I evaluate, *Am I interested in that? That's intriguing, and is that something I want to pursue?* But I never look at it like *I have to pursue this because that person did*," she tells me. Being intentional and asking ourselves what *we really want* (free from outside noise) also helps us evaluate the rest practices we need to service that goal. And I admit, as a nondisabled, neurotypical woman in my late thirties, my rest practices and requirements will look different from someone who is disabled, neurodiverse, and/or older.

We can also be guided by Spoon Theory, a concept introduced by writer Christine Miserandino and now used more broadly by the chronically ill and by disability-justice activists. Essentially, Spoon Theory tells us to view our energy in finite units of "spoons," and once they're used up, they're gone. For people who are chronically ill or disabled, the same task—such as taking a shower—could use up four spoons on one day and one spoon on another. If we could imagine our energy as twelve spoons in a day, how could we spend them more mindfully? If halfway through our day we've expended all twelve spoons of energy, how many of us are forced (or put the pressure on ourselves) to continue on producing without capacity? When we don't factor in our rest—and push through exhaustion, burnout, or illness— we uphold competition and ableism. When nondisabled people choose to hustle and ignore signs from our bodies that we need to slow down, we're signaling to our disabled and chronically ill peers, "Your bodies that can't keep up with this hustle aren't worthy."

As a caregiver for a young child, I know there are some caregiving tasks I *must* save spoons for—which has helped me evaluate more intentionally what I have the energy to say yes to and decline everything else. As La'Kita herself has often guided me in our coaching sessions, the best way to assess whether to accept or decline an opportunity is to seek signals from my body. She's taught me to try to listen for any messages I'm getting internally that say yes. And if I can't hear them loudly: "If it's not a 'hell yes!,' it's a no."

EXPLORE EMBODIMENT PRACTICES IN WORK AND LIFE

It's a powerful act of resistance when we model embodiment practices in our workplaces that make it safe for our peers to choose to honor their bodies, too. It's especially meaningful when leaders engage in practices signaling to those around them that success doesn't have to come at the cost of their mental, physical, or emotional health.

As an entrepreneur with a team reporting to me, that has meant pushing back against unreasonable client deadlines, sometimes even opting out of projects, and being clear with clients, peers, and my team about when I'm out of office and uncontactable by email. Given that 81 percent of business owners check emails on vacation and six in seven business owners who check emails on vacation still feel burned out after taking time off, I know this is rare. I spent most of my career and entrepreneurial journey believing that if I took time off or asked for more time to complete a project, I'd lose opportunities. And I want to be clear that our hustle-always culture promotes this scarcity thinking, so it's not unfounded. But this is precisely when those of us with privilege—like me, as my team looks to me for guidance around work-culture norms—can take a stand. I know I've made some progress because more members of my team feel empowered to set better boundaries by asking for realistic deadlines, figuring out what to prioritize, and never letting vacation days go unused. I acknowledge that this can be hard early in your career or if you're far from the top in a hierarchical organization. But as I know firsthand, it can also become the default not to set boundaries around work even if you're in a more senior position or you're the boss. This is where slowing down the autopilot approach to ignore stress, pain, nonwork commitments, or other signals to keep working is so necessary.

Workplace leaders who are white, male, wealthy, and nondisabled: Your part in this is crucial. When we see you listening to (and taking corresponding action) to honor your body, it can create paradigm-shifting ripple effects for all those around you. One of the research-backed ways that leaders can create gender equity in the workplace is to safeguard against an "always on" culture of overwork, which makes it safe for caregivers (overwhelmingly women) to balance caregiving duties with work. When male leaders visibly and audibly take time off for caregiving, vacations, and illnesses, they strongly signal that this behavior is encouraged and accepted. When leaders work through vacations, sickness, and nonwork commitments (like childcare or eldercare), it signifies to others that work takes precedence over everything else and that those who don't follow suit will be less successful at the organization.

When leaders honor their bodies, the consequences are far-reaching regarding creating a culture where people don't feel like they will "lose out" unless they're constantly pushing to their maximum physical and mental limit. This is particularly key to organizations seeking to create a human-centered culture that makes it more than OK for employees at any level to listen to what their bodies are telling them.

Another unusual but highly effective embodiment practice I've developed is to prioritize taking a lunch break in the workday. Sixty-two percent of Americans eat lunch at their desk, and I found myself doing the same when I worked in corporate America. I often worked through lunch even when I started working for myself—again, the scarcity mentality of "missing out" or "falling behind" if I took time for myself. Shunning breaks isn't great for our mental or physical health. Coming from Singapore, which has a rich "eat lunch with your co-workers" work culture, I knew I had to make a change. Part of my practice has become deliberately scheduling time for lunch in the middle of any workday. When I pack lunch, I'll be sure to eat it away from my desk—whether at a park, weather permitting, or in a communal indoor space away from my phone and laptop. I try to prioritize meeting one of the amazing women in my life for lunch or spending time with my partner, all of which helps me feel more embodied.

I've also deliberately sought out embodiment practices outside of work. Recently, I became certified to teach yoga after completing two hundred hours of training. Indeed, the time spent in achieving this goal meant time off work, which as a parent and an entrepreneur was hard to do. But I became convinced that I needed to develop a somatic practice that would help me slow down my impulse to always be working, not only as a business owner but also the shift I put in round-the-clock once my son is home. My aim wasn't to become a yoga instructor or find ways to further my career, which is how the "old me" would have justified taking time off from work and investing time and money in pursuit of the yoga certification. My sole aim was to have the tools to be more present in my own body, after coming to the training burned out and exhausted, realizing that I had spent most of my life disassociating from my body. For people who are type A overachievers, disassociation and dysregulation are so common that most of us would rather live in pain than choose to find ways to reconnect with our bodies.

Whether it's meditation or any type of slowing down, somatic practice feels particularly challenging for people like us. Of course, ancient scholars of Eastern traditions knew that meditation was really challenging, often referring to our restless minds as variations of the "monkey mind." Even so, most ancient meditation (or meditation-like) practices were developed so long before the current pace of life and the internet that I believe the pioneers could never have fathomed the ubiquity of distraction and disassociation that would become commonplace in our lives. The world we live in makes it impossible to find quiet from external stimulation and to connect our minds and bodies. I won't rehash the data I've shared in previous chapters about how social media companies benefit or the widespread issue of mental health challenges, but we know that it's an epidemic.

Despite the incredible two hundred hours of learning from my yoga teacher, I am no closer to developing a daily meditation practice. This chapter isn't designed to shame and blame you for not meditating, as do so many media articles that tell us meditation is the success secret of CEOs. (Competition over who can meditate the most? Um, OK. Not the point!)

But I do know that to uncompete, to approach the world with abundance, inclusion, solidarity, collaboration, and radical generosity, we must start by being grounded in our bodies. We can do this by developing our own practices that help us find that grounding.

I intentionally chose to learn about the philosophy of yoga, of which the asana movement practice is a small part, with Ashish Arora, an Indian teacher. However, I have seen competition and oppressive ideals proliferate even in wellness industries, perpetuating exclusion and bias—in fact, many somatic practices rooted in or derived from ancient Asian cultures have been co-opted, commercialized, and even made exploitative in the West. For example, yoga in the West has become mostly disassociated from the deep philosophies derived from Vedic traditions that specifically emphasize nonviolence, nonjudgment, and compassion to ourselves and others, and has instead devolved into who can do handstands and the highest number of poses. The archetype of the ideal yoga practitioner in the West—young, female, white, and small-bodied—is completely different from the inclusive, nonjudgmental place that this ancient tradition stems from.

So when I say we must develop an embodiment practice, it is with the caveat that we must find what works best for us, and if we find that a practice causes us stress or pressure to perform and compete, then that's a strong sign we need to seek an alternative. (Relatedly, any somatic practice that requires exorbitant amounts of money or shames you for not engaging with it at a certain frequency and intensity with the latest expensive gear should absolutely be discarded.) That is the difference between real, transformational self-care and faux self-care, as Pooja Lakshmin's transformational book, *Real Self-Care*, highlights: "Real self-care . . . is not a one-stop shop like a fancy spa retreat or a journaling app; it's an internal process that involves making difficult decisions that will pay off tenfold in the long run as a life built around the relationships and activities that matter most to you."

It often requires us to make difficult decisions like opting out of overwork, deciding not to compete in another marathon with an injury, or choosing to take a thirty-minute lunch break when everyone around you brags about how they didn't even have time to eat because they're *so very busy*. It is a practice to eschew grind culture, not co-opt to the default.

I'm concerned that post-pandemic return-to-office mandates will make it harder to find ways to be in our bodies as we once again face stressors like commutes, long hours in the office, and lack of flexibility. This is again where leaders can—and must—model what it looks like to take breaks and rest.

Rest itself is an expansive concept and central to liberating our bodies. Saundra Dalton-Smith, a physician and author who pioneered the Seven Types of Rest framework, provides a beautiful way to view types of rest as an embodiment practice. Below are the seven types of rest she outlines, each worth reflecting on in terms of how we can incorporate it into our lives.

1. **Physical rest.** Physical rest involves helping your body recover and maintain its functionality. Physical rest can be passive, like napping or sleeping, or active, like stretching, yoga, foam rolling, or getting a massage.

2. **Mental rest.** Mental rest gives your brain a break from racing thoughts, ruminations, endless to-do lists, or work. Types of mental rest include meditation, short breaks from work, and relaxing hobbies.

3. **Sensory rest.** Cell phone notifications and the sounds of our coworkers chatting are examples of sensory stimulations that can overwhelm our brain. To counteract overstimulation and get sensory rest, Dalton-Smith recommends closing your eyes momentarily, using noise-canceling headphones, or, if possible, spending a few minutes alone in a dark, quiet room.

4. **Creative rest.** Some sources of creative rest might include spending time in nature, pursuing a creative project, or filling your workspace with objects that spark joy, wonder, and curiosity.

5. **Emotional rest.** As a recovering people pleaser, I know firsthand what it's like to be emotionally drained from my people-pleasing tendencies. Emotional rest requires us to set boundaries with others and honor them.

6. **Social rest.** Consider a few of the most important relationships in your life: Which relationships give you energy? Prioritize spending some time with those who uplift you or fill you with positive emotions. Rest doesn't always have to mean solitude, and it's important to know which people charge you back up.

7. **Spiritual rest.** Spiritual rest, according to Dalton-Smith, is "the ability to connect beyond the physical and mental and feel a deep sense of belonging, love, acceptance, and purpose." We can implement spiritual rest through prayer, volunteering, or joining a spiritually minded community.

I want to reemphasize because it's so important that none of these embodiment practices are about being more productive or "resting today to work harder tomorrow." Instead, when we prioritize being in our bodies through deliberate, regular practice, we signal to ourselves and others around us that our bodies are more than just tools of production. No awards, bragging rights, or slowing down just to speed up more. We slow down to slow down because we believe in honoring and listening to our bodies. Our radical actions to honor our bodies in a world that doesn't model this allow others around us to feel empowered to do the same. Only then do we begin to uncompete for the long haul. Only then can we uncompete at scale.

A COMMUNAL APPROACH TO EMBODIMENT AND WELL-BEING

We rarely think of wellness as a communal, public health issue and instead are likely to blame illness on individual choices. But rejecting the pernicious idea of "worthiness through productivity" and the ensuing dismissal of the wisdom inherent in our bodies cannot be done alone. We can learn to feel well, whole, and present in our bodies only when we approach embodiment with a community-care lens.

When we are present in our bodies, we become more able to operate from a place of compassion and care for others. I've deliberately made it a practice to recommend other people by name when I can't take on new career opportunities, as I've outlined in previous chapters. But I didn't come to that by happenstance—it took intentional tuning in to my health at any given time and understanding that I couldn't possibly take on everything that came my way. Stepping back when we need rest offers a natural space for others to step into. For so many FODs, working ourselves to the bone affects our health—but it also prevents us from passing the baton on when it's time. We can operate from abundance, solidarity, inclusion, and collaboration when we reframe urgency culture to reject taking on every single thing that comes our way. By believing and acting as if our health and the health of those around us matter, we create opportunities for people beyond just us as individuals. We take turns taking care of each other, ramping up when we are well, ramping down when we are ill or approaching illness, knowing that no one person can—or should—do it all.

I've surmised that curating and creating a community that practices uncompeting around bodies and wellness has had a big part to do with how I feel about myself. When surrounded by people who actively compete, compare, and comment on bodies, I'm immediately drawn back to how that showed up earlier in my life. We have ways to go around fully liberating our bodies, and I want to give us permission to take the time to get there. Black and brown bodies have been denied the right to our bodily autonomy for centuries, and even some progress we have made is under threat. But being in community with leaders like La'Kita, guided by the work of scholars like Tricia Hersey and Saundra Dalton-Smith, reaffirms to me that choosing to liberate my body from constant productivity and learning to see it as worthy even at rest are both radical and my birthright.

In fact, my ancestors left me a blueprint, which I didn't even recognize until I began writing this book. Growing up, sometime between one and three o'clock every afternoon, silence would descend over my house. My mother would go into her bedroom, draw the curtains, shut the door, and take a thirty-minute rest. A post-lunch rest—sometimes a nap, sometimes just a "rest-my-eyes break," as Mum would call it—was so much part of our family's ritual that I just never thought much about it. When I visited my grandparents in Mumbai, Naniji and Nanaji, they would do the same. As a hyperactive child, I despised coming to a rest, but I knew it was a sacred time for all my elders and quickly became silent to honor their space. It was clear that whoever was at home at that moment—family members and guests alike—was invited to rest. It was a communal activity.

As the years went on and I went to Western colleges and then entered the corporate workforce, I never thought much about this afternoon ritual, nor did I compare notes on whether other families engaged in it. All I knew was that as I became an adult, my work peers and I would all complain about mitigating the exhaustion we felt in the afternoons at work by downing two to three cups of coffee. As I progressed in my career, that afternoon slump felt even more pronounced for me. The demands of (badly) juggling my career with motherhood took over, and the afternoon fog just kept getting worse. Seeing how overwhelmed I was, my mum kept encouraging me to take a twenty-minute "eye break," and I kept ignoring her. It's only now that I realize how much wisdom was passed down from my own ancestors, who found their own resistance to colonial and capitalist oppression by taking breaks, saying no, and learning to listen to what their bodies told them—in whatever ways they could.

As I write this, another five emails pop up in my inbox. New work opportunities beckon, but I can feel myself on the brink of exhaustion. "I am my ancestors' wildest dreams," I repeat as a mantra in my head. "I can do this. I can make the space for it." But then I think of my Naniji and the wisdom of those afternoon naps that were just for her. No one could take away that time from her. Space carved out just for her within long days that never really belonged to her and the women in our lineage.

I know for certain that if she could see me now, she would be astounded by the way I nourish my body and have so much more autonomy to decide how to move or rest based on how I feel that day. All privileges that were unfathomable for women like her, but built on the foundations they laid for me.

"I am my ancestors' wildest dreams, and that's why I choose rest," I say to myself, closing my inbox and my eyes.

CHAPTER NINE

Redefine Success
on Our Own Terms

M ost people say they don't consider themselves successful. If I'm brutally honest, it's hard for me to say I am. There's always so much *more* I could achieve. I interviewed hundreds of corporate leaders in my former life as a journalist—including people in C-suite roles—and I can't remember one who seemed entirely convinced that they were successful. Many admitted to having a lot more to accomplish before they could definitively declare success. The idea that there's always a higher peak to climb is pervasive.

Professional success is usually defined as making more money or getting new titles, promotions, or awards. The most acceptable way to measure success is by your salary or your job title, but rarely do we take a moment to reflect whether these are metrics of success we set for ourselves or part of a path where the goalposts were already laid out for us.

Of course, I know intimately what it's like to live a life based not only on my parents' definitions of success (which, as you've likely ascertained, were quite different) but also on what the larger community told me to do. And that definition itself was also complicated for me by gender—because I am a South Asian child of immigrants, success was measured by prestigious education that would lead to getting an influential job and becoming wealthy. But because I'm also a South Asian woman, it meant being married to a man, raising children as a primary caregiver, keeping a beautiful home with delicious meals, while also maintaining strong relationships with my family and instilling cultural values in said children. I'm exhausted just typing that out, and as you might have guessed, it's taken me a long time to understand that this wasn't my own definition of success.

Our ideas of success and the steps we need to take to get there are based on other people's expectations. It's also why so many of us in the professional world are completely thrown for a loop when we don't get a promotion or get laid off, or, for entrepreneurs, when we lose a big client or project. It threatens our very sense of self. When we walk on paths chosen for us by others, it can totally shake us up if the results don't show up as expected; the thought is "I followed the instructions, so why weren't the outcomes as promised?"

And in today's unpredictable environment, that's so often the case; hard work alone doesn't determine a linear outcome. I've read that as many as half of US college graduates today are underemployed, despite college degrees long being considered the surest way to get a high-paying job. Working round-the-clock is no longer (if it was ever) a sure path to promotion. There are so many variables beyond our control—not to mention class and racial privilege—that affect how work rewards us. If we don't take the time to define success for ourselves, without the noise of "shoulds" and expectations around us, we'll never fully be able to find it. That target will constantly move because it's not one we've deliberately chosen.

Defining how we want to live our lives on our own terms, measured by what makes us feel whole, is the only way to break this cycle. We must be embodied and fully present while figuring this out for ourselves. If we take a long-term view, success, at its core, is about creating a life well lived. Being intentional about what matters most to us, then setting about to create it, in community, is the only way we can begin the healing. My mum often says, "None of the five fingers on one hand are the same size, yet united together, they make a strong fist," a Hindi proverb. Yes, we must see ourselves as part of the collective, but we must also know that a singular definition of success—or a life well lived—simply can't fit everyone. We can begin this journey by exploring **play**, **possibilities**, **patience**, and **kindness**.

PLAYING TO (RE)DISCOVER WHAT MATTERS MOST TO US

When I moved to the United Kingdom as an eighteen-year-old university student, I was surprised to meet several people with different definitions of success than the ones I was conditioned to have. Anyone I knew who wasn't following the narrow definition of success prescribed by my community on an age-appropriate schedule was spoken about with pity or as a warning about what happened if you weren't "focused" (read: competitively working to achieve these goals).

Even so, in London I met, for the first time, people who weren't pursuing goals to be "successful"; they were defining success as being able to play and pursue their pleasures. I met a male dancer who taught pole-dancing classes at a small, nondescript studio near my university *just for fun.* No performances, no big studio attached to his name. His main goal was to help people who came in for lessons feel good about themselves and move their bodies. Sure, he had other gigs to help pay the bills, but the way his eyes lit up when he talked about *this* endeavor made it a lightning moment for me. I was inspired and exhilarated while also knowing that this definition of success or joy wasn't for people like me. My family had expectations; they'd made sacrifices; people would be judging us by my career *and* being married "at the right age." But in the years since, I've seen the innate wisdom, freedom, and even radical resistance in embracing unconventional notions of success. Not everyone has the luxury to discover and play—much less those of us who've been historically denied the opportunity to—but when we're moving from the mindset of scarcity to abundance, we must claim play for ourselves.

I've learned tremendously from people who define their lives by finding the most authentic version of themselves rather than climbing a ladder of success—financial or otherwise—that was programmed for them. Unfortunately, it often takes an amount of privilege to live life in this way. But I also find many of us who do have some financial privilege, like me, are still too stuck in fear to veer off script. Because having privilege is not the only factor, although it helps immensely—it also takes deep courage and strong self-worth to reject traditional notions of success and write our own. Particularly for those of us who've never seen it modeled in our own communities.

So often, the conventional metrics of success are tied to money and status. These are easy to quantify, so it makes sense—they're measurable, universally recognizable, and signal where we are in a perceived linear path through life. As I've described throughout this book, when we embark on a true commitment to uncompete, we can often, even contrary to what the prevailing narrative tells us, find financial success and status. All of this can help us build broad and sustainable wealth—from a stronger community to measurable financial abundance. But financial abundance just for us alone is a narrow and incomplete definition of success. There are so many ways to succeed in work and life, and only in critically examining the options, choosing what appeals to us, and rejecting what doesn't can we move away from a limited view of a successful life.

As I've written before, financial stability and living an ambition-fueled life both matter greatly to me. I'd be hypocritical if I suggested we give up on these goals if they matter to us. But in my journey to uncompete, I'm trying to examine more closely where and when those traditional markers of success encourage fierce competition for limited resources, or comparison thinking around titles, or are chased only to win approval from others.

Often, "successful careers" are externally defined as ones where someone can climb the ladder, get awards, receive salary bumps, manage a large team, and get a job title that sounds impressive to others. But if we stop and evaluate the moments that really felt meaningful to us, it would likely be when we were working on worthy endeavors, mentoring someone one-on-one toward their own growth, and having enough energy to live a full life outside of work. It should go without saying that multiple markers of success may intersect—perhaps our high-paying job can help us derive meaning. But if that's not the case, if you know deep in your bones that your joy lies elsewhere, then un-competing makes it more than OK to seek measures of success that are meaningful to you.

Being more discerning about what success constitutes to us on our own terms will release so much of the pressure that comes from living up to others' expectations. For women of color who face extreme ex-haustion and loneliness in jobs, it can help more of us feel empowered to walk away from jobs that might look great on paper but are soul-sucking when we're constantly the "only." Empowering each person to define their own success allows us to stop ascribing value to humans based on our yardstick of success. It's painful to see how society treats (and pays) service workers, care workers, and, broadly speaking, many people who were considered "essential workers" during the COVID-19 pandemic but quickly lost that status once we were out of lockdown.

Maybe the barista at the coffee shop is living their best life where they're able to work in a job that gives their life value and meaning—whether at work or outside of it. Maybe we'll stop idolizing and com-paring ourselves to famous people once and for all if we begin to realize that the cost of fame—such as giving up privacy—is incompat-ible with our definition of a well-lived life.

To begin this discovery requires you to open your imagination to all the ways that your work, and your life, could feel successful beyond the status quo. This is again how cultivating play can be informative. There's no singular way to do this, but I find that reflecting on a time when I felt free to do as I pleased, before expectations were placed on me, offers some clues.

Could you reflect on such a time, ideally from your childhood, and recall what you felt drawn to do? *What would you do when no one told you what to do? What activities were you drawn to? Where did your mind natu-rally wander to when you were alone? Where did you feel most comfortable and safe?* More people are (re)discovering hobbies and activities that were once meaningful to them but that they were forced to abandon in ex-change for "grown-up" jobs and responsibilities. I never harbored any aspirations to write books, although I loved writing as a child and would even write my own books of imaginary stories complete with drawings and stapled bindings. But as I grew older, I stopped reading books for pleasure—it was academic or work-related texts, or nothing. My excuse was that unless it was "improving" my career (or later, my parenting skills) in some way, there wasn't time in the day for it.

I've come back to reading fiction again only during the past five years. In fact, when I was knee-deep in research while writing my last book, I would read romance novels before bed as a counterbalance to all the nonfiction I was reading during the day. As I discovered a world of authors beautifully diversifying the genre in ways I never read grow-ing up—from Jasmine Guillory to Nisha Sharma to Akwaeke Emezi—I began to rediscover a part of myself that I'd buried: the child and then the teenage Ruchika who loved to read for pleasure and was sur-rounded by books. Now, if I can't take even five minutes of a day to read a novel, I feel less like myself. For me, this has become a measure of success—do I have time to engage in play, in what makes me feel most like myself? Reading fiction certainly does.

This kind of play is available to all of us, maybe not always and not in large quantities, particularly for those of us who are caregivers. Even so, the exploration and reflection can help us find out when we feel most aligned with "us" versus outside definitions of success.

BOLDLY CARVING OUR OWN PATH

Meaningfully engaging in this journey requires audacity. You will face resistance. One of the most toxic ways I've seen a competition mindset show up in our relationships is when we belittle, invalidate, or criticize someone else's choices because we believe that these choices are throwing shade on us, the way we live our lives, and our definition of success. When I first became a journalist, I met several professional South Asian people who would undermine me and my choice of profession. Some would make comments about how little money I was making, others mentioned that I was "lucky to work in a nonstressful job," and others pointedly avoided asking me about work, preferring to talk about how important their jobs in technology or finance were. In those moments I felt slighted and angry. But as I've begun my own healing, I see that my "nontraditional" career path and definitions of success for my life that weren't dependent on making money (find me anyone who goes into journalism to make money!) or bragging that I worked at a Fortune 500 company felt like an affront to them. It challenged their notion that success was narrowly defined in the ways they were taught—for example, personal fulfillment or social justice was not part of the success equation. It wasn't even in their realm of possibilities. Of course, I've noticed that judgment immediately comes up when women, people of color, and others from historically excluded identities defy societal expectations unapologetically in any way. Our conforming to narrow definitions of success and the threat we feel that others are better achieving these expectations are ever looming. We've generally seen people like us rewarded only for conforming to an already trodden path. By no means do

I have success figured out or perfectly mapped out for myself. But I do know it takes commitment and courage—quite like the work to liberate our bodies—to embrace what success means to us, especially when we face resistance from others for choosing it. To uncompete, we must continually and critically examine what our definitions of success are, how they came about, and who told us we needed to achieve a certain checklist by a certain age.

Notice how I didn't write "assess whether we are happy or unhappy." In much of the literature I've read about happiness, I've come to realize that trying to "always be happy" is usually the cause of great sorrow. Instead, I've learned that all the above components come together to create a life that can feel purposeful and worthy, even if you're facing sorrow, illness, or injustice. And when we don't feel like we have any agency over these areas, it can breed insecurity and exacerbate a scarcity mindset and a default approach to be competitive.

What I think we all know but don't always internalize is that others' choices don't define our success. When we feel like we have endless possibilities—abundance—in front of us, we're more likely to be able to cheer others on when they're exploring and finding possibilities to live their best lives. When we feel stuck and limited in what we can do, we resent others for taking a different path.

I think it is particularly tough in communities whose possibilities have been limited by others' imaginations because they've faced bias and white supremacy. As I work toward my own healing, I can begin to empathize with (if not forgive) other South Asian people for belittling the choices I've made to pursue career paths that weren't considered "successful" and "worthy" in our communities. Journalism, consulting, and writing all required me to create new paths when new possibilities and opportunities came my way. That I didn't consider money as the top metric of success in my career was also seen as breaking the mold. I can now see how my choices may have felt like a challenge to the only way those people felt they could be respected in our South Asian community and as immigrants in the West. We say competition is about standing out, but really, it's about who conforms the best to standards that are leveled against so many in the first place. The only way to resist is to wholeheartedly commit to discovering all the possibilities that lie ahead of us. To resist being restricted by others' expectations, we must carve our own way.

Alok Vaid-Menon (ALOK) is an example of someone who exemplifies this in every way. ALOK is a poet, comedian, public speaker, and actor who constantly questions and explores the gender binary in every way, especially through their appearance and style. ALOK frequently posts on social media the criticism (unfortunately, sometimes vitriolic) they receive about their appearance. The nasty comments are so telling of the policing we do of one another's conformity (or not) to existing standards of "normalcy," and the responses are telling of how much courage and self-worthiness it takes to chart your own definition of success.

In August 2020, ALOK shared this reflection on receiving negative comments:

> i used to be so self hating: my internalized homophobia/transphobia/misogyny/racism made me feel like i had to disappear myself in order to be worthy, made me distance myself from everything different, lash out at any perceived threat to my normalcy. it was a hollow life—one where i sought the myth of

sameness as if it would keep me safe. but it didn't. nothing i could do was ever enough. i was always wanting, aspirational, remiss.

it was only through the care and compassion of my friends that i began to embrace self-acceptance. and through self-acceptance i began to accept that everyone is different from one another and that's totally rad, not a threat to my identity. the more i work on my self-healing, the more love i have for everyone and everything!! it's overflowing out of me! i have so much hope, so much faith, i am overwhelmed by the beauty around me. i am so thrilled to be alive! not just to exist: but to be alive.

i believe now in the potential for transformation, our continual becoming, because i have experienced it firsthand.

to my haters: i love and need you! i am fighting for you, too! i am sorry that you have been misled to target me and not address the crises you're going through. i am sorry that you can't see me outside of your anxieties and insecurities. when we take off those projections the world is so much more vibrant and three dimensional, i promise. i know that you've probably been so hard on yourself and been made to feel like you weren't enough, but you are. and have always been. i believe you are worth more than conditional acceptance! you don't have to be strong here. you don't have to play pretend here. you are special and worthy of community who loves you for you, not your disappearing act!

I dream of a world where all of us can have such brave self-compassion: It naturally flows into acceptance and compassion for others, particularly those exploring paths of success and possibilities that are completely different from ours.

HOW TO UNLOCK
POSSIBILITIES IN YOUR LIFE

Sometimes, imagining greater possibilities for success doesn't have to mean doing more or putting more on your plate. Sometimes, success can be learning to step back.

I take a lot of inspiration from one of my childhood idols: Monita Rajpal, a life coach who was previously a CNN International television anchor. After almost two decades at CNN, Monita left at the height of her career to prioritize her health and her family, while also seeking a slower pace of life. That's no small feat in an industry where women of color are scarcely in front of the camera, and certainly not in the 1990s and 2000s, when she was on TV. When I asked her if she's ever regretted her decision to leave a glamorous television job (she's interviewed every famous person of her time!) and move to the rural English countryside with her husband and young son, she told me, *"Never, never, never."*

In a blog post about her decision to leave her news career, she wrote this:

> One of my leading values is to feel free, free to design my day
> and my life my way. I work from home which I absolutely love.
> I am not without my worries—no one really is but when we feel
> we are not living someone else's definition of success, we have
> so much more fuel within to find solutions to our challenges.

Seeing Monita live a beautiful, restful life after decades in the public eye has reiterated for me that you are your ancestors' wildest dreams when you get to choose the possibilities for your own life.

Here are some ways you can dream up possibilities just for you:

1. **Reflect on your values.** Take time to identify and reflect on the values that guide your life. What principles do you hold dear? What matters most to you in your personal and professional endeavors? Understanding your core values will provide clarity and direction as you navigate your journey toward success.

2. **Explore what actually makes you want to get up every morning.** Delve into activities, hobbies, and interests that ignite your enthusiasm and bring you joy. What activities make you lose track of time? What topics do you find yourself continuously drawn to? Exploring these will uncover hidden talents and strengths, and will reveal what truly resonates with your soul.

3. **Set *personally* meaningful goals.** Define clear and achievable goals that align with your values and the possibilities ahead for you. Start small. Ask yourself, "What do I aspire to achieve in my personal and professional life? How do I envision my ideal future?" Setting meaningful goals will empower you to take purposeful action and make tangible progress toward realizing your dreams.

REDEFINING SUCCESS AT SCALE

Sometimes I'll hear from leaders that although in theory they'd love to expand how success is defined at their workplace, in practice it feels impossible. I understand this, particularly as we are all wrapped up in structures of capitalism and exploitation.

I am slowly beginning to see bigger organizations set success goals differently from conventional markers. I think of real-estate developer Lake Union Partners, which sold units of a development in Seattle's historically Black Central District back to Black business owners. On its website, the firm describes itself as "experienced developers who create places with design integrity, intentionality, and sensitivity to local neighborhoods." By moving away from a purely profit-driven motive as is expected, particularly of real-estate developers, they could measure their success by contributions made to propelling Black economic and cultural wealth.

When I was on the founding team of the women-run-and-founded media company The Establishment, the other founders and I were aligned on the fact that our success wouldn't be measured by audience engagement alone and that our core mission was to cover stories that needed to be told. To do this, we decided to do away with online comments in order to protect our writers, who were overwhelmingly from historically marginalized backgrounds and had often faced trolling when writing for other sites. As any media person will tell you, online comments generate revenue—in fact, the more engaged a comments section of an article is, the longer readers tend to spend on your website. (Which is also why social media posts that incite strong emotions tend to go viral compared with posts that don't.) Still, when we were able to state that success would be measured by the impact our stories would have on readers and didn't pay writers based on how many clicks they got, we were able to create a one-of-a-kind publication that told daring stories about women. (The company has since closed but has inspired more legacy media publications to focus on gender coverage.)

I'm also finally seeing a shift in my home country of Singapore. Despite the importance of beating out the competition, of rankings, and of materialism stressed as success markers for most Singaporeans while I was growing up, a 2023 report from its government found that those definitions were now outdated. A majority of two hundred thousand Singaporeans surveyed said they looked for meaning and purpose in their careers beyond financial compensation. Several government initiatives supporting the changing definition of success have been announced in Singapore, from more government-funded financial support for new parents to funding higher starting salaries in nondegree jobs. I'm inspired by the example of how Singapore is instituting a progressive wage model for people who work as elevator and escalator technicians. There's been more focus on getting people to value technical jobs and other careers that don't require a college degree so that people aren't judged or penalized for not having high-paying jobs. From my vantage point, this is a huge undertaking and would be revolutionary if achieved!

I believe we'll see many, many, many more examples of people working on innovative solutions to big-picture problems once society begins to make it viable and possible for its citizens to think about success differently. Imagine how many more of us would choose a different career path or even a whole different life if we were encouraged to discover success on our own terms.

PATIENCE: HOW WE CAN REDEFINE FAILURE

A few months before my friend Soraya turned forty, she spent every evening on LinkedIn obsessively comparing her career path to others she knew. She would scroll to calculate when people graduated college—trying to figure out whether they were about her age—and then start to berate herself for not getting as far ahead in her career. She did this without fail right up until the big 4-0. She tells me that overnight, something flipped. Turning forty made her realize she had spent close to four decades seeking to be perfect and was tired of it—no, exhausted. She wanted to let go of perfectionism and embrace whatever her path looked like, even if it was completely different from what she—and others—expected of her. In the years since, she's never gone back to compare on LinkedIn again.

In a competitive society, anything outside of a prescribed, conventional definition of success is defined as failure. I've seen pressures to "never fail" take shape in extraordinarily damaging ways among my female and nonbinary peers, particularly in our appearance, in our caregiving abilities, and in the workplace. We must be unflappable and never make a mistake. Of course, this makes sense in a system where room for error and second chances are egregiously low for women of color. Journalist Zulekha Nathoo interviewed me about why many white men get to "fail up" whereas women and people of color are severely penalized for small mistakes, according to a recent study.

We've normalized a definition of success where failure is not an option because it wasn't an option for us. We saw people who looked like us reprimanded, punished, and denied opportunities because of the slightest mistakes. These "failures" in a competitive society include things like divorce, infertility, losing a job or being unable to get one, having to close a business, and being broke. But in my journey to uncompete, I have met many women who are embracing "failures"—really just the unexpected twists of life, of which there are many—and have carved a path that's authentic and powerful for them.

Perhaps that's why the greatest inspiration in my life—and the permission to *fail* that I deeply ached for as a child—came from my mother's decision to divorce my father at age fifty, after twenty-eight years of being married. In the eyes of so many in our community, her divorce was seen as a massive failure, and many people I grew up with—literally, whose homes I slept over at as a child—never even bothered to check in on her or us after the divorce. The narrative was clear: She—and, by extension, we—had failed by not staying married to my father, no matter how much those years had broken her. But seeing my mum choose her joy, redefining her success to *embrace* the failure of a marriage that wasn't serving her, has been the goalpost I've aspired to ever since.

It's allowed me to finally let go of the toxic ways I would talk to and treat my body, embracing the "failure" of eating what gave me pleasure and not punishing myself when I "failed" to work out. It allowed me to have brutally honest conversations with my partner when I realized that I needed so much more support than I was getting and was willing to have my own marriage "fail" if that's what it would take to get that support. We're still married, but it took the realization that I was *willing* to fail at it for our relationship to evolve into an equitable, joyful one. Only without the fear of failure can we get closer to our own definition of success—which can, and will be, different from others' definitions of success.

In fact, I want our definition of success to include failure. Not in a "get up and try again so you can succeed next time" way (see below for my thoughts on resilience), but rather that when we give ourselves the grace to fail, we can finally stand in our power. Because when we compete for "perfectionism" as our goalpost for success, there will always be someone who will be closer to "perfection" than us. But if we allow ourselves to fail, to fully embrace failure as the very essence of being human, I believe more of us will be able to let go of the insecurity that derives from the pressure to never fail.

Here are three ways I've begun a path of recovery from a lifelong focus on trying to be perfect, being extremely unkind to myself when I deviated, and cycling on repeat:

1. **Take a long-term view.** Failures are hard at best, devastating at worst, and, of course, tough as hell to navigate in the moment. This is turbocharged for those of us who also have others' expectations thrust upon us: A bad grade or job rejection or being fired doesn't just feel like our failure but also a failure for those who were looking to us to succeed. While toxic positivity–ing through it doesn't work, what does work is *feeling* the emotions and doing what you need to process. A big cry. Ranting to friends. Therapy. More crying. But as you get some space from the failure, begin to reframe it as a setback for now, not forever. Take a long-term view that whatever went off the track for now doesn't mean your whole life is a failure. And yes, some setbacks are much harder to bounce back from: A job rejection isn't the same as an acrimonious divorce that also hurts the kids and other family members. But failures often allow us to refocus on what matters most to us. When I look back at doors that slammed in my face, I now realize that they wouldn't have been the right path for me anyway. I felt terrible in that moment, sometimes for years on end, but hindsight made it obvious it was a blessing in disguise. That's the view I try to take nowadays when I fail.

2. **Surround yourself with your community.** I know I've talked about community and collaboration ad nauseam, but research backs up how much it helps to turn to others when you're navigating failure. At work, when people feel like they can take risks, fail, and still be valued, they're likely to have a high level of psychological safety. High psychological safety is linked to innovation and growth, according to Amy Edmondson from Harvard Business School, which is why more organizations are trying to cultivate a culture that makes it safe to fail. On a per-

sonal level, having a close circle of trusted folks to lift you up and remind you that one failure doesn't mean *you're* a failure can help turn it around. When we're vulnerable with people we feel safe with, it helps create a deeper connection—all par for the course when we're trying to uncompete.

3. **Practice doing something you're *not* great at.** Most perfectionists try hard to avoid activities they're not good at. Take it from me: I wouldn't raise my hand to speak in a meeting unless I was sure I had the right answer—which meant that someone else almost always got to speak before me. But now as an adult, I've tried to tell myself that not having a fully formed idea before I speak up or even making a mistake when I'm in a meeting doesn't mean I'm terrible at life. It contextualizes that I'm going to fail at some things no matter how hard I try, and even if I improve partially, am able to give myself grace, laugh it off, and try again, this is good enough. I've noticed that some of this attitude has started carrying over to more regularly being OK with things not going according to plan. Like if I lose a client I've spent a long time preparing to pitch or have to break up with a friend whose values don't align with mine any longer. Getting better at failing helps us develop kindness toward ourselves and others, as well as often brings us closer to what really matters most to us.

KINDNESS TO
OURSELVES AND OTHERS

Speaking of kindness, I'm coming to realize how many of us are surrounded by nice people, not kind ones. In 2021, Black queer Seattleite Jordan K. Green posted this on X (formerly known as Twitter):

> When I describe East Coast vs West Coast culture to my friends
> I often say "The East Coast is kind but not nice, the West Coast

is nice but not kind," and East Coasters immediately get it. West Coasters get mad. 😂😂😂

The post sparked a debate, with commenters trying to discern the difference. Having lived on both coasts, I know exactly what he meant.

"So often, we West Coasters think that showing *sympathy* or feeling *empathy* is an act of kindness. Sadly, it's really just a nice act," he went on to explain. Bicoastal wars aside, Jordan was onto something I think many of us struggle with no matter where we live. We often think that just being nice to someone in passing is good enough but that we are not responsible for helping others or understanding their needs. To be nice would be to say to a friend who is shivering, "Sorry you're cold," then move on with our day, or to place a "Black Lives Matter" sign in our yard without ever trying to understand how anti-Blackness shows up in ourselves and others, and how to take steps to address it.

On the other hand, kindness would be, for example, lending your friend your coat or giving them a ride home in your warm car instead of waving them off at the bus stop. Being kind would mean doing the hard work of addressing anti-Blackness in yourself and the institutions around you. More of us can benefit from assessing if and how we are kind to others. How much do we feel responsible for others' needs and find ways to address them? Instead of offering what we think they need, do we step back to ask them *What do you need from me?* And then take necessary action based on what we've heard?

Kindness to ourselves and others is a measurement of a life well lived and a successful life as defined by the principles of uncompeting. I've deliberately left it to this point of the book to address it because I don't think we can fully develop and practice kindness without taking all the steps I outlined earlier. This is likely the hardest part and the one that can transform a society that has for far too long prioritized competition over empathy and financial success at the cost of human and environmental suffering. I also want to acknowledge the challenge here of asking women, people of color, and people already marginalized and excluded in society to "practice more kindness to others." Of course, we need people with the most resources available to them to practice kindness. Yet we can't opt out because we've been hurt or had our kindness exploited as weakness. As poet June Jordan wrote, "We are the ones we have been waiting for."

Indeed, it is in our communities, with those of us we are most intrinsically linked with, where we can begin the work of practicing kindness. I think of it as concentric circles—kindness to ourselves, then to those most immediately in proximity, then outward. As Australian writer Randa Abdel-Fattah writes, "Sometimes it's easy to lose faith in people. And sometimes one act of kindness is all it takes to give you hope again." Given her Palestinian heritage against the backdrop of the horrific genocide in Gaza in 2025 as I write this, her words carry more meaning.

A NOTE: BEWARE OF RESILIENCE AS A MARKER OF YOUR WELL-LIVED LIFE

The idea that you must suffer for success and overcome extreme hardship is a false narrative that bolsters a competition mindset and keeps us perennially in distress. We applaud those who have overcome poverty, addiction, or abuse to build stable lives and financially viable careers. We call them "resilient" without investigating *why* we have a system that makes it so hard to overcome that hardship in the first place. It's a narrative that is especially pernicious for women of color, but looking at adversity and suffering as ennobling is extremely commonplace in America. And this narrative works well to hide the continued erosion of collective support that directly results in people having to overcome unspeakable adversity. This is why, although I encourage a wide-open definition for success, I still reject models and definitions of success that require us to suffer.

One of the areas around competition that I've struggled most with is what to "teach" my son about it. From my own father I learned that I was unworthy of attention or love if I didn't produce and didn't compete with and outrank my peers on various metrics of traditional success. He told me that hardship was a building block of success; if you told children you loved them, you were making them soft. Physical affection was frowned upon. His favorite lines were "You gotta be tough" and "In the world, there are sharks and fish. You must be a shark." The idea that teaching kids to opt out of competition, to pursue their joys and passions, to measure success by kindness and values was largely a foreign concept to me. Even though my mother privately told me versions of this, away from my father's ears, the world at large reemphasized in hundreds of small and large ways that the only way to be successful was to struggle relentlessly—and then inflict the same struggles on the next generation.

The worry that I'll make my son "too soft" to survive in this winner-take-all world is a conflict I often have with myself. I want him to be curious and pursue what he's passionate about. But I do also want him to be self-sufficient and independent. I believe in abundance and the pursuit of joy and in rest as a human right. I want him to push himself and learn, but not to believe that acute struggle is just part of being human, like I did. Of course, I don't want him to crumble if life throws him hardships. It's a conundrum I don't have a definitive answer for. But if we applaud only "success" that is forged through acute suffering—a result of an unequal, racist society that works tirelessly to beat down the people most downtrodden by these systems—then *that* is not the resilience I wish for him or for anyone's child. Our elders, whose ancestors faced colonization, enslavement, brutality, and disrespect, should not wish for us to be brutalized by the same systems.

I no longer look at media articles about financially successful, fancy-titled career women with multiple children who also serve on multiple boards who also have beautiful homes who also give back who also have a "hobby" as a marathon champion as my inspirations for success. I want ease. I want a life well lived on my own terms. I no longer compare my achievements to those of people who have sacrificed the most sacred parts of themselves for visible titles. I'd rather not be tested any more in my life to earn "resilience" stripes; I had a childhood that was eroded in many ways by this narrative. And as I see firsthand how narrow definitions of success exacerbate toxic masculinity, I've grown more concerned for boys, men, and people socialized as male. Of course, toxic masculinity can have disastrous consequences for girls and women, but we are finally having nuanced discussions about how it affects boys' and men's lives, too.

When my son was born, my mum gave me a lovely coffee mug that had the words "Always Be Extraordinary" written on it. Over the next few years, I'd sip my afternoon green tea from that cup, reminded that even in the face of challenges—raising a small human, building a business, navigating health challenges, being a present mother, daughter, wife, friend, sibling, and community member, all in the face of global devastation from ongoing wars, a xenophobic-misogynist US presidential administration, then a once-in-a-lifetime pandemic—I could, and should, *always* be extraordinary.

But over the last few years, the "Extraordinary" has faded entirely from the cup through repeated washings. Only the words "Always Be" remain. If I'm to think of a practical definition of what it means to uncompete, it basically guides us to be *exactly* who we are, without any additional qualifier to help us stand out, get ahead, or push others out of the way in a competitive world. To be successful, we don't *need* to be extraordinary, powerful, brave, or *insert any other aphorism* that requires us to add an armor to who we are. We must give ourselves the permission to just be. And in "just" being, we give permission for others to just be, too. We invite them to bring their unfiltered, unvarnished, authentic selves to their community. In turn, we begin the revolutionary work to create a community that doesn't define its members' success by how remarkable they are and how much they produce even through hardship, but rather by how liberated they are to *be*.

For my son, I wish for gentleness and ease. I wish for a brown boy *not* to be measured by his grades, job title, earning capacity, how much he's sacrificed to prove that "kids of immigrants get the job done," or ideals of toxic masculinity that don't encourage him to explore his value and worth outside of producing and earning. I want him to take risks and know that he will still be loved if those risks don't work out and he fails. The next time anyone—even me—tells him what his life should look like, I want him to be able to articulate what feels right for him inside, if it doesn't match. I want him to have the agency to create his own vision for success and joy. I want him to make decisions based on how it feels in his body. I want him to know that he doesn't have to "Always Be Extraordinary" but can simply "Always Be" and be worthy of extraordinary kindness and love.

CHAPTER TEN

Seek Peace

As I began the journey to write this book over two years, the universe sent me infinite examples of women of color who boldly, unequivocally, unapologetically prioritize their mental peace over all else. I'm thinking of the incredible Latinx leader who walked away from working for a household-name celebrity's team because no amount of money was worth the disruption that the always-urgent culture demanded of her. That and the lack of tranquility that came from navigating racial bias as the "only" at her workplace. The Black woman who worked in a big technology company and took a massive pay cut to work at an organization that aligned with her goals to create a more antiracist, socially just world. The Indian woman who left a lucrative but all-consuming job after battling years of chronic illness to honor her own body. The many, many, many brave souls agitating and advocating for racial, LGBTQ+, and gender justice in their organizations in the face of ever-deepening resistance who eventually walk away from corporate advocacy to other forms of resistance so they can sleep well at night. It continues to inspire me when I make decisions now—who to take on as clients, what issues to work on, what to spend time on, and who to spend time with—by answering this question: "Will this bring me toward peace or take me away from it?"

I recognize how so many of us have been denied from seeking peace, kept on a short leash and made to feel like choosing any other path would leave us financially and otherwise desolate. As I reflect back on the traits I thought were necessary to be "successful," it breaks my heart to imagine myself as a child internalizing the message that peace is a foolhardy goal. The problem with this approach is it asks us to bottle up and force ourselves to go against our very human instincts to collaborate, build community, and celebrate others. Albert Einstein is sometimes attributed as saying that "if you judge a fish by its ability to climb a tree, it will live its whole life believing that it is stupid." I'd go one step further and say not only would the fish doubt its competence, but it would also spend its whole life struggling to breathe. It would live its whole (short) life without peace. In struggling to fit into boxes never quite made for us, we will never find liberation or justice.

The absence of personal and societal tranquility that we endure today as a result of competitive, exploitative systems is one of my most enduring concerns and the most compelling reason for why I want us to uncompete at scale. Without peace, there's no way we will be able to find the strength to challenge entrenched, toxic systems of oppression—from racism to poverty to inequality writ large. We may feel bitter and resigned, thinking, *What's the point anyway?* We may have even temporarily benefited from these systems. So why bother changing them?

But how can we even begin to reconcile the push for change we need everywhere with the existential dread, the overwhelm, the exhaustion, the loneliness, the powerlessness, the chronic stress that we've come to normalize in our society? If our hard work and outsmarting the competition aren't helping alleviate the acute struggles that most of us face daily, what will?

Peace. Prioritizing mental peace over competition and scarcity will allow us to fully benefit from the creation of healthier environments in personal, corporate, and societal spaces that will inspire collaboration, abundance, inclusion, solidarity, and radical generosity. As we've learned, the foundation and the roof—the entire house of uncompete—are built on and around *unlearning* the chaos of competition, seeking to uncompete as a choice guiding our actions, and allowing us to resist what's hurting us individually and collectively. When we operate from a place of peace, we're able to disengage from the vicious cycle of constantly trying to prove ourselves and feeling beaten down, and, as a result, having no spaciousness in our lives to engage in what truly matters to us. We go on to bequeath that hurt to others. To seek peace, we can benefit from mindfully finding balance, creating rituals, and choosing integrity.

FINDING BALANCE

My mum's name, Seema, means "boundary" in Sanskrit. But her modus operandi is "balance." Growing up in a household where my father largely opposed rituals and religion, I viewed my mother's practice of spirituality as anti-Western and antiscience, and therefore not one I thought would be worth getting to know better. After all, in the school I was attending, Western science was promoted as the most civilized way to be.

And the dogmatic version of the Hindu religion practiced in the community I grew up in didn't quite resonate either. I saw more focus on grand gestures of outward piousness (like always going to the temple or spending a whole weekend in group prayers) or shaming people for not being devoted enough—my family was chided for being non-vegetarian, even by some people who secretly ate meat! Members of my community growing up often engaged in competition to demonstrate who was more religious by spending more money on hosting the biggest religious ceremonies.

It's only now that more of us are seeking the ancient wisdom of traditions that existed around us all along, looking specifically for guidance in reconciling the fracture of feeling unmoored despite checking off all the measures that were supposed to define a successful, happy life. Many, like me, are on a spiritual path that isn't based on dogmatic practices and strict adherence but is inclusive of all and emphasizes the belief that every person has the right and agency to choose what's best for them.

Around the world, there's a growing community of young people who are turning to spiritual traditions to reconcile the ruptures between the competitive world around us and a yearning for peace and balance. It's not becoming a better version of you to get more; it's becoming the most *true* version of you so you can fully embrace and enjoy what you already have. To feel more present in assessing which new opportunities or endeavors to take on rather than just adding more to your already overflowing plate.

I interviewed Ananta Ripa Ajmera, author of *The Way of the Goddess* and teacher of Ayurvedic and Vedic traditions. (These are predecessors of Hinduism, which became defined as such only during the British colonial rule of India.) Ananta herself walked away from a corporate job to follow a spiritual journey. She grew up in the United States, born to Indian parents who wanted her to pursue Western definitions of success: making money and getting a corporate job. Finding herself torn between their definitions of success and an inner calling that her life's purpose was to be in service of others, she began a spiritual journey in India. Despite opposition from her family members when she left her corporate job, she eventually became a practitioner of Ayurveda, a three-thousand-year-old holistic health and medicine practice.

For Ananta, success is a harmonious alignment of all aspects of her life—body, mind, soul, and senses—guided by the ancient wisdom of Ayurvedic and Vedic teachings. True success to her is rooted in living with purpose and integrity (*Dharma*), striving to create abundance that benefits all beings (*Artha*), and embracing joy, creativity, and playfulness along the journey (*Kama*). Ultimately for her, success is about achieving a state of inner freedom (*Moksha*) where she is liberated from limiting emotional and mental patterns, allowing the soul to shine in its fullest expression and show others what is possible for them by personal example.

I asked Ananta how the pursuit of abundance, which we largely interpret in our modern world as *financial* abundance—could be positively reconciled with spirituality, especially when there's so much hoarding and greed around. She replied that the idea of abundance in Vedic traditions is defined as getting to a place where *you* believe that what you have is greater than what you desire. Wow.

Is there a way to manifest and live a life where you're exceeding what you want and surrender to the purpose you were put on this Earth to fulfill? What I've found—just as many ancient traditions educate us—is that it's only when you believe you already have everything you need that you begin to start seeing new opportunities come into your life. And only from a space of calm and abundance can you even begin to evaluate choices: *Is this opportunity right for me?*

When uncompete was a seed of an idea, still germinating in my mind as a response to the constant envy and overarching belief that I wasn't enough the way I was, that there was always a "better" version of me to be molded, hustled toward, and outcompeted to become, speaking to Ananta clarified much of what I was grappling with. Her explanation of abundance seems to perfectly capture what it means to uncompete. TL;DR: *You do you.*

In 2019 I received an unsolicited offer from an outside investor to expand my business. It was flattering and, of course, a "dream" next step for any entrepreneur who has grown a business to a certain level. But when I sat and reflected on what mattered most to me, how I wanted to live my life and how I wanted to *feel* every day, the type of impact I could make in keeping the company small versus hiring and growing quickly, I realized that the prevailing definition of success to grow at all costs would deplete me.

Sure, it was hard to move away from the possibility of more money, which is traditionally done through growing exponentially. But as I shared in earlier chapters, I realized that wasn't the singular pursuit of the abundance I was seeking. I was largely content with where I already was, having blazed a trail to open a company as the first woman in my family to do so. Most of all, my true dream—though hardest to admit to myself as an ambitious woman—was to live a peaceful life where a business expansion wouldn't come at the expense of time with my then three-year-old son.

It took months of deliberation and questioning. Eventually, I declined the offer and chose my peace. For the record, I will never discourage anyone's dreams to grow, make more money, and become a world-renowned business owner or anything similar. To uncompete isn't about playing small. To uncompete is to reflect on what playing big means *to you*, not what you're told to do or what is expected of you. To uncompete is to *play big on your own terms.*

Much to my surprise, bigger opportunities and contracts began to appear after I declined the investment. The endeavors I could take on felt more aligned with creating the balance I craved instead of the growth that would mean more travel, more time away from my family, more stress, and less time to spend on my health. Ananta nodded when I relayed the surprise I felt, now that I can look back on how this played out years after I made the decision. Spiritual teachers like her believe that when you are really aligned with your purpose—your *why was I put on this planet*—and anchored to a higher ideal, then your work becomes more powerful, your influence becomes deeper, and your mind becomes calmer and more content. Even when you say "no," if that decision comes from a place of abundance, not scarcity, it often leads to bigger and better achievements. There's no limit to what you can achieve, according to the Vedic and other spiritual traditions, but it's always from a place of where your current happiness is and not dependent upon the *next* thing you acquire.

Vedic spirituality encourages us to enjoy life to the fullest, but in a way that we don't become dependent upon any of these things to feel a sense of fulfillment. Any approach to acquisition—getting or making more—must come from a preexisting sense of abundance rather than looking for abundance in the form of an object or acquisition. In the modern world, we equate success, abundance, and pleasure as coming to us from the next external source, such as making more money, finding a partner, gourmet food, or luxury travel. When we uncompete, we don't reject material goods, but we don't base our definition of success or fulfillment on acquiring them.

I saw (and continue to see) my mother living in this way, which is how I started recognizing what it looks like to uncompete in every facet of your life. I've seen her closing her eyes with satisfaction and joy as we tucked into packed lunches around the giant trees at Seattle's Volunteer Park. She was clearly more contented there than at the fancy restaurant where we had her birthday dinner later that week. I've seen her relish quiet time with herself and show equal delight with the cacophony made by her three grandchildren. She dresses beautifully and elegantly, sometimes in an expensive sari or intricate dress if the occasion calls for it, but is equally at home in a simple cotton dress. It's an inspiration for me to see her live unapologetically in a society that forces women to constantly be seeking to either look younger or become invisible.

On the other hand, the competition mindset never left my father in all the years I knew him. What I witnessed was a person who was always unhappy, always searching for something better or comparing himself with someone who had what he didn't have. I recall sitting in Michelin-starred restaurants—something my father believed he needed to do to elevate his status among his colleagues—and hearing him express dissatisfaction with every part of the experience. He was never at peace or content, believing there was a better wine out there than what the sommelier recommended, that the food was better at the restaurant we *didn't* end up going to, that the table next to us ordered a better entrée, that the service was never up to par. In him, I saw the deep discontent that comes from believing that there's always something better out there, so you can't enjoy what you have in front of you. There's no balance in life because you're constantly striving to find the next thing to fulfill you. But when you get that object, experience, or acquisition that was meant to unlock some promised happiness, you can't ever feel it. When competition is the only thing you know, there's really no way to feel like you've won, even if by every measure you have won. Perhaps the greatest lesson I learned from observing him is that a competition mindset erodes every little sliver of the potential to experience contentment because there's never a sense of balance or peace with what you already have.

FOSTERING RITUALS

In 2013, when I first moved to Seattle, I met a gorgeous woman wearing a colorful neck scarf who had a honeyed, breathy voice. One of the first few things I learned about her is that she was from Turkey and loved to host communal Sunday brunches that were inspired by her childhood in Istanbul. In the past decade-plus, that person, Ekin Yasin, has become one of my closest friends, and she made good on her offer of hosting Sunday brunch (and dinners, and my baby shower, and so many other amazing meals!) at her house, where she cooked intricately plated dishes that spanned the length of a dining table for twelve (or fourteen or twenty!). We've been in each other's lives through birth, loss, grief, and many, many big and small moments. It's not an exaggeration to say that had our friendship not blossomed over the years, I wouldn't feel nearly as content to call Seattle home for more than a decade.

In 2019 Ekin unexpectedly lost her mum, Ulker, a fiery, generous woman with a loud, extraordinary laugh who we were fortunate enough to meet over amazing meals she hosted when visiting from Istanbul. I felt the grief deep in my heart and, back then, couldn't imagine how the loss would affect Ekin's tenacious spirit. But in a way that is truly Ekin, she created a unique ritual to keep alive her mother's incredible memory and legacy of hosting meals by inviting friends to a weekly "Pasta Sunday." This ritual is inspired by the communal "drop-ins" that Ekin's parents would host for friends every Sunday in their Istanbul apartment, something that is largely absent in Westernized dual-income families.

Every single Sunday since Ulker's passing, Ekin pays homage to and celebrates her mother's incredible life—sometimes by inviting friends to eat pasta with her, other times eating with just her wonderful husband, Matt. It's not that grief lessens, as anyone who has experienced this very universal emotion will tell you, but sharing it allows us to remember that we are connected in our humanity and you don't have to suffer through hard times alone. There is a sense of peace that comes from the solidarity we share even when our hearts are breaking.

As more people have gotten to know about Pasta Sunday, Ekin has heard from distant connections and even strangers about how her ritual to honor her mum has inspired them to come up with their own rituals to honor people they've lost in their lives. A ritual must be accessible to you—it shouldn't intrude on your well-being—and sustainable, a practice you can carry on doing (not a one-off event), Ekin tells me. It's how she's kept Pasta Sunday alive for over five years, no matter where she is in the world.

Ekin processing her grief in such a visible way through the Pasta Sunday ritual, in the context of a Western culture that often demands that we "keep on going" (I've literally met people who've been expected to go back to work and function "normally" a day or two after a loved one's funeral), her intentional celebration of her mum's life, week upon week, year upon year, is an act of resistance. Witnessing Ekin's thoughtful ritual up close, truly honoring both her mother and herself, made me realize how rituals can help us create a meaningful life that can ground us in our purpose and allow us an abundance mindset. Rituals have gotten a bad rap in religious and cult circles (nothing wrong with a religious ritual that's not harming anyone, to be clear), but a ritual can be anything meaningful to you that marks and celebrates a passage of time.

I feel the necessity of rituals more than ever in a competitive society, especially because according to the typical calendar of milestones, I've already celebrated all the ones expected of cis, straight women—I got a degree, got married, and had a child. As far as society is concerned, there's nothing really worthy of celebration anymore in my life, certainly not unless I win some big award or achieve any other milestone that requires toil, sacrifice, and, of course . . . beating out my competition.

But when I create my own rituals, I'm signaling to myself and others that my life is worthy and meaningful, no matter what I achieve. I encourage all of us to find and foster community rituals. However, the point of these communal rituals is not to separate people based on faith or identity but rather to find ways to bring people together to realize how much more we have in common than not. In other words, solidarity building.

Rituals can be created at no cost; I try to ritualize sending my loved ones who live far away a monthly update about my life over WhatsApp, for example. I'm trying to be more deliberate about honestly sharing the hard things, the exhaustion of being a woman of color in this world, the parts of working motherhood and people pleasing that are considered mundane in this world but are often the biggest parts of my day. I see vulnerability as the antidote to a competition mindset—softness in a world that tells you that winning means domination.

My mum's ritual of writing her three children letters and cards by hand is one that I believe really helped all of us find our way in the dark times within our childhood that were tainted by her toxic marriage. When we were younger, the letters would be more frequent, especially after we would have typical mother-child disagreements. The ones I remember the most are the letters after we disagreed on "teenage" things like who my friends were or the secrets (and lies) that many of us inevitably learn to keep from our parents. I would lament about not being understood; in one, I distinctly remember writing, "I have to put on different masks, one for school and one at home. It's so hard and painful." At fourteen, I was describing the code switching that so many children of color learn to do in a whitewashed world where we often feel like we're never living up to anyone's expectations—

we're not "cool" enough to be like the white kids, but not studious (or religious or cultural) enough to fulfill our community's expectations. After tears and heated debates with us, my mother would write beautiful letters sharing her point of view, her fears, and, above all, how much she loved us.

The ritual continues to this day, particularly when we have spent time together at my home or hers and are about to part; letters are snuck into luggage before we head to the airport, tearstained, to be read on the long flight home. My siblings and I try to keep this ritual alive (a reminder of how steadily our handwriting has deteriorated in the age of devices), a special way to process our feelings and remind one another that even though we live on three different corners of the Earth, there's a level of solidarity and support that transcends borders. I truly believe that this ritual has helped bind us against the type of rivalry that can fracture or even destroy sibling relationships. To be sure, rituals take time to honor, time that competition and capitalism tell us we should be spending working or "hacking" our lives to become more productive, or healthier, or more _____. But rituals allow us to reclaim our time and remind us that we are part of a larger ecosystem than just ourselves—critical to uncompeting. That we are enough, just as we are, and get to choose to spend our time on what nourishes and rejuvenates us. And what brings us peace.

CHOOSING INTEGRITY

There's another aphorism my mum often says to me in Hindi: "To cover up one lie, you have to tell a hundred more. Truth doesn't require any memory." My mother has lived her life with incredible integrity, and I've found that even in the most painful and chaotic moments of her life, she could find inner peace because she always was guided by her integrity.

As I write this, there's a horrific war going on in Gaza in which over fifty thousand lives have been senselessly lost, the vast majority of whom are women and children. Yet so many powerful people have chosen to remain silent or "neutral" on calling for a ceasefire for fear of losing public support (if they're in the public eye), positions (if they're leaders of organizations), or opportunities. There are very real structural barriers imposed on many people when they speak up against injustice; a person who would have to live in poverty if they lost their job shouldn't be the one risking their job to speak out, although I've met several people I admire greatly in this situation. But for many people, the cost to speak out isn't very high *and* their words could materially aid a ceasefire, and their silence is painful. Many of us choose silence against injustice to maintain the status quo because competition tells us we'll "lose our place" if we speak up. That acting with integrity is for the foolish.

We are reaching an urgency like never before for the ultrawealthy and the ultrapowerful (people usually sit at the intersection of both) to operate with more integrity. There is a lack of benevolence among the very wealthy today, as Italian economist Guido Alfani argues in a *New York Times* essay. Historically, the superrich have stepped up financially when their communities were in crisis, whether during past pandemics, the Great Depression, or past wars. But during the COVID-19 pandemic, not only did many superrich people *not* give more money to governments and aid agencies to help alleviate the crisis, but many also became even wealthier than they were at the start of the pandemic.

It's undeniable that rich people are becoming more selfish: We see an increase in the use of private jets (disastrous for the environment) and other extravagances at the same time as a steep increase in childhood hunger in the United States. Again, I think this is where a competition mindset fueled by individualism has a huge part to play. The antidote requires a widespread belief that we are all intrinsically linked and that our responsibility is to ensure that our entire community thrives, not just us as individuals. That we must operate with integrity and responsibility rather than exploit and hoard.

When I looked for corporate leaders for inspiration and examples of integrity beyond just PR stunts, I came up woefully short. Patagonia, the American outdoor retailer, was the name that kept cropping up in my research as an outlier where profit and integrity seemed to align. (To be clear, I've seen smaller examples of this, including how I now run my own company, but there's a belief that larger organizations can't be purpose driven, despite what their corporate values statement would say, because profit maximization is still what drives all for-profit companies.)

"A company that aims to be socially and environmentally responsible has the same primary duty as any other company: to pay its bills on time. It cannot honor its other responsibilities unless it meets its first responsibility: to be financially fit. That said, shareholder return shouldn't be piratical," write Yvon Chouinard and Vincent Stanley in their book, *The Future of the Responsible Company: What We've Learned from Patagonia's First 50 Years.* (Chouinard is the founder of Patagonia, and Stanley is its director of philosophy.) Profit as the sole enterprise isn't good for the health of the planet or the business, as it depletes investments into employees, systems, and innovation.

"You can't do what lazy companies do: bleed suppliers for cost reductions to achieve greater efficiency or use cheaper but more environmentally harmful, often labor-exploitative, materials," Chouinard and Stanley write. Patagonia's drive to be environmentally responsible initially hurt the company's bottom line but eventually made it more profitable: "Doing the right thing made money, just not the next day."

I'm encouraged by any example of how we can lead with integrity even if our goal *is* to make a profit. As a business owner in a capitalistic system, I don't want to run a company at a loss. But we *can* choose to create "profit, but not at all costs, and never without care to other humans and the planet," as Patagonia does.

On a smaller but no less impressive scale, I'm seeing many more women-of-color-founded enterprises operate similarly. One such example is Chef Asma Khan's London restaurant, Darjeeling Express, which employs only immigrant women with no formal culinary training in its kitchen in order to challenge the traditionally pale, male, and elite culinary traditions of fine dining.

How I've thought about living my life with integrity, or what I believe the reason is for me being born in this body, is dictated by what I've learned about the theory of karma. I was eleven or twelve years old, sitting in my Naniji and Nanaji's (maternal grandparents') small flat in Mumbai, India, when my Nanaji took out a weathered book titled *Theory of Karma*. One of the central tenets of Hinduism, Buddhism, Jainism, and a few other religions, karma now has been enshrined in pop culture, including as the title of a popular Taylor Swift song. But the meaning goes well beyond the simplistic "what goes around, comes around" explanation. As my Nanaji explained to me that day, karma refers to every thought and intention having a corresponding external action. Please excuse my simplistic description of karma—it's such a beautiful and profound idea—but in essence, karma teaches us that every thought, feeling, and then action will have a consequence, so it's important to live our life with good thoughts, feelings, and actions to attract good energy back into our lives. Karma goes beyond (the Western *mis*understanding of it) the idea that one bad action will immediately have the universe doling out a punishment to you for it. Instead, when we align with our soul's purpose (or *dharma*, as Ananta explained), we are more likely to incur beneficial karma, which brings peace, opportunity, and liberation.

Actions that we take daily compound and constitute our lives in the long run—not just one large donation to a nonprofit or writing a recommendation letter for someone we know seeking a job. To uncompete relies on us consistently taking actions with intentionality and purpose. We realize that our life isn't about comparing ourselves to others or behaving in ways that could cause harm to others but benefit us.

In fact, now that I've spent time learning more about karma (since Nanaji gave me a book on it all those decades ago!), I truly feel that even if I "win" what I want in the short run by outcompeting someone else, the victory is short-lived if I didn't act with honor and integrity during the process.

This also helps us identify others who believe in uncompeting. It's when you meet someone who seems to be in perfect alignment between their purpose and acting in ways that inspire, uplift, and help others, which attracts good energy and positivity around them. None of these concepts say that only good things happen to good people. I'm sure we can think of many examples of people who we've seen behave with dishonor and lack of integrity but still materially prosper. In fact, in the world we live in, that seems too often to be the formula to build wealth and power. But those who believe in the theory of karma say that those gains are often short-lived and that material (or financial) success ultimately doesn't beget happiness or peace. In addition, karma is about the long view in life—not just an immediate action and consequence, but the accumulation of generations of actions (and if you believe in it, even lifetimes). Karma is also communal and intrinsically community linked. So it's not just a matter of what you do and put out into the world, but your karma is also influenced by the intentions and actions of people around you.

Because the theory of karma shows us how we're interconnected and interdependent as a community, wanting to attract "good" karma isn't just about amassing things for yourself but also about improving the health of your community. This philosophy has connected deeply with me as I think about what it means to uncompete—it has made it clear to me how much my life's focus is on building communities where everyone, particularly those who have been marginalized and excluded, can thrive. It's also made it easier to step away from Western ideas of individualism and meritocracy; I see it as my responsibility to ensure that I drop off food to sick friends, refer others for opportunities, and actively use my privilege to uplift others. I recognize how much that joy and, yes, karma are linked to how others in my community are doing. To engage with integrity with others to build trust.

Moreover, karma allows us to separate from the idea that only we are inherently deserving of the abundance in our life and therefore should hoard it for ourselves. Not only has karma taught me how the good actions of my ancestors (particularly my mum's) have brought in so much abundance, but also that my karma is linked to my life's purpose to help others. In most situations, we have a choice on how to act or react. To compete with someone or not. To put down someone who has spoken ill of us or not. To be unkind and ungenerous to ourselves because that's just what people expect us to do ("Ugh, I'm so bad for eating cake—look at my thighs") or not. To stand up in solidarity against racism and injustice or not. When we believe in karma, we have a road map of how to make those choices with intention. And from those choices and actions unfold our lives and those of people in our community.

PEACE AND RELEASE

One of the ways I've made peace with the pain of my childhood—of feeling torn between the competition-to-conquer approach I saw in my father and the uncompeting that I saw in my mother—is by actively, vocally saying to myself, especially in moments of chaos and turmoil, "I *choose* peace." Competition robs us of our inner peace. When we uncompete, we are more likely to find (or return to) a peaceful mental state.

Our existing system rewards people who undercut others at all costs, particularly megalomaniacs and narcissists. That's one of the reasons that peace feels so out of reach—because people in leadership positions prioritize self-interest, selfishness, and even destruction over peace. We live in a world where it feels impossible to find peace, personally or in society. When I encountered the work of Ramani Durvasula, licensed clinical psychologist and author of multiple books on narcissistic people, it stopped me in my tracks.

As Durvasula herself cautions, not everyone with some narcissistic traits is a narcissist, and not all abuse is narcissistic abuse. Yet when I dug deeper into her work, which not only focuses on the narcissist (which, as a society, we are so intrigued by) but also the hurt and trauma experienced by those who survive relationships with a narcissist, as my family has in dealing with my father, it all clicked into place for me. I had witnessed all four pillars of narcissism she describes in her work: lack of empathy, grandiosity, a chronic sense of entitlement, and a chronic need to seek out admiration and validation from other people. I finally made a connection between why competition was such a toxic mainstay of my early life and how I would find inner peace only once I could name, confront, and finally let go of all that had been modeled by my father as the way to live a successful life. As Durvasula said in an interview on the *Minimalists* podcast,

> Narcissistic people are the ultimate capitalists because they want to win. They're very competitive. They like hierarchies. . . . So they will unrelentingly go for success. They don't care who they have to hurt, who they have to throw under the bus. They're going to get it because it's supply for them, but then that attracts people to them. And so what we need to do is rewrite our paradigms and get away from the charm, charisma, confidence, success, the checklist model, and really have people reflect: "Do I feel respected? Do I feel safe? Does this feel compassionate? Does this feel empathic?" The fairy tales aren't

about that. They're about whose flashiness got them a castle, versus about some ordinary dude with empathy.

Durvasula also is frequently quoted as saying how narcissists are disproportionately represented in leadership and powerful positions because our competitive, winner-take-all system rewards narcissists. (Can you think of any?)

I've seen a lack of empathy (which is taken to the extreme by narcissists) become normalized in our competitive world; it's even often described as a justifiable price to pay for success. I refuse to accept that. Choosing to uncompete usually means choosing to be an "ordinary" person with empathy. The mental peace that flows from that choice is worth it, as I've learned. When I choose to prioritize peace by uncompeting, it doesn't mean that I take bad behavior lying down or don't protect myself but that I prioritize peace by not slinging mud or, more importantly, losing my faith in humanity.

Because it's so easy to believe that everyone is out to get you, that every strike should be counteracted with a blow twice as hard. That the world is only made up of sharks. But when I think about how this approach and mindset make me feel in my body—tense, angry, stressed, clenched, constantly in "fight" mode—I know that this isn't healthy for me physically or emotionally. Imagining a world where the people who are compassionate, collaborative, and uncompeting outnumber those who are competitive and vengeful is the only way I can navigate this time of turmoil.

Choosing mental peace and setting boundaries with those who constantly compete is so deeply necessary when we are faced with competition at every turn. I believe that only when we choose peace as our ultimate goal are we able to actively resist systems of oppression. This may read as counterintuitive, but when we don't choose the path of peace and we're constantly in "fight" mode, we become bitter. I think it's one of the reasons more of us get caught in a cycle of competition and comparison, which robs us of our peace. By uncompeting, we can achieve the greatest benefit of physically and mentally healthier, interconnected, and joyous societies. We can finally invite peace into our lives by trusting those around us, believing that others have our "backs" and that we don't always have to keep proving our worth by producing and accomplishing.

I am deeply inspired by activist Anita Hill. Despite experiencing the failures of a system that confirmed Clarence Thomas to the US Supreme Court in 1991, even after her impassioned testimony that he had sexually harassed her, she has led three decades of change for gender equality. Speaking at Stanford University in 2024, Hill called gender equality not a "sprint or marathon, but a relay race."

This is precisely what it means to uncompete: Even in the face of systemic failures designed to breed mistrust, we must choose to see one another as collaborators, not competitors. We don't give up because of one setback or challenge, no matter how big it is. We realize that the greatest change comes from working together to resist that which harms us. That as we use our voices to speak up not only for our rights, but also for the rights of others who have been marginalized, this advocacy compounds and creates opportunity for other marginalized people to also experience justice and liberation. We believe that passing the baton to future generations isn't done to earn us publicity points but is central to our mission to make social change. We can't lose hope or compromise our peace.

It is precisely because we've experienced so much unrest in our lives that we aren't naturally encouraged to collaborate. It is because we've been taught that competition matters more than peace that we haven't resolved conflict. It is the absence of peace in our personal, professional, social, societal, and even environmental ecosystems that has left us gasping, alone, sick, isolated, and powerless. That's why, even though seeking peace may seem like an impossible endeavor, it is a powerful and necessary foundation on which to build all our biggest dreams: equality, justice, solidarity, and connectedness.

Seeking peace isn't just a dreamy statement; it's dogged resistance against systems that tell us we don't deserve peace. That we aren't worthy of it. That the world can never be peaceful. But we recognize that our liberation is interconnected and that without each of us experiencing peace, none of us will be truly peaceful.

Seeking peace as a goal to uncompete is radical and revolutionary. It requires us to not be passive bystanders but active creators and leaders of our lives, in community with others. For all of us who ever felt like there wasn't an answer to the restlessness and despair we've been feeling, we must know it was always inside us. Ours to choose and unlock and unleash. When we uncompete, we find redemption. We create justice. We begin the healing we are so desperately seeking for ourselves and others.

When we uncompete, we thrive. Each and every one of us.

Becoming a Good Ancestor

I n 1955 Jonas Salk unveiled a vaccine for poliomyelitis, an infectious disease that disproportionately affected children under the age of five. He did not patent his vaccine, responding when asked why not, "Could you patent the sun?" His contribution was so valuable that he knew patenting it for a profit would never achieve the impact he had set out to make—to save the maximum number of lives possible. Since the vaccine was introduced just under seventy years ago, polio has mostly been eradicated. To uncompete, at its core, requires us to deeply reflect on how we can conduct our lives in a manner that could create the greatest good for the highest number of people over and beyond our lifetimes. Or, as Salk himself advised, "Our greatest responsibility is to be good ancestors."

I first heard of the idea of being a good ancestor from globally renowned antiracism educator Layla F. Saad, who aptly titled her podcast *Good Ancestor*, where guests talk about how to show up in the world in a way that honors those who have come before us and serves those who will come after we're gone. When we compete with an individualistic, winner-take-all, zero-sum approach in our lives, we have little hope of changing the world or of leaving a legacy that can inspire the generations who come after us.

Competition at all costs has us playing and staying small because we remain limited in how much good we can do in the world. We become beholden to what I call "power with a small *p*," which is snatched, forced, or wielded over. To step into the greatest Power we have within ourselves, we work tirelessly to uncompete and to fulfill our greatest responsibility to be good ancestors. We take the long-term view in any situation, asking ourselves, "Is competition the right approach here, or collaboration? Am I operating from a scarcity mindset or an abundance mindset?"

To uncompete means to prioritize being at peace with yourself and your decisions, knowing you have done the best you can in any situation. From believing you have what you need, not always seeking more. In an era where dating apps make it seem that there's always a better choice a swipe away, restaurant lists that make it impossible to make a definitive choice on where to eat, social media platforms making it seem like everyone has a better life than you, it feels radical to internalize the idea that you are enough, that you have enough, and that the choices you've made are good enough. Some people may willfully misconstrue what I'm saying to mean that I don't advocate for self-improvement, ambition, or growth. That without a competitive mindset, we can't improve society. I disagree. What we need more of isn't competition or zero-sum thinking. What we need is the capacity for greater imagination. For more of us to believe and see, deep within ourselves, a world of abundance where we can all win. Where we can all succeed. For us to collaborate and propel each other toward this audacious future. I would argue that the greatest change makers in the world had radical effects precisely because they had learned to access an inner light and peace. Even in the darkest moments of my childhood, I could see an inner light radiate so brightly from my mother that it became a powerful antidote for the darkness I saw around me.

I've seen people most marginalized by society dig deep into their inner reserves to agitate for radical change outside. Each of them believes that a rising tide lifts all boats and that the work is not just about gaining personal power, recognition, or money.

When we uncompete, we build not for today or tomorrow but for generations to come. As good ancestors, we can make decisions that affect not only our own lives and the ones around us but also generations beyond our own. We engage in our civic responsibility and actively uphold justice for all and democratic ideals. We live the truth that what we do today has ripple effects all around us and for the long term. To uncompete offers an alternative where we are empowered, grounded, and forward-looking. We move from believing we have no agency to knowing that we can make choices to change our lives and the lives of those around us. To uncompete is to invest in building a beautiful, thriving future for all.

Acknowledgments

This is the hardest part to write; I've written a whole book about recognizing others and how interconnected we are and how we should always give others their flowers, but I'm so fearful I'll forget someone here. Any omissions are my error alone, and I hope you'll forgive me, knowing my permanent status of being undercaffeinated and overwhelmed on deadline!

This book wouldn't be possible without my incredible mum, Seema; the blessings of my maternal grandparents, Kusum Nani and my late Nanaji, R. P. Agarwal; and all the ancestors in my maternal lineage. Mum, there really aren't enough words to describe the depth of your love or the strength of your soul. I hope I captured a tiny bit of your essence in these words.

This book is also only in your hands because of Maile Beal, who saw in me something I hadn't even dreamed of in myself. Maile, you're a star and the best agent-champion-friend I could ask for. Thank you

Acknowledgments

to the entire ARC team for being so excited when *Uncompete* was a seed of an idea and for all your championing since!

Thank you to my incredible editor, Emily Wunderlich, who opened me up to a higher and deeper level of writing than I ever thought possible. Thanks for your gentle and firm edits throughout this process. I'll always be grateful that I got to bring this book to life with you. I am also deeply grateful to the team at Viking and all the amazing people who have supported me in this process.

Thank you to Martha Burwell, whose immediate support for the ideas of uncompete and rigorous collaboration on the "uncompete" survey (along with many, many years of partnership) have been invaluable. My deepest gratitude to Jen Jarnagin and Marisol Del Valle, who both had such keen insight with their research on this book.

I'm grateful to the team at Meghan Stevenson Books, particularly Claudia Gabel, who was a solid partner as I panic-worked through early edits. Appreciate your reminders to keep calm and write on!

Thanks to Ayanna Meyers, whose partnership on formatting endnotes ensured we came with receipts.

I am deeply grateful to everyone at the Candour and collaborating teams for all the support over the past many years, most of all to Vanessa Arias, whose encouragement and meticulousness has kept me on track! Thanks to Marie and the Incontrera Team, Eva Jannotta and the Medusa Media team, the team at Stern Strategy, and Jasmine Barta.

La'Kita Williams gets a special mention, not only as someone who so generously allowed me to share parts of her story, but also for inspiring me in so many ways that I can't even begin to capture here. May we always have fancy meals and plenty of toasts forever!

Acknowledgments

I'm also very, very grateful to all who shared their stories and insights with me for this book. I built this on the foundations laid primarily by Black and brown leaders, activists, thinkers, and doers.

Thanks especially to all my incredible friends and the community of women the world over who have cheered me on. I will *definitely* leave folks out, so—though it takes a *village* to do this—I'll highlight just a few book-related names: Deepa (Book Aunties United!), Ekin (thanks for the celebratory lunch on the day I landed the book deal!), Jamie, Amy Gallo, Bindiya, Ijeoma, Sonora, Aarti, Shroo, and Shar. To *all* the magic people around the world who have modeled the principles of this book in so many ways, visible and invisible, I am eternally grateful.

Thanks to my son's teachers and caregivers over the years, particularly Gloria, Portia, and Mahtab.

To my loving family-in-law: Mom and Papa, Katie, Russ, and S. Thank you for all your encouragement and blessings.

To Ra + Sameer, it means the world to have navigated this journey with y'all in different ways and at different stages. Thank you for holding me steady as we lived through it all, then began the work of healing through it all. I love you both incredibly much. Human nature is such. (Too soon? LOL!)

To Rahul, A + A: May my sweet nieces always find a world that champions them and a community that is centered on uncompeting and a dad who is a wonderful model. <3

To P: The one who showed me that love is a verb, not a noun. You've modeled what it means to support, champion, celebrate, and propel in ways I can't describe. And thanks to that first Scrabble game

Acknowledgments

you made me lose, I'll always know that one can lose at games and still win at life. This book is very much fueled by your magic coffee. :)

To V: Becoming your mother was the strongest lesson that our liberation lies in community. You are everything. May you always know how proud I am to be your mum.

Notes

Chapter One: Competition Is the Water We Swim In

23 **from Malaysia in 1965:** Lucian W. Pye, review of *From Third World to First. The Singapore Story, 1965–2000*, by Lee Kuan Yew, *Foreign Affairs* 80, no. 2 (2001), www.foreignaffairs.com/reviews/capsule-review/2001-03-01/third -world-first-singapore-story-1965-2000.

23 **It was just the only way:** "The World Bank in Singapore," World Bank Group, accessed January 29, 2025, www.worldbank.org/en/country/singa pore/overview.

27 **key factor of their business success:** Jeff Bezos, "How Amazon Thinks About Competition," *Harvard Business Review*, December 21, 2020, https://hbr.org /2020/12/how-amazon-thinks-about-competition.

32 *Rediscovering Our Common Humanity:* Brian Hare and Vanessa Woods, *Survival of the Friendliest: Understanding Our Origins and Rediscovering Our Common Humanity* (Random House, 2020).

33 **Silicon Valley technology entrepreneurs:** "Competition or Cooperation? Fostering a Collaborative Workplace," Stanford Institute for Research in the Social Sciences, January 5, 2021, https://iriss.stanford.edu/news/competition -or-cooperation-fostering-collaborative-workplace.

34 **"more whites and fewer nonwhites":** Zack Beauchamp, "Trump and the Dead End of Conservative Nationalism," *Vox*, July 17, 2019, www.vox.com /2019/7/17/20696543/national-conservatism-conference-2019-trump.

35 **analogy of a game of Monopoly:** Annie Reneau, "She Summed Up the Economic Legacy of Black Americans in One History Lesson and Monopoly

Metaphor," *Upworthy*, June 9, 2020, www.upworthy.com/woman-puts-protests
-into-historical-context.

36 **sought-after fields:** "What Is the Impact of Stress in the Workplace?,"
Talkspace, accessed January 29, 2025, https://business.talkspace.com/articles
/the-negative-effects-of-stress-in-the-workplace.

37 **how we can minimize them:** Thomas Gerding and Jun Wang, "Stressed at
Work: Investigating the Relationship Between Occupational Stress and
Salivary Cortisol Fluctuations," *International Journal of Environmental Research and Public Health* 19, no. 19 (2022): 12311, https://pmc.ncbi.nlm.nih.gov
/articles/PMC9564551.

37 **"anger, anxiety, and being overwhelmed":** Gerding and Wang, "Stressed at
Work."

38 **a growing epidemic:** Office of the Surgeon General (OSG), *Our Epidemic
of Loneliness and Isolation: The U.S. Surgeon General's Advisory on the Healing Effects of Social Connection and Community* (US Department of Health and Human Services, 2023), www.hhs.gov/sites/default/files/surgeon-general-social
-connection-advisory.pdf.

38 **takes an antidepressant:** Jamie Ducharme, "America Has Reached Peak
Therapy: Why Is Our Mental Health Getting Worse?," *Time*, August 28,
2023, https://time.com/6308096/therapy-mental-health-worse-us.

38 **30 percent since 2000:** Ducharme, "Peak Therapy," 2023.

38 **two decades prior:** Ducharme, "Peak Therapy," 2023.

39 **member of the Nazi Party:** *Knowledge at Wharton* podcast, "Remembering
the Dark Side of the Space Race," Wharton School of the University of
Pennsylvania, July 26, 2019, https://knowledge.wharton.upenn.edu/pod
cast/knowledge-at-wharton-podcast/macdonaldbook-secret-history
-space-race.

39 **incredible Black women:** Margot Lee Shetterly, *Hidden Figures: The American
Dream and the Untold Story of the Black Women Mathematicians Who Helped Win
the Space Race* (William Collins, 2016); and Hidden Figures, directed by
Theodore Melfi (20th Century Fox, 2017).

39 **compared with their male and white peers:** Bas Hofstra et al., "The Diversity-
Innovation Paradox in Science," *Proceedings of the National Academy of Science of
the United States of America* 117, no. 17 (April 14, 2020): 9284–91, https://www
.pnas.org/doi/abs/10.1073/pnas.1915378117.

40 **commit future crimes than white defendants:** Michael Totty, "How to Make
Artificial Intelligence Less Biased," *Wall Street Journal*, November 3, 2020,
www.wsj.com/articles/how-to-make-artificial-intelligence-less-biased
-11604415654?mod=article_inline.

41 **a similar proportion of men:** Kerri Smith, "Women's Health Research Lacks Funding—These Charts Show How," *Nature*, May 3, 2023, www.nature.com /immersive/d41586-023-01475-2/index.html.

42 **early brain development, and cognitive ability:** Clancy Blair and C. Cybele Raver, "Poverty, Stress, and Brain Development: New Directions for Prevention and Intervention," *Academic Pediatrics* 16, no. 3 supplement (2016): S3036, www.ncbi.nlm.nih.gov/pmc/articles/PMC5765853.

43 **only the "best" make the cut:** Anna Esaki-Smith, "Harvard Accepts 3.59% of Applicants, Highest Rate in 4 Years," *Forbes*, updated March 29, 2024, 9:43 a.m. EDT, www.forbes.com/sites/annaesakismith/2024/03/28/harvard-accepts-359 -of-applicants-highest-rate-in-4-years.

43 **Manhattan private preschools:** Gretchen Morgenson and Patrick McGeehan, "Wall St. and the Nursery School: A New York Story," *New York Times*, November 14, 2002, www.nytimes.com/2002/11/14/business/wall-st-and -the-nursery-school-a-new-york-story.html.

47 **household income than your education:** Joint Economic Committee Democrats, *Education Can Help Narrow the Racial Wealth Gap, but Structural Solutions Are Needed to Close It* (Joint Economic Committee, October 1, 2021), www.jec.senate .gov/public/index.cfm/democrats/2021/10/education-can-help-narrow-the -racial-wealth-gap-but-structural-solutions-are-needed-to-close-it.

48 **major divergence on policy preferences:** Joel Achenbach, "Science Is Revealing Why American Politics Are So Intensely Polarized," *Washington Post*, January 20, 2024, www.washingtonpost.com/science/2024/01/20/polarization -science-evolution-psychology.

Chapter Two: What It Means to Uncompete

54 **the community, *and* to society:** Wikipedia, "Competition," last edited January 7, 2025, 05:36 (UTC), https://en.wikipedia.org/wiki/Competition.

54 **Aiko Bethea says:** Brené Brown, host, *Dare to Lead* podcast, "Aiko Bethea on Creating Transformative Cultures," Parcast Network, February 8, 2021, https://brenebrown.com/podcast/brene-with-aiko-bethea-on-creating -transformative-cultures.

54 **critically acclaimed book *Emergent Strategy*:** adrienne maree brown, *Emergent Strategy: Shaping Change, Changing Worlds* (AK, 2017).

57 **just as competitive as men:** Selin Kesebir, "Research: How Women and Men View Competition Differently," *Harvard Business Review*, November 6, 2019, https://hbr.org/2019/11/research-how-men-and-women-view -competition-differently; and Kyle Mittan, "Study Casts Doubt on Theory

That Women Aren't as Competitive as Men," University of Arizona, November 1, 2021, https://news.arizona.edu/news/study-casts-doubt-theory-women-arent-competitive-men.

58 **"the tuned-out, indifferent bitch"**: Olga Khazan, "Why Do Women Bully Each Other at Work?," *Atlantic*, updated August 3, 2017, www.theatlantic.com/magazine/archive/2017/09/the-queen-bee-in-the-corner-office/534213.

60 **"your sense of worthiness"**: Sahaj Kaur Kohli, "Cultural Experiences That Reinforce Scarcity Mindset," *Culturally Enough*, March 10, 2023, https://culturallyenough.substack.com/p/cultural-experiences-that-reinforce.

61 **in his health advisory**: Office of the Surgeon General, *Parents Under Pressure: The U.S. Surgeon General's Advisory on the Mental Health & Well-Being of Parents* (US Department of Health and Human Services, 2024), www.hhs.gov/sites/default/files/parents-under-pressure.pdf.

61 **Daniel Markovits in *The Atlantic***: Daniel Markovits, "How College Became a Ruthless Competition Divorced from Learning," *Atlantic*, May 6, 2021, www.theatlantic.com/ideas/archive/2021/05/marriage-college-status-meritocracy/618795.

64 **highest salaries are overwhelmingly white:** "Our Workforce Data," Amazon, updated June 17, 2024, www.aboutamazon.com/news/workplace/our-workforce-data.

64 **spending the most on health care:** Justina Petrullo, "US Has Highest Infant, Maternal Mortality Rates Despite the Most Health Care Spending," *American Journal of Managed Care*, January 31, 2023, www.ajmc.com/view/us-has-highest-infant-maternal-mortality-rates-despite-the-most-health-care-spending.

64 **babies are delivered vaginally:** Emily Oster and W. Spencer McClelland, "Why the C-Section Rate Is So High," *Atlantic*, October 17, 2019, www.theatlantic.com/ideas/archive/2019/10/c-section-rate-high/600172.

65 **to benefit Republican candidates:** Daniel Medina and Bob Ortega, "Emails Show How a Right-Wing Group Steers GOP Leaders on Major Policy Issues," CNN, updated March 18, 2024, 10:58 a.m. EDT, www.cnn.com/2024/03/17/politics/dark-money-fga-ashcroft-invs/index.html.

65 **carbon-dioxide emissions:** "Causes and Effects of Climate Change," Climate Action, United Nations, accessed January 30, 2025, www.un.org/en/climatechange/science/causes-effects-climate-change.

66 **according to the United Nations:** "Facts and Figures," Act Now, United Nations, accessed January 30, 2025, www.un.org/en/actnow/facts-and-figures.

71 **innovators, artists, and political leaders:** David Robson and Alessia Franco, "Montessori: The World's Most Influential School?," BBC, January 31, 2023,

www.bbc.com/future/article/20230131-does-the-montessori-method-actually
-work.

71 **a smaller elite:** Matt Beard, "Montessori Education Could Reduce the Advantage Gap Between Rich and Poor, but It's Only Available to the Rich,"
Guardian, January 19, 2020, www.theguardian.com/commentisfree/2020
/jan/19/montessori-education-could-reduce-the-advantage-gap-between
-rich-and-poor-but-its-only-available-to-the-rich.

72 **Brazil, Australia, and Canada:** Richard Schuster et al., "Vertebrate Biodiversity on Indigenous-Managed Lands in Australia, Brazil, and Canada Equals
That in Protected Areas," *Environmental Science & Policy* 101 (November
2019): 1–6, www.sciencedirect.com/science/article/pii/S1462901119301042.

72 **within Indigenous territories:** Julia E. Fa et al., "Importance of Indigenous
Peoples' Lands for the Conservation of Intact Forest Landscapes," *Frontiers
in Ecology and the Environment* 18, no. 3 (2020): 135–40, https://esajournals
.onlinelibrary.wiley.com/doi/full/10.1002/fee.2148.

Chapter Three: Reset Our Mindset

83 **"skills in how to cooperate":** Tema Okun, "White Supremacy," in *Dismantling
Racism: A Workbook for Social Change Groups*, ed. Kenneth Jones and Tema Okun
(ChangeWork, 2001), www.thc.texas.gov/public/upload/preserve/museums
/files/White_Supremacy_Culture.pdf.

84 **lawsuit of its kind in professional sports:** Jeff Carlisle, "USWNT, U.S. Soccer
Federation Settle Equal Pay Lawsuit for $24 Million," ESPN, February 22,
2022, www.espn.com/soccer/story/_/id/37625711/uswnt-us-soccer-federation
-settle-equal-pay-lawsuit-24-million.

93 **$19 billion to 2,450 nonprofits:** Yield Giving, accessed January 23, 2025,
https://yieldgiving.com.

95 **"come together and take collective action":** Leah Hunt-Hendrix and Astra
Taylor, *Solidarity: The Past, Present, and Future of a World-Changing Idea* (Pan-
theon, 2024).

95 **established in American society:** Lynda Lin Grigsby, "Black Couple Rented to
a Chinese American Family When Nobody Would. Now, They're Donating
$5M to Black Community," *NBC News*, March 6, 2024, www.nbcnews.com
/news/us-news/black-chinese-family-coronado-california-rcna140717.

96 **going to people of color:** "Corporate America Promised to Hire a Lot More
People of Color. It Actually Did," Bloomberg, updated September 26, 2023,
11:00 a.m. EDT, www.bloomberg.com/graphics/2023-black-lives-matter
-equal-opportunity-corporate-diversity.

Notes

Chapter Four: Reframe Comparison

104 **psychiatrist Sue Varma:** Mayesha Soshi, "Why We Can't Help but Compare," *Juggernaut*, September 24, 2024, www.thejuggernaut.com/why-south
-asian-parents-compare-their-children.

106 **benign and malicious:** Jens Lange and Jan Crusius, "Dispositional Envy Revisited: Unraveling the Motivational Dynamics of Benign and Malicious
Envy," *Personality and Social Psychology Bulletin* 41, no. 2 (2015): 284–94,
https://pubmed.ncbi.nlm.nih.gov/25534243.

108 **separately with two groups:** Niels van de Ven et al., "Why Envy Outperforms Admiration," *Personality and Social Psychology Bulletin* 37, no. 6 (2011):
784–95, https://journals.sagepub.com/doi/abs/10.1177/0146167211400421.

111 **substance abuse, stress, and suicide:** Ujala Zubair et al., "Link Between Excessive Social Media Use and Psychiatric Disorders," *Annals of Medicine and
Surgery* 85, no. 4 (2023): 875–78, https://pmc.ncbi.nlm.nih.gov/articles/PMC
10129173.

111 **psychologist Nicholas Kardaras:** Nicholas Kardaras, *Digital Madness: How Social Media Is Driving Our Mental Health Crisis—and How to Restore Our Sanity*
(St. Martin's, 2022).

114 **how hard it is:** Zoe Blaskey | Motherkind (@ZoeBlaskey), www.instagram
.com/zoeblaskey; Mary Catherine Starr (@MomLife_Comics), www.insta
gram.com/momlife_comics; Not Safe For Mom Group (@NotSafeForMom
Group), www.instagram.com/notsafeformomgroup.

114 **promote body confidence:** Brown Girl Therapy (@BrownGirlTherapy),
www.instagram.com/browngirltherapy; Lizzo (@LizzoBeEating), www
.instagram.com/lizzobeeating; Alex Light—Body Confidence (@AlexLight_
ldn), www.instagram.com/alexlight_ldn.

114 **provide antiracist content:** POCIT (@POCInTech), www.instagram.com
/pocintech; DecolonizeMyself (@DecolonizeMyself), www.instagram.com
/decolonizemyself.

116 **A short list includes:** Center for Humane Technology, accessed January 23,
2025, www.humanetech.com; Organization for Social Media Safety, accessed
January 23, 2025, www.socialmediasafety.org; National Cybersecurity Alliance, accessed January, 23, 2025, https://staysafeonline.org/resources/social
-media.

117 **others are engaging in:** "How FOMO Became a Fixture," Alumni, Stories,
Harvard Business School, May 11, 2023, www.alumni.hbs.edu/stories/Pages
/story-bulletin.aspx?num=9169.

117 **"from which one is absent":** Andrew K. Przybylski et al., "Motivational,
Emotional, and Behavioral Correlates of Fear of Missing Out," *Computers in*

Human Behavior 29, no 4 (2013): 1841–48, www.sciencedirect.com/science
/article/abs/pii/S0747563213000800?via%3Dihub.

117 **Mayank Gupta and Aditya Sharma:** Mayank Gupta and Aditya Sharma,
"Fear of Missing Out: A Brief Overview of Origin, Theoretical Underpinnings and Relationship with Mental Health," *World Journal of Clinical Cases* 9,
no. 19 (2021): 4881–89, https://pmc.ncbi.nlm.nih.gov/articles/PMC8283615
/#B8.

118 **"you constantly struggled with them":** Patrick McGinnis, "FOMO: The
Surprising History of the Meme That Started It All," Patrick J. McGinnis,
accessed January 23, 2025, https://patrickmcginnis.com/wp-content/uploads
/2021/07/History-Of-Fomo.pdf.

118 *Technological Forecasting and Social Change:* Anushree Tandon et al., "Dark
Consequences of Social Media-Induced Fear of Missing Out (FoMO): Social Media Stalking, Comparisons, and Fatigue," *Technological Forecasting and
Social Change* 171 (October 2021): 120931, www.sciencedirect.com/science
/article/pii/S0040162521003632.

118 **"Our digital habits":** Kristen Fuller, "JOMO: The Joy of Missing Out," *Psychology Today,* July 26, 2018, www.psychologytoday.com/us/blog/happiness
-is-state-mind/201807/jomo-the-joy-missing-out.

Chapter Five: Choose Joy

129 **children experience childhood trauma:** "The Prevalence of Adverse Childhood
Experiences, Nationally, by State, and by Race or Ethnicity," Child Trends,
February 12, 2018, https://www.childtrends.org/publications/prevalence
-adverse-childhood-experiences-nationally-state-race-ethnicity.

130 **author Adia Gooden:** Dr. Adia Gooden, accessed January 23, 2025, https:
//dradiagooden.com.

130 **In her TED Talk:** Adia Gooden, "Cultivating Unconditional Self-Worth,"
TED Talk, DePaul University, Chicago, May 2018, 15 min., 21 sec., www.ted
.com/talks/adia_gooden_cultivating_unconditional_self_worth.

130 **"To take up space":** Adia Gooden, "How to Cultivate a Sense of Unconditional Self-Worth," TED, November 18, 2020, https://ideas.ted.com/how
-to-cultivate-a-sense-of-unconditional-self-worth.

132 **Gooden makes four:** Gooden, "Unconditional Self-Worth," 2020.

135 **the German word for joy:** Juli Fraga, "The Opposite of Schadenfreude
Is Freudenfreude. Here's How to Cultivate It," *New York Times,* updated
November 28, 2022, www.nytimes.com/2022/11/25/well/mind/schaden
freude-freudenfreude.html.

136 **in a *New York Times* interview:** Fraga, "Freudenfreude," 2022.

138 **Chambliss also encourages:** Catherine Chambliss, "The Role of Freuden-freude and Schadenfreude in Depression," *World Journal of Psychiatry and Mental Health Research* 2, no. 1 (2018): 1009, www.remedypublications.com /open-access/the-role-of-freudenfreude-and-schadenfreude-indepression -277.pdf.

140 *Make—and Keep—Friends*: Marisa G. Franco, *Platonic: How the Science of At-tachment Can Help You Make—and Keep—Friends* (G. B. Putnam's Sons, 2022).

141 **another way to cultivate freudenfreude:** Fraga, "Freudenfreude," 2022.

142 **facing bias in the workplace:** Ruchika Tulshyan and Jodi-Ann Burey, "Stop Telling Women They Have Imposter Syndrome," *Harvard Business Review*, February 11, 2021, https://hbr.org/2021/02/stop-telling-women-they-have -imposter-syndrome.

143 *Creating Connection and Bridging Divides*: Geoffrey L. Cohen, *Belonging: The Science of Creating Connection and Bridging Divides* (W. W. Norton, 2022).

144 **Laura Morgan Roberts and her team write:** Laura Morgan Roberts et al., "An Antidote to Microaggressions? Microvalidations," *Harvard Business Re-view*, May 15, 2023, https://hbr.org/2023/05/an-antidote-to-microaggressions -microvalidations.

145 **"Joy is your birthright":** Tanmeet Sethi, *Joy Is My Justice: Reclaim What Is Yours* (Hachette Go, 2023).

Chapter Six: Create an Abundant Community

149 **within our workplaces:** Denise McLain and Ryan Pendell, "Why Trust in Leaders Is Faltering and How to Gain It Back," Workplace, Gallup, April 17, 2023, www.gallup.com/workplace/473738/why-trust-leaders-faltering -gain-back.aspx.

150 **work leads to better performance:** Sarah Brown et al., "Employee Trust and Workplace Performance," *Journal of Economic Behavior & Organization* 116 (August 2015): 361–78, www.sciencedirect.com/science/article/pii/S0167 268115001365.

150 **researching trust at work:** Paul J. Zak, "The Neuroscience of Trust," *Har-vard Business Review* (January–February 2017), https://hbr.org/2017/01/the -neuroscience-of-trust.

156 **economist Sylvia Ann Hewlett:** Sylvia Ann Hewlett, accessed January 30, 2025, www.sylviaannhewlett.com/books.

157 **a 2016 Lean In/McKinsey report:** *Women in the Workplace 2016* (LeanIn .org and McKinsey, 2016), www.mckinsey.com/featured-insights/diversity -and-inclusion/women-in-the-workplace-archive#section-header-2016.

157 **companies said they had sponsors:** Sylvia Ann Hewlett and Kennedy Ihezie,

"20% of White Employees Have Sponsors. Only 5% of Black Employees Do," *Harvard Business Review*, February 10, 2022, https://hbr.org/2022/02/20-of-white-employees-have-sponsors-only-5-of-black-employees-do.

161 **"You may take your business":** Rosalind Chow, "Don't Just Mentor Women and People of Color. Sponsor Them," *Harvard Business Review*, June 30, 2021, https://hbr.org/2021/06/dont-just-mentor-women-and-people-of-color-sponsor-them.

164 **Wikipedia entries of women:** Donna Ferguson, "'Why Are They Not on Wikipedia?': Dr Jess Wade's Mission for Recognition for Unsung Scientists," *Guardian*, October 1, 2023, www.theguardian.com/science/2023/oct/01/why-are-they-not-on-wikipedia-dr-jess-wades-mission-for-recognition-for-unsung-scientists.

166 **I often turn to:** Tina Opie and Beth A. Livingston, *Shared Sisterhood: How to Take Collective Action for Racial and Gender Equity at Work* (Harvard Business Review Press, 2022).

169 **"By coming together":** Koritha Mitchell, *From Slave Cabins to the White House: Homemade Citizenship in African American Culture*, The New Black Studies Series, edited by Darlene Clark Hine and Dwight A. McBride (University of Illinois Press, 2020); and Koritha Mitchell, *Living with Lynching: African American Lynching Plays, Performance, and Citizenship, 1890–1930*, The New Black Studies Series, edited by Darlene Clark Hine and Dwight A. McBride (University of Illinois Press, 2011).

170 **mobilizing for Harris:** Koritha Mitchell, "Identity Groups Are Mobilizing for Kamala Harris. That Shows Progress," *Time*, July 29, 2024, https://time.com/7005092/kamala-harris-identity-groups-zoom-calls.

170 **"your job is to empower somebody else":** Pam Houston, "The Truest Eye," *O: Oprah Magazine* (November 2003), www.oprah.com/omagazine/toni-morrison-talks-love/1.

Chapter Seven: Build Collective Power

175 **in college admissions:** Students for Fair Admissions, Inc. v. President and Fellows of Harvard College, 600 U.S.181 (2023), www.supremecourt.gov/opinions/22pdf/600us1r53_4g15.pdf.

176 **worth $3 billion:** Nick Thompson and Diana Magnay, "Oprah Winfrey Racism Row over Switzerland Shop Incident," CNN, updated August 11, 2013, 10:32 a.m. EDT, www.cnn.com/2013/08/09/world/oprah-winfrey-racism-switzerland/index.html.

176 **shoplifting in a New York deli:** "Report: Forest Whitaker Says He Was Wrongly Accused of Shoplifting in Deli," *CBS New York*, February 16, 2013,

www.cbsnews.com/newyork/news/report-forest-whitaker-says-he-was
-wrongly-accused-of-shoplifting-in-deli.

176 **janitorial and administrative staff:** Joan C. Williams et al., "Double Jeopardy? Gender Bias Against Women in Science," *UC Hastings College of the Law,* January 2014, https://worklifelaw.org/publications/Double-Jeopardy
-Report_v6_full_web-sm.pdf.

178 **"the conception of power-with":** Pamela Pansardi and Marianna Bindi, "The New Concepts of Power? Power-Over, Power-To and Power-With," *Journal of Political Power* 14, no. 1 (2021): 51–71, www.researchgate.net/publication
/350807403_The_new_concepts_of_power_Power-over_power-to_and
_power-with.

178 **corresponded with power-with:** Hannah Arendt, *On Violence* (Harcourt Brace, 1970).

178 **"serves as a subterfuge":** Audre Lorde, *I Am Your Sister: Collected and Unpublished Writings of Audre Lorde,* ed. Rudolph P. Byrd et al., *Transgressing Boundaries: Studies in Black Politics and Black Communities Series,* ed. Cathy Cohen and Fredrick Harris (Oxford University Press, 2009).

179 **Aruna Rao and David Kelleher:** Just Associates, accessed January 30, 2025, https://justassociates.org/big-ideas/power1.

180 **"what I think I am capable of":** "Stacey Abrams on Writing Herself into the Story—and History," *CBS News,* May 9, 2021, www.cbsnews.com/news
/stacey-abrams-on-writing-herself-into-the-story-and-history.

182 **a little more than $192,000:** Jack Caporal, "Average Net Worth by Age, Education, and Race," *Motley Fool,* updated March 18, 2024, 3:19 p.m., www
.fool.com/research/average-net-worth-americans.

183 **more than $284,000:** All figures in this paragraph are from Caporal, "Average Net Worth."

191 **bettering each other's lives:** Aminatou Sow and Ann Friedman, *Big Friendship: How We Keep Each Other Close* (Simon and Schuster, 2021).

197 **achieving all our financial dreams:** Rachel Rodgers, *We Should All Be Millionaires: A Woman's Guide to Earning More, Building Wealth, and Gaining Economic Power* (Harper Collins Leadership, 2021).

198 **"associate, or board member?":** pam_boy (@pam_boy), "Beyoncé can find 24 black trombone players, but your company cannot find a single black intern, associate, or board member?," Twitter (now X), September 28, 2020, https://ifunny.co/picture/pam-boy-beyonce-can-find-24-black-trombone
-players-but-5r60Z3418.

199 **2023 Eras concert tour:** Melody Chiu and Jeff Nelson, "Taylor Swift Gave a Whopping $197 Million in Bonuses to Eras Tour Performers, Crew on Top of Their Salaries (Exclusive)," *People,* updated December 9, 2024, 1:22 p.m.

EST, https://people.com/taylor-swift-gave-eras-tour-crew-usd197-million
-in-bonuses-exclusive-8758216.

Chapter Eight: Liberate Our Bodies

208 **"There was time now"**: Tricia Hersey, *Rest Is Resistance: A Manifesto* (Little Brown Spark, October 11, 2022). Emphasis mine.

210 **all their paid time off**: Shradha Dinesh and Kim Parker, "More Than 4 in 10 U.S. Workers Don't Take All Their Paid Time Off," Pew Research Center, August 10, 2023, www.pewresearch.org/short-reads/2023/08/10/more-than-4-in-10-u-s-workers-dont-take-all-their-paid-time-off.

210 **one in four US mothers**: Sarah Kliff, "1 in 4 American Moms Return to Work Within 2 Weeks of Giving Birth—Here's What It's Like," *Vox*, updated August 22, 2015, 1:40 PM EDT, https://www.vox.com/2015/8/21/9188343/maternity-leave-united-states.

210 **we need embodiment or rest**: Organization for Economic Cooperation and Development, "PF2.1 Parental Leave Systems," OECD Family Database, accessed January 30, 2025, www.oecd.org/content/dam/oecd/en/data/datasets/family-database/pf2_1_parental_leave_systems.pdf.

211 **"bad for your health"**: "Health Disparities Between Blacks and Whites Run Deep," Harvard University, T. H. Chan School of Public Health, April 15, 2016, www.hsph.harvard.edu/news/hsph-in-the-news/health-disparities-between-blacks-and-whites-run-deep.

214 *The Body Is Not an Apology*: Sonya Renee Taylor, *The Body Is Not an Apology: The Power of Radical Self-Love*, 2nd ed. (Berrett-Koehler, 2021).

216 **filmmaker Shonda Rhimes**: Shonda Rhimes, *Year of Yes: How to Dance It Out, Stand in the Sun and Be Your Own Person* (Marysue Rucci, September 13, 2016).

216 **hundred episodes each**: Lesley Goldberg, "With 'Scandal,' Shonda Rhimes Notches Rare Third 100-Episode Milestone," *Hollywood Reporter*, April 13, 2017, www.hollywoodreporter.com/tv/tv-news/scandal-shonda-rhimes-notches-rare-third-100-episode-milestone-993523.

220 **disability-justice activists**: Christine Miserandino, "The Spoon Theory," But You Don't Look Sick, 2003, https://butyoudontlooksick.com/articles/written-by-christine/the-spoon-theory.

222 **I know this is rare**: Emma Parker, "The Business of Breaks," Time Off Report 2024, Clarify Capital, updated March 27, 2024, https://clarifycapital.com/business-of-breaks.

223 **when I worked in corporate America**: Maria Wollan, "Failure to Lunch," *New York Times Magazine*, February 18, 2016, www.nytimes.com/2016/02/28/magazine/failure-to-lunch.html.

226 **"activities that matter most to you"**: Pooja Lakshmin, *Real Self-Care: A Transformative Program for Redefining Wellness (Crystals, Cleanses, and Bubble Baths Not Included)* (Penguin Life, 2023).

226 **rest as an embodiment practice**: Dr. Saundra Dalton-Smith, accessed January 30, 2025, www.drdaltonsmith.com.

Chapter Nine: Redefine Success on Our Own Terms

243 **"not your disappearing act!"**: Alok Vaid-Menon, "every time i receive hateful reactions to my appearance i remember how grateful i am that i have access to friends who helped me transform my pain and resentment into poetry and resplendence," Facebook, August 6, 2020, www.facebook.com /AlokVMenon/photos/every-time-i-receive-hateful-reactions-to -my-appearance-i-remember-how-grateful-/2381138338848612.

244 **"solutions to our challenges"**: Monita Rajpal, "How to Prioritise Between Life and Career: Making Conscious Decisions for Success," *Monita Rajpal* (blog), September 5, 2024, updated December 19, 2024, www.monitarajpal .com/single-post/choosing-conscious-decisions-over-having-it-all-the -power-of-prioritizing-life-and-career.

246 **"sensitivity to local neighborhoods"**: Lake Union Partners, accessed January 23, 2025, https://lakeunionpartners.com.

247 **those definitions were now outdated**: Forward Singapore, accessed January 30, 2025, www.forwardsingapore.gov.sg/.

248 **men get to "fail up"**: Zulekha Nathoo, "'Failing Up': Why Some Climb the Ladder Despite Mediocrity," *BBC*, March 3, 2021, https://www.bbc.com /worklife/article/20210226-failing-up-why-some-climb-the-ladder -despite-mediocrity.

248 **penalized for small mistakes**: Christy Glass and Alison Cook, "Performative Contortions: How White Women and People of Colour Navigate Elite Leadership Roles," *Gender, Work & Organization* 27, no. 6 (2020): 1232–52, https://onlinelibrary.wiley.com/doi/epdf/10.1111/gwao.12463.

250 **makes it safe to fail**: Amy C. Edmondson, "Leading in Tough Times: HBS Faculty member Amy C. Edmondson on Psychological Safety," Harvard Business School, November 22, 2022, www.hbs.edu/recruiting/insights -and-advice/blog/post/leading-in-tough-times.

252 **"West Coasters get mad"**: Jordan K. Green (@jordonaut), "When I describe East Coast vs West Coast culture to my friends I often say 'The East Coast is kind but not nice, the West Coast is nice but not kind,' and East Coasters immediately get it. West Coasters get mad. 😄," Twitter (now X), January 21, 2021, https://x.com/jordonaut/status/1352363163686068226.

Notes

253 **"the ones we have been waiting for"**: June Jordan, *Directed by Desire: The Collected Poems of June Jordan*, ed. Jan Heller Levi and Sara Miles (Copper Canyon, 2007).

253 **"give you hope again"**: Randa Abdel-Fattah, *Does My Head Look Big in This?* (Orchard, 2005).

Chapter Ten: Seek Peace

263 **British colonial rule of India**: Ananta Ripa Ajmera, *The Way of the Goddess: Daily Rituals to Awaken Your Inner Warrior and Discover Your True Self* (Penguin Random House, 2022).

272 **argues in a *New York Times* essay**: Guido Alfani, "What Happens When the Superrich Are This Selfish? (It Isn't Pretty.)," *New York Times*, November 19, 2023, www.nytimes.com/2023/11/19/opinion/rich-billionaires-philanthropy-covid.html.

273 *Patagonia's First 50 Years*: Vincent Stanley and Yvon Chouinard, *The Future of the Responsible Company: What We've Learned from Patagonia's First 50 Years* (Patagonia Works, 2023).

274 **traditions of fine dining**: Hugh Tucker, "Asma Khan: A Force for Women in Food," BBC, March 7, 2024, www.bbc.com/travel/article/20240307-asma-khan-a-force-for-women-in-food.

278 **validation from other people**: Audrey Hamilton, host, *Speaking of Psychology* podcast, episode 37, "Recognizing a Narcissist, with Ramani Durvasula," American Psychological Association, May 2016, www.apa.org/news/podcasts/speaking-of-psychology/narcissism.

278 **interview on the *Minimalists* podcast**: *The Minimalists* podcast, episode 431, "Healing from Narcissistic People," Patreon, February 19, 2024, www.youtube.com/watch?v=cLoTJ8EdY3A.

280 **"but a relay race"**: Angelica Puzio Ferrara, "'Not a Sprint, but a Relay Race': Anita Hill's Politics of Hope," Stanford University, Clayman Institute for Gender Research, January 29, 2024, https://gender.stanford.edu/news/not-sprint-relay-race-anita-hills-politics-hope.

100 YEARS of PUBLISHING

— ◇ —

Harold K. Guinzburg and George S. Oppenheimer founded Viking
in 1925 with the intention of publishing books "with some claim
to permanent importance rather than ephemeral popular interest."
After merging with B. W. Huebsch, a small publisher with a distinguished catalog, Viking enjoyed almost fifty years of literary and
commercial success before merging with Penguin Books in 1975.

Now an imprint of Penguin Random House, Viking specializes
in bringing extraordinary works of fiction and nonfiction to a vast
readership. In 2025, we celebrate one hundred years of excellence in
publishing. Our centennial colophon features the original logo for
Viking, created by the renowned American illustrator Rockwell
Kent: a Viking ship that evokes enterprise, adventure, and exploration, ideas that inspired the imprint's name at its founding and
continue to inspire us.

— ◇ —

For more information on Viking's history, authors, and books,
please visit penguin.com/viking.